M000187133

Daughters of Parvati

CONTEMPORARY ETHNOGRAPHY

Kirin Narayan and Alma Gottlieb, Series Editors

A complete list of books in the series is available from the publisher.

Daughters of Parvati

Women and Madness in Contemporary India

Sarah Pinto

PENN

UNIVERSITY OF PENNSYLVANIA PRESS

PHILADELPHIA

Copyright © 2014 University of Pennsylvania Press

All rights reserved. Except for brief quotations used for purposes of review or scholarly citation, none of this book may be reproduced in any form by any means without written permission from the publisher.

Published by
University of Pennsylvania Press
Philadelphia, Pennsylvania 19104-4112
www.upenn.edu/pennpress

Printed in the United States of America
on acid-free paper

10 9 8 7 6 5 4 3 2 1

ISBN 978-0-8122-4583-7

A catalogue record for this book is available from the Library of Congress.

For Dennis,
and to the memory of Nirmala

All I can do is tell the truth. No, that isn't so—I have missed it. There is no truth that, in passing through awareness, does not lie. But one runs after it all the same.

—Jacques Lacan, The Four Fundamental Concepts of Psychoanalysis (1978)

Sometimes it is necessary to restore the lost parts, to rediscover everything that cannot be seen in the image. . . . But sometimes, on the contrary, it is necessary to make holes, to introduce voids and white spaces, to rarify the image, by suppressing many things that have been added to make us believe that we are seeing everything.

—Gilles Deleuze, Cinema 2 (1989)

May words cease to be arms; means of action, means of salvation. Let us count, rather, on disarray.

—Maurice Blanchot, The Writing of the Disaster (1995)

Contents

Note on Transliterations

In transliterating spoken Hindi in this text, I have taken the simplest approach, though it has meant diverging from technically precise transliteration. For smoother reading, I have avoided diacritical markings and have not differentiated between long and short vowels, dental and palatal fricatives, and so on, maintaining only the most basic conventions. Where names are concerned, I have transliterated according to convention rather than followed transliteration guidelines (therefore, Pooja or Puja instead of Pūjā or Puujaa).

Introduction: Love and Affliction

Late, by myself, in the boat of myself,
no light and no land anywhere,
cloudcover thick. I try to stay
just above the surface, yet I'm already under
and living within the ocean.
　　　　　—Jalal ad-Din Rumi, "Saladin's Begging Bowl" (1995)

January in north India is a strange kind of cold for someone used to Boston winters, to piercing air and eclipsing snowfalls. It is milder, but demands more effort—spreading quilts, seeking sunlight, finding warmth outdoors. On such mornings, after wiping the dust off my daughter's mary janes, disciplining a scarf around her braids, and seeing her to school, I set off for a chilly interior, a space heavy with the difference between inside and outside. In a locked inpatient unit of a small, private psychiatric clinic, I visited with a woman I call Sanjana, a middle-class housewife about my age. As we sat on her bed shelling peanuts, she talked about her young son, her ex-husband, her doctors, her sadness, her anger, her desire to find a job in one of the new call centers. When she got out of the hospital, she said, she would move to a different city, start a job and a new life. In the meantime, she paced the short width of the ward, beads in hand and prayers on her breath, keeping warm and filling hours with a metric of longing and devotion. When I asked what she and the other women talked about, she said, "We talk about the only thing there is to talk about: getting out."

What was temporary and what was permanent were unclear for Sanjana. They were unclear categories for me as well. The word "visit" intercedes in my accounts of this winter and the months and years before and after it. It describes many of my activities, though I called what I was doing "research" as I passed through the halls of hospitals and clinics. I broke up long stretches in the city where my daughter and I were living (but really just visiting) with journeys north, to a smaller city near the mountains. Small treasures in large expanses of time, those visits took us to Ammi, or Mother, as everyone called her, a woman living in deep psychosis in a spacious house her son had built for. She had spent nearly three decades inside the infamous Agra Mental Hospital (as it was then called), a period punctured by infrequent though regular visits from her son and daughter-in-law. Now, they visited Ammi in her new home, traveling from their own home overseas. Her ex-husband also visited for weeks at a time. Though he said little to her, Ammi called him the Librarian and every morning went to his room to receive a book. She pressed it to her forehead, then returned to her room in the servants' quarters.

Much later, after summer heat ruptured that short, unsettling winter, I visited another psychiatry ward—this one with open doors—where a goddess spoke through a young mother, entering the inpatient unit as a passenger in her skinny limbs and wild eyes. She shouted accusations at her doctor, "You are God. You have everything, I have nothing." A younger woman a few beds down had been sent to the ward by court order. She insisted to her doctors that she would like to remain married to the two men she was involved with, while her mother argued that these men were taking advantage of her daughter's mental illness. Signs of past abuse went unacknowledged by the otherwise attentive young doctors who saw to her diagnosis.

Through a winter, many hot months, and two monsoons, I met with women in circumstances that defied connection. All the while, I was creating for my daughter and myself a series of homes out of what were really just visits, building small worlds and little stabilities far from the New England home where my life and family were dissolving behind me. I left those dissolutions for the security of anthropological research and the promise of purpose it offered, occupying with my four-, then five-, then six-year-old daughter an ever-expanding constellation of people, gestures to family, to connection. The things I encountered were anything but solidifying, though. Instead, they were undoing. This book is an account of that time and those moments of undoing. It is also an account of efforts to make something out of them.

In homes and wards, I found situations that were radically different but shared the presence of things both true and untrue, evident and fantasy astute and wild; things about men and women, parents and children, the mind and its afflictions. Each situation held signs of delusion as well as things that were telling and real. In each was a crisis in how people treated each other. And in each, those same elements, approached from a different angle, were just things that were. These situations happened in different cities, decades, and social classes, but all had places in the history of global psychiatry, in shifts from institutionalization to community care, from theories blaming families toward ideas about the biology of illness, from government medicine to privatization, and toward ever-increasing reliance on pharmaceuticals. They also shared the thread of troubled marriage and contested love, and the ways intimacy is organized in the north Indian Hindi belt. They shared the figuring of divorce, among other breaks in relationships, and the social burdens it generates, burdens that that fall heavily on women. This, too, involves a history of changes—in the ways women are considered individual entities or symbols of the groups of which they are part, in the ways they are more and less dependent on fathers, husbands, sons, and brothers.

Many situations I encountered seemed to reverberate with elements of familiar crises, such as women abandoned to psychiatric wards, cast out by families, or medically diagnosed for making unusual decisions. While not entirely the same as their older counterparts, these new conditions did not make for altogether new dilemmas. The question arose: should ways of naming "what is wrong" remain the same? And the diverse circumstances I encountered shared an ethical paradox. That paradox is the theme of this book. At blurry boundaries between truth and something to the side of it, this paradox involves the way categories of ethical evaluation—the good and the bad—collapse in medicine and human relationships, and in what a terser language calls the "management" of mental illness. For instance, abandonment, an important term in critical perspectives on mental illness, might typically be opposed to care. Likewise, freedom might be imagined in opposition to constraint. Both scales help us evaluate practices like commitment proceedings or conditions in homes and hospitals. But I encountered many situations in which those spectra operated simultaneously, their terms overlapping, even collapsing in the work of everyday ethics. In committing a family member to inpatient care, or managing a loved one's medications, or bringing a family member "home," or making a new home for oneself when things have come undone, care became—necessarily—indistinguishable from constraint; freedom felt a bit like abandonment. In the nexuses of care and constraint, and freedom and abandonment, I strug-gled, as did the people involved, not only to respond to crises but also to recognize a crisis in the first place, to differentiate what was inevitable from what was unjust. What might be learned in these moments? What language might suit them?

I have found these questions to be dense and troubled when thinking about love and kinship. And I have found them to be weighty in psychiatry units and households where, in one way or another, medicine's attention to minds is part of a family story. A similar uncertainty pressed on me when I felt my anthropological approach was both a lens and a blinder. As I moved from thinking about midwives and childbearing—topics of my earlier research—to mental illness, doctors, and drugs, these questions led me away from dominant critiques of global medicine, those that focus on the systematic exclusion (from families, from societies, from what it means to be human) of those deemed unfit or abnormal, and toward an ethic that did not always align with the arrangement of ideals underlying global psychiatric practice and policy, or with scholarly critiques of them.

This ethic focuses on relations, especially their undoing. I call it an ethic of dissolution. I find in it upended distinctions between agency and interdependence, a spectrum that orients many thoughts about the right, best, or good enough way to practice psychiatry and live life with others. This book is a description of those spaces of ethical grappling at the overlap of crises—crises of mind, crises of relatedness, crises of intimacy, crises of medical care—and the decisions, assertions, compromises, and actions that happen there.

This is also a book about gender and the particular considerations that thinking from the perspective of women brings to medical practice. Observers of medical history have long taken notice of the effects psychiatry has had on women, in particular in Europe and North America. These effects include constrictions, regulations, and abuses, and the ways bodies and desires are policed, ideas about gender enforced, and misfit women cast out, locked away in attics, asylums, and wallpapered rooms, or forced to change their ways. At the same time, the systematic suffering of women in relation to psychiatry is not to be separated from the ways women have benefited from the develop-ment of sciences of the mind. Both sides of the equation show psychiatry's unique relationship to women's lives, a relationship that has produced a cas-cade of effects—social critiques, new theories, and changes in the ways medi-cine is practiced and psychiatry thinks about bodies and selves.

As a gendered reading of psychiatry in India, what follows considers the ways gendered crises in psychiatry overlap with other kinds of problems—problems of a social and epistemological nature, that is, problems of relating and knowing. I have framed my account in this way not because India has more gender crises than other places but because it is a rich setting in which to ask what makes a social crisis out of a medical situation—a treatment, system, language, or bodily effect—or to ask how we know a problem when we see it. That India, like much of Asia, is represented in the broad strokes of the global imagination as a place replete with both gender problems and gender strategies gives us many layers to quilt together and pull apart. So too does the fact that so many vital and globally relevant understandings of gender, critiques of social inequality, and forms of intervention have originated here in terms resonant with the economic and cultural conditions that bind much of the world.

This book is also about another kind of crisis, another kind of paradox, one that overlapped, in my observation, with gender crises. In the households, clinics, inpatient units, and shrines through which I witnessed women passing, settling in, staying, and moving on in the flux of distress, crises in selfhood and psychiatric caregiving tended to coincide with crises of narrative: unfinished and unfinishable stories, dilemmas of representation, disjunctures in perspective or coherence, and destabilizations of truth telling. In other words, gender crises in Indian psychiatry seemed to converge with crises in narrative and storytelling. Why was this so? What was its effect on people's lives?

If anthropology is interested in the points at which meanings, values, and languages that attend to human life are shored up, it is also interested in the way that shoring up happens against the possibility that things are not as stable as they seem, that something powerful happens in the instability of categories (Sedgwick 2003; Strathern 2005). This is as true for science as for other domains of life, and medicine's apparent certainties can rest on things that are ever disintegrating and being remade—ideas, knowledge, moral paradigms. Crises of narrative that coincide with medical crises and kinship crises are a telling place to find things dissolving (and reconstituting) or disintegrating (and reintegrating). Amid conditions pertaining to economic structures, knowledge practices, and material demands (elements of postcolonial, neoliberal subjects), crises in caregiving happen and are responded to at points of disintegration—of selves, relationships, social orders, and certainties. Ethics involve negotiations in the space of dissolution,

processes that pertain equally to medicine, kinship, and narrative and involve the work of undoing, unmaking, and breaking down as much as
efforts to solidify, stabilize, and shore up. This is an ethnographic space—
ethical practices in and of dissolution can reveal details about specific times
and places, specific ways people think about themselves as entities in relation to others, and particular human interactions that defy spectra of separation and togetherness, agency and constraint. That this appears to be
gendered territory seems important.

It would be easy enough to attribute crises and boons in the care of
women with mental illness to distinctly "Indian" elements—gender structures, cultural and religious models, forms of healing, and ways of thinking
about the body, the psyche, and the self. But while medicine, love, and stories
are part of constellations of social life in India, they also point us, Southern
Cross-like, toward axes more universal and patterns less local. What happens
in the spaces in which I spent time involves processes that converge in other
places too. For one thing, medicine always happens in a context, meaning
that there are multiple, perhaps innumerable, possibilities for a global practice
like psychiatry. In north India, the main point of difference is not between
"Indian culture" and "the West," however each may be defined. Though
these terms are vivid imaginaries, they are rooted in a social landscape that
is, in fact, remarkably diverse. India can be—and often is—characterized by
its pluralism. This includes a plurality of medical practices; of nonmedical
forms of healing and non-Western forms of medicine; of cultural habits,
power arrangements, legal structures, religions, and ideas about what it
means to be a woman or a man, sick or well, mad or sane. India is also a
place in which being "global" has long been a fact of life. India is not a
branch of globalization; it is one of its roots. The long presence of psychiatry
in India makes the "Western" in Western medicine a clumsy imaginary. This
means that what we find there about psychiatry may tell us something about
what we might expect to find elsewhere, in one shape or other, even as what
we find there may also unsettle things about psychiatry (or medicine, or
power, or love, or family) we assume to be true everywhere.

As an effort to find my way through the ethical thickets I encountered
in households, hospitals, and inpatient wards, this book is at first glance
about the social life of medicine, the effects of psychiatry on the lives it
touches or that reach for it. It asks how medicine takes part in people's
everyday struggles and explores the specific, pedestrian existence of sciences
that offer themselves as universal.

At second glance, it is about love, marriage, and family. It is, especially, about the violence and undoing that are part of their makeup, the way bonds are unpurled and knitted into new designs much like sweaters I once watched village women unravel and remake to fit the shapes of growing children. Received wisdom—reinforced as much by Bollywood movie plots as by Western fantasies—says that the Indian family and Indian marriages are defined by their stability; they are built like fortresses, not rebuilt like shanties. This is a false ideal. There are, of course, many lives, marriages, and families in India that are precisely shantylike, not because they involve new or unconventional ways of being a family but because they happen to fall apart and get patched up. This book is about the shanties—the falling apart and rebuilding. It is less an account of new or old sciences, policies, practices, or technologies, or their clash or cohabitation with traditional practices, than it is about the ways medicine unmakes bonds between people. In particular, it is about the way that in psychiatry's treatment of women, much clinical work echoes the very nonclinical work of inhabiting new worlds when things fall to pieces—things like love and the transactions of desire, labor, and selfhood that are the mortar of family life.

At third glance, or maybe at first, this is a story about stories, about the ways they, too, come undone. It struggles with the moments in which language's ability to tell the truth reaches its end. This happened a lot in the cases I encountered. It also happens in what we might call research or ethnography, or arguments and theories, as well as in the common and fantastical things people tell themselves in order to get on with life.

My own story is, for better or worse, indelibly stamped into my impressions of clinics and wards. My work—the research activities that morphed into something harder to name—spread over several years, beginning with a return to a city I knew well but had not lived in for some time. I wanted to look into the ways Indian psychiatry, in that little corner of the world, might play a role in the everyday lives of women, in the "houseflows," to use Valentine Daniel's term (1987), that shape lives, offer meaning, and matter for women in a complicated, changing world. It was not an easy endeavor. For one thing, I had brought my daughter Eve. This was, of course, more blessing than hindrance. I saw familiar scenery through new eyes. I watched the astounding process of a child acquiring a new language—spoken words and bodily movements—and becoming a new kind of creature (a small-town north Indian girl). I was and continue to be surprised by her observations, ones I never could have made myself.

Where earlier fieldwork had placed me in households, where children were an expected presence, this work was different. It involved hospitals and doctors' offices, workplaces and places of healing. And Eve had to go to school—an adventure in new bodily habitations, new forms of care and discipline. Instead of bringing her with me everywhere (though we did our share of that), I now had to carve out time and space without her in a city in which childcare outside the family is all but unheard of, and a woman alone with a child is an anomaly with a base note of danger.

Also, unlike in fieldwork I had conducted about childbirth, this time the stories people told were vague and slow to emerge. Language was slippery. People were cagey. This was shadowy territory. It would seem reasonable enough to gloss these blurred pictures as evidence of stigma, but that would be too easy. People are cagey and evasive about many things, and we use language in multiple and creative ways. That this was so in the context of illness and affliction was not necessarily evidence of cultural attitudes about what is abnormal. It may have been that, but it may have involved something else as well—the extension, perhaps amplification, of more everyday, let us call them normal, ways of living in a world with others.

Through sheer accident I found myself working in the locked female ward of a new private psychiatric hospital at the edge of the city. I found there what seemed to be a disproportionate presence of women at the edges of marriage—divorced, divorcing, coming out of broken relationships, or in relationships of which their families disapproved. These facts appeared to be not only noteworthy but woven into patterns of treatment. These women's situations gutted me, and, so, I turned my attention toward marriage and its ways of ending, the stakes of divorce for women, and the impacts these elements may have had on afflictions and treatment.

I returned a year later to the same place profoundly changed—indeed, undone. I came back with Eve again holding my hand or, when my hands were full, the hem of my shirt. But I saw our world through a new and cracked lens, reeling from a separation from Eve's father, carrying the weight of that grief and of a season of lies and anxiety from an ill-timed and ill-chosen affair. This journey extended a year already dominated by confusion over the difference between leaving and returning, between what was lost and what gained, between being free and being lonely. I had left one home for a series of temporary ones, one street, one city for another, a mortgage for rent, and, finally, Boston for India.

After a departure that can only be described as traumatic, during a stopover in Delhi, for five straight days I did not sleep. While Eve, snoring off her jet lag, did not need my sanity, I pulled myself weeping to my friends' breakfast table. I could not hold still, in mind or body, and felt I was collapsing into a tiny kernel from a point beneath my ribs. I was desperate to get us to our adopted city, a short flight away. The morning we left Delhi, our flight was delayed for hours. In the terminal, wobbly with sleeplessness, I watched spots move in the thick air. Eve was an oblivious angel, playing with the dolls she carried in a little metal box, making first a school, then a Harvard Square out of the black vinyl seat. I was grateful when the woman next to me leaned over to talk, lashing me back to the world with language of everyday things. It wasn't until arriving in our familiar old apartment that I found sleep. There, over the garage of a guesthouse in the home of Mrs. M., an elderly widow, in a neighborhood of grand homes gone to seed, I began to feel the ground beneath my feet.

I ran away from a lot in bringing us back to "the Annexie," the name for that rambling apartment, to its loose delineations of inside and outside, to the kites (the kind on strings) competing with kites (the kind with wings) for altitude above our roof, and to the people I knew and loved in this, our shadow life. In the years since I first started coming here, the city had rolled well over the waistline of its river, consuming mango orchards and turning villages into urban neighborhoods. Learning how to reinhabit not only this space but any home space, how to make and populate a warm, secure world for Eve, how to reknit an unraveled life by moving slowly through the days—these were the first order, though I may not have realized it. I felt daily the sting of the question "Where is her father?" and the dizzying compression of a lie, or partial truth, in my protective response, "He is working in the U.S." I slowly disarticulated myself from the shambles that was my new relationship, and from the obsessive thoughts, guilt, and panic it wrought. And I returned to the clinic where I had begun my work a year before, a space I call Moksha. The measure of women's days there influenced the pace of my own. The place felt like a vortex, only rather than sucking me in, it seemed that its effects expanded outward to other aspects of my life. But I was lucky—I could leave. Its effects for me were temporary, illusory.

As our life slowed into routine, I built my days around the stuff of a mother's life—early morning school preparations, afternoons keeping partial track of Eve's movement through her delineated neighborhood—she was allowed no further than the *paan* stall on the corner, where she bought bubble gum on credit—and evenings orchestrating the small universe of a household of two. I grew closer to Mrs. M. as we settled into the Annexie, a high-ceilinged space with chipping paint, a rooftop veranda, and a precarious, crumbling staircase leading to a side yard. We had tea with Mrs. M. most evenings in the fading light of the main courtyard or the tremble of her bedroom's tube light. Mrs. M. poured extra sugar for Eve, taught her the appropriate phrases for summoning the cook for more biscuits, and told us what it was like to be in the first class of women at Benaras Hindu University, or to give birth during Partition, or to take "four children, two dogs, and a mother-in-law" in a Studebaker to a holiday in Kashmir.

I punctuated my weeks with Thursday evening visits to Sufi shrines, feeling the welling up of my own sorrows while, around me, women in varying conditions of longing and distress went into trance at the tombs of saints. I had never noticed all the tombs in the city, the shrines grand and humble, but suddenly I was aware that they were all around me. When this period was over, with sadness and expectation, we went back to Boston, where I resituated Eve in her American world. She adapted quickly. I had a harder time.

I returned to India a month later, this time by myself, back to my shadow life. I moved into a smaller room in the same house, nostalgic for my apartment, which another family of foreign researchers now occupied. Instead of going to the private ward, I spent my days in the psychiatry unit of a large government hospital (which I call Nehru Hospital), a setting flush with sound, aroma, and movement. Most important, it was thick with people. The two scenes could hardly have been more different. Not only were the government inpatient units open (that is, doors were literally open and people moved freely through spaces), the government hospital was populated with families. Where most of the residents of Moksha's locked female ward were middle-class, and many at the margins of marriage, women in Nehru were from a range of social classes and backgrounds. Most were married women or girls too young to be married. In both settings, scrutiny of intimacy, especially married life, was central to clinical technique, but to different ends. Moksha was what I came to think of as a space of heartbreak; Nehru was a setting in which bonds were stitched back together, often with coarse thread. Each had its own crises. In Moksha, in the worst cases, women were held for long periods of time, years into decades, often against their will. In Nehru, suffering came in the ways family relations were reinstated as part of therapy, even when those relations were part of the problem. In better or more middling situations, circumstances fell somewhere to the side of these points, and, of course, neither gloss was true for every case, and my observations were as prone to whims of time and chance as is life in any complex setting. Nonetheless, I was struck by the different stakes of kinship and its dissolutions in each setting.

My days unfurled differently as well. In the late afternoons I seldom got home in time for tea with Mrs. M. At night I was too exhausted or busy to visit shrines. I had notes to write up. I had books to read. Days boiled by rather than dripping like honey. I did not sleep much. I wrote up multiple book proposals—shamefully prematurely. In the first week in the government hospital I met at least five times the number of doctors, patients, and families I had met in eight months at the private clinic.

In many ways this book, and what I have to say about Indian psychiatry, is divided according to these two phases and the spaces they represent, the ways of being and sense of time I felt in each. The Moksha phase, and the space it occupies in this book, was, for me, characterized by a sense of immobility, of stasis and long stretches of slow-moving, undoing time. This was the phase of remapping a familiar landscape through the location of its shrines, and of stepping with acute and often painful awareness through mundane minutia of living a life. Research was slow; I wrote endless, descriptive notes on brief patches of time and small interactions. I painted word murals with long accounts of places. When there was nothing to write about I wrote poetry, mostly about our home and neighborhood. This was the phase of kitchens, children, and buckets of laundry, and of my near-constant household companion Prem, the young woman who helped me cook, clean, locate Eve, and manage the hordes of children who crashed like waves through the house. It was the phase of summer turning into winter, of pushing back the furniture at night so we could dance to keep warm. It was the phase of sadness, and most of all it was the phase of Eve.

The Nehru phase was a time of busyness and motion, of frenetic and swiftly moving time, of hand-scrawled notes too extensive to make it into my computer, single notebooks filled in a day of work, daily trips to the heart of the old city rather than its newest fringes, and the constant appearance of new faces, new names, and nameless patients with ailments that needed to be named—diagnosing being the main work of the psychiatric residents with whom I spent my days. Ants infested my computer, pouring out of its tiny openings every time I turned it on, getting out of the way, it seemed, for the onrush of bytes. This was winter turning into summer in a rapid descent, not a slow climb. It was bracketed by flights rather than train journeys. Sitting in packed outpatient clinics through eight hours of constant interaction, I learned in the first two weeks the multiple trade names of drugs, which had baffled me for months. I forgot to return phone calls. I did not go to religious ceremonies. There was no time for poetry and no place for sadness. This phase involved a vertiginous freedom of movement unthreaded from the eyelets of domesticity, and at the same time an ache—comforting at times, excruciating at others—for my little girl and our empty afternoons.

Throughout it all I thought I was doing research. I was not, or only partially was. This was especially true in the locked ward of the private clinic. The dynamics of the place seemed to undo so much; among other things, they swept away, in their rush of intense human interaction, the securing distance of a research agenda, the comfort of being on the opposite side of a lens. Throughout my fieldwork, but especially in that space, the stories of love and madness I took note of were as much stories about me. I write this with little pride and much embarrassment, but it is important to acknowledge it, lest I seem to speak for others when I speak about them. What follows has arguments and theoretical musings, it makes a stab at articulating what might be in crisis about Indian psychiatry and in psychiatry more broadly, and at identifying strategies people and families use in dealing with suffering. It makes an even more tentative effort to craft a language of ethics where existing ones, to my mind, fall short. But it also represents, in many places, something other than research and makes no claim, or little claim, to authority, scientific or otherwise, and especially not to that juggernaut, generalization, which federal guidelines in the United States use to define research as research. It is the barely ripe fruit of an effort to capture, for a moment, a sense more than an interpretation of layered dissolutions—of minds, selves, bonds, families, clinical certainties, stories, anthropological argument—and of the presence of those dissolutions in efforts to bring things back together again, to "rehabilitate" or "articulate," in the strict senses of those words.

I have struggled to name the result; it cannot be called research results or witnessing, nor anything equally heroic, and neither can it be called ethnography entirely, or memoir. It may, however, be something not unlike the imperfect and incomplete things that the people I met did every day in struggling to describe their own histories, something that is at once interpretive and represents the limits of interpretation, narrative and at the limits of storytelling, true and a mere effort to reach for truth. Maurice Blanchot has a passage that captures a descriptor I struggle to locate. He writes, "May words cease to be arms; means of action, means of salvation. Let us count, rather, on disarray. When to write, or not to write makes no difference, then writing changes—whether it happens or not; it is the writing of the disaster" (1995: 11).

Writing down the disasters and the mundane, then and now, in notes or chapters or poetry, was a kind of asylum, offering the embrace of narrative and confining messy realities into the square walls of meaning, offering, that is, both refuge and violence. In this and other ways, the asylum—and the idea of it—shadowed me as I moved through days of research into days of writing. It certainly trailed the lives of the women I met in wards and clinics. Figuring out how that was so remains important, as does determining what its implications might be for understanding the ways medicine is a form of power. The asylum has long been iconic of a certain kind of historical disaster. It has represented the exclusion from social life of people deemed unfit for humanity and stood for forms of social regulation beyond asylum walls. It has also represented psychiatry's long phase of custodial care and institutionalization and the abuses it involved. And it has stood for an irony that moves across times and settings—representing confinement, exclusion, discipline, and abandonment, and at the same time safety and protective harbor.

When I spoke with doctors about Indian psychiatry's history, I was often told about "dumped women"—a social and medical crisis iconic of the asylum era. These were women who were left by families in government asylums (men have been "dumped" too, but the burden of symbol and statistic falls on women). The scandal of dumped women was, like the asylum, a social crisis that may have remained in postinstitutionalization psychiatry, in spite of longstanding legislation requiring families to care for their sick, but, as I spent time in wards, clinics, and homes, how it did so and whether women were still dumped became less clear. But the *idea* of dumped women is part of how people have come to understand contemporary Indian psychiatry and address its current crises and darker past.

Abandonment is an orienting idea for understanding how the power structures established in psychiatry's asylum era persist in other models of treatment and care. Michel Foucault described the asylum as both agent and end point of discipline, establishing structures in which care might become synonymous with regulation to the point of social exclusion, even death. In Europe, in the nineteenth century, a system was established in which kin performed the work of surveilling norms, turning over their abnormal members to catchment spaces and zones of discipline (Foucault1988). For Foucault, the psychiatric patient, or madman, became a focus of modern power and the asylum integral to a disciplinary network that depended on the family as object and agent of weeding out (2003a: 93). Asylum and family "lean on each other," Foucault wrote, creating "a discourse of truth" that is both about "the family" and takes shape through it (2003a: 94).

A Foucauldian sense of abandonment is also an orienting idea for anthropologists, especially those interested in medicine and therapeutics, the politics of intervention, movements of people and populations, and relationships between individuals and institutions. As a sign and symptom of the history of the asylum in structures of caregiving, the concept of abandonment allows critics to expose the stakes of political and economic arrangements, neoliberal and otherwise, things that seem well beyond asylum life, strictly speaking, but can be shown to retain its ways of knowing, normalizing, and excluding. "Abandonment" also provides an ethical language for responding to such crises. In keeping with its Foucauldian affiliations, it is associated with normativity and regulation, surveillance and definitions of "the human," or "life," as well as their alternatives—"the ex-human," "letting die." At the same time, its association with late capitalism finds abandonment—and anxiety about it—to be a symptom of contemporary Western forms of life and governance. Its iconic sites are clinics and prisons, and the household and family are its shared secret and imaginary other, their covert accomplice and dream of refuge. Abandonment is understood in reference to other terms, like confinement, as well as liberatory alternatives like freedom and care. Its sense of liberation is a state of belonging. (There are a great many texts to cite for this literature, most ranging from the early 1990s to the present; a few key ones include Salerno 2003; Agamben 1998, 2005; Nancy 1993; Biehl 2005; Povinelli 2006, 2011; Rose 2007.)

The idea, if not always the fact, of the asylum was a seam in the lives of many women I met. So was abandonment. But neither term was stable;

neither idea held the same place or had the same effect in women's lives. Where notions of abandonment and its iconic architecture, the asylum, assume a grid of evaluation, a moral judgment—who is normal and who is not, who is fit and who is not, who is contagious and who is not—in many cases, even those in which abandonment seemed a potent reality, such a grid was not always apparent. One woman's confinement in a private ward representing (or intending to represent) contemporary outpatient-oriented, community-based psychiatry, and another's freedom in an isolating home space after decades in an institution suggested that while the asylum may be a movable idea in women's lives and psychiatric practice, it did not necessarily depend on moral evaluations about what is normal or human and what is not. The idea that contemporary psychiatry incorporates families into its work of adjudicating fitness for humanity envisions the asylum as a set of social practices alive and well in contemporary medical practice and, indeed, in family life. My sense is that the latter may be so in India— social crises that defined asylum life persist, though not always in the former terms—as a series of efforts to normalize. A question underlying much analysis of contemporary psychiatry is, then, the extent to which we have reached the end of the asylum, well after the era of deinstitutionalization, and how the *idea* of the asylum and its effects continue to infuse everyday life. People still joke, after all, about sending (or being sent by) their loved ones "to Agra" when they act a little bit crazy.

The history of the asylum is a global history. Indian psychiatry is at once part of that history and departs from received wisdom about the place and persistence of the asylum in medicine. Indeed, the history of psychiatry in India has long explored the question of just how universal psychiatric models are. The young doctors with whom I spent time in Nehru's in- and outpatient wards often spoke comparatively, describing what was "different" about psychiatry in India, what was particular to its sciences, what new shape universal ideas took there, and in what ways it was inflected by culture. This was true of diagnostic categories, symptom presentations, treatment regimes, doctor-patient relations, and other aspects of clinical practice.

It would be patently false, however, to attribute any sort of difference to psychiatry's newness in India. Psychiatry has existed on the subcontinent for nearly as long as it has existed anywhere. At the dawn of the discipline, the time of alienists and asylums, psychiatric scholarship in and about India was a means for British assertion of moral and scientific superiority. At the same time, it offered a forum for validating, experimenting with, and learning from practices considered distinctly Indian. In the mid-nineteenth century, both Indian and British doctors treated patients in a busy marketplace of ideas and techniques, and care of the mad was dominated by private practitioners and large institutions. The latter housed British and "native" patients separately, reproducing complex social stratifications in which Indians were divided into classes and castes in native asylums while members of the Indian elite were cared for in English institutions (Ernst 2007). Though accomplishing racial separation through physical distance, psychiatry in India did not aim for the goals of social control of native populations accomplished in Europe or other colonies (Ernst 2007). In India, colonial authorities discouraged rising admissions into institutions and saw the burden of responsibility for the native mad as resting on native communities, families, and native-run asylums (Ernst 2007: 223). While nineteenth-century Indian asylums were, like their Western counterparts, "arbiters of sanity" in which reason and character were gold standards of wellness (Mills 2006; quotation from Kapila 2005: 154), their disciplining capacity was of limited reach. When approaches for dealing with the mad shifted from moral therapies oriented around the management of daily life to medical notions of illness and treatment, India rapidly adjusted, as the demands of administering to the Indian population made medical approaches, with their less intensive needs for institutional care, more expedient (Ernst 2007).

Upon its arrival in India, psychoanalysis was a field for debating difference, often in starkly colonial and subtly anticolonial terms. While the asylums were in full operation, European and Indian psychoanalysts debated whether Freud's ideas reflected universal realities or offered local explanations about European psyches adaptable to Indian conditions. Even as British doctors used Freudian models to assert European superiority and promote negative views of colonial subjects, the nature of those subjects and their societies seemed to demand revision of those models, particularly for Indian analysts. Psychoanalysts like Girindrasekhar Bose were able to claim the social legitimacy offered by the medical profession even as their revisions, many of which drew on Hindu philosophy and mythology, undermined medicine's claim to universality (Nandy 1995; Hartnack 1999). After Independence, though psychoanalysis went into decline as a practice in India, it remained an important tool for articulating the uniqueness and validity of Indian culture. Scholars exploring "the Indian psyche" used psychoanalysis to frame difference and discern the impact of colonialism on Indian selves (Kurtz 1992; Kakar 1981; Roland 1991; Nandy 1983).

Throughout the twentieth century, psychiatry in India remained oriented around large, centralized institutions. After Independence, the former asylums (renamed mental hospitals) remained the central nodes of caregiving until the 1960s and 1970s, when a shift away from this system involved first an increase in hospital psychiatric units, and later changes to mental health policy that brought global aims of deinstitutionalization into the Indian context. In many settings deinstitutionalization was already being tested by Indian doctors, who saw opening asylum doors and returning patients to families as a benefit to patients' well-being. Indeed, though large-scale shifts toward deinstitutionalization did not begin until later (in India and elsewhere), the beginnings of community care in India date to the 1950s and the experiments and innovations of specific doctors (Jain and Jadhav 2008).

During this period, psychiatric units in hospitals were expanded and psychiatry began to move more systematically beyond the asylums. The length of inpatient stays decreased, though according to observers, many families continued to see mentally ill family members as burdens (Jain and Jadhav 2008: 567), a view that meshed with philosophies of long-term institutionalization and limited patient-family interaction. In the 1970s, following new World Health Organization (WHO) guidelines, India embarked on incorporating psychiatry into basic health services, a process that would take several decades and far-reaching economic shifts to accomplish. Implementation of WHO policy had an ironic quality, however. Ongoing efforts in India to address a lack of basic provisions by building up infrastructure clashed with international goals of shifting mental health care out of specialized settings and into basic health provision; in other words, doctors in India were struggling to build up the structures being dismantled in other countries (Jain and Jadhav 2008: 569).

Soon, changes to policy would further question the value of large custodial institutions. In 1982, the new National Mental Health Programme (NMHP) explicitly stated the aim of promoting community participation. First implemented in Karnataka in 1984, the NMHP was not particularly successful in its early years, lacking both funding and "clear objectives" (Jain and Jadhav 2008: 573). In 1987, the Mental Health Act replaced the Indian Lunacy Act of 1912, though much of the original language remained. New policies aimed to address abuses in the asylum system and shortage of practitioners, and formulas for overseeing institutions aimed to prevent forcible admission and long-term incarceration—hallmarks of the asylum era.

In India, deinstitutionalization did not mean the end of the asylums. Though names were changed and systems restructured, institutions remained. Testimony to Indian medicine's ability to reinvent itself, these edifices became centers for mental health care in India, vital and vibrant settings of treatment, research, and training. Restructuring began in the 1990s, when, following lawsuits over abuse and poor treatment, mental hospitals were restaffed, reorganized, and given new models of treatment, and their relationship to the state was modified, if not entirely severed. These former asylums became sites to train doctors in efforts to respond to scarcity, and new hospital faculty attempted to reunite "dumped" patients with families. At the same time, as such flagship institutions were few and far between, burdens intensified for hospital psychiatry wards and, as general medical infrastructure grew (though slowly), mental health was increasingly located in the domain of primary care. Economic liberalization and the restructuring of health care meant the appearance of more private facilities catering to mental health.

New policies have not necessarily meant new realities. According to critics, community psychiatry in India remains "a top-down endeavor" with little interest in local practices (Jain and Jadhav 2008: 562). Mental health care is highly diverse or, one might even say, patchy. Most cities have a dire shortage of psychiatrists but no lack of other practitioners, legitimate and otherwise, willing to treat psychiatric ailments. Alongside general practitioners, these include other medical specialists, pharmacists, and uncertified practitioners. A range of options and standards offers a bewildering field of more and less accessible opportunities, even as psychiatric facilities are few. The research and teaching institutions housed in the old asylums are heavily attended and often overcrowded, as are psychiatry wards in government hospitals. It is not unusual to hear of large outpatient clinics seeing up to five hundred patients per day. At the same time, private clinics may lack patients and struggle to survive. Transitional residency and day care structures are all but absent for those lacking support networks or requiring more intervention than families can provide. In this context, patients and families may see multiple doctors in the course of seeking treatment. What some might describe pejoratively as "doctor shopping" may in fact be careful and extensive efforts as families navigate a complicated and uneven system.

One of the most striking features of contemporary Indian psychiatry is its overwhelming orientation toward pharmaceuticals. Received wisdom and most observation holds that drugs are by and large the only treatment offered or available (with some exceptions in larger cities and for more elite patients), and most prescribing is done not by psychiatrists but by doctors in other specializations or pharmacists. In most settings, psychotherapies remain out of reach for most patients due to lack of practitioners, time, and resources. However, in my observation, even in the briefest clinical sessions, microencounters oriented around diagnosing, prescribing, and tweaking prescriptions, doctors offer patients and their kin advice about how to change behavior, interact, cope with stress, and deal with difficulty. Though brief and piecemeal, something akin to nonpharmaceutical therapy is included in processes dedicated to prescribing.

Nonetheless, distress of varying levels of severity is treated with medication, and many drugs may be prescribed at once. High rates of prescribing are in part due to drugs' accessibility, relatively low cost, and wide availability due to lax regulation (Nunley 1996). Some psychiatrists I spoke with felt that drugs were more culturally appropriate for their patients, and that psychotherapeutics imposed Western ideas about the self and assumed daily realities incompatible with Indian life. For patients, drugs—and more of them—may be evidence of decent, attentive care and may seem to offer more immediately evident results (Nunley 1996).

In the heavy reliance on pharmaceuticals, observers have found traces of the asylum, asking what medications accomplish socially as they transform the chemistry of the body. Underlying these queries is a sense that drugs enact power systems on and through patients in the same way asylums once did, as forms of control, normalization and containment. In this view, drugs serve multiple purposes of governance in Indian psychiatry, regulating and enforcing ways of being. They may communicate medical authority or materialize knowledge systems for which there is no obvious or immediate cultural referent, establishing patients as subjects of knowledge politics in contests over who has the authority to know (Jain and Jadhav 2009). They may offer social belonging in impoverished settings in which people are portrayed by intervention schemes as "deprived" by lack of access to drugs (Ecks 2005). Psychotropics may be a way of maintaining order in households or coping with medical care of uncertain quality, critical and binding forces in "local ecologies of care" by which people negotiate material constraints while making sense of their worlds (Das 2004; Das and Das 2006).

Most importantly, drugs involve more than doctors and patients. Like all medical care in India, psychiatry is a family matter. Kin (or friends, neighbors, even coworkers) accompany people to the doctor, often speaking on their behalf, answering questions, and narrating histories. Two, three, even four people may gather around a patient, producing stacks of carefully folded prescriptions, slips of paper that offer histories of care and family life. Family members may purchase drugs for a patient, manage medications, and interact with doctors on the patient's behalf. As pharmaceuticals enter social worlds, new ways of being a family, new kinds of bonds, and new forms of intimacy emerge. A father's careful management of his daughter's complicated regimen of antidepressants, anxiolytics, and vitamin supplements may be part of their daily routine; a wife's administering of drugs to her elderly husband may extend the care she has offered through decades of meals prepared and served; a son may describe the time he takes away from work to purchase the right medications as a way of protecting bonds of reciprocity with his mother.

The same is true of inpatient care. Medicine in many settings depends on the presence of kin. In government hospitals, families stay on the wards with patients. One person may stay at night, another may come in the morning, yet others may gather in the afternoon, preparing and bringing food and taking care of daily needs. In former asylums and private clinics this is less likely to be the case. Families may be permitted only during visiting hours and contact may be limited for therapeutic as well as practical reasons. The role of families in patients' lives and care is, like so much in Indian psychiatry, enormously variable, making different medical settings vastly different social scenes. In some cases, people are separated from family, in others family dramas are relocated to the clinic.

Also plural are ways people think about what it means to suffer, understand affliction, and seek to heal it. Indeed, in my observation, except for doctors, people seldom experience psychiatry as distinctly Western or see it as conflicting with other models of care. Many who come to clinics also seek the services of religious practitioners, visit Hindu temples and Sufi shrines, and integrate religious frameworks into their understanding of distress (Flueckiger 2006; Corin, Thara, and Padmavati 2004). Though faith-healing centers come under scrutiny in government efforts to rationalize healing, for sufferers religious contexts exist unproblematically alongside the idea that healing comes via needles and pills (Fabrega 2009; Halliburton 2009).

At the same time, conditions in outpatient psychiatry demand approaches best described as pragmatic (others have used this term as well, extending it into an ethical model for care; see Sousa 2011). In the government clinic where I worked, time was short and facilities ranged from the air-conditioned offices of higher-level physicians to the dusty rooms of the outpatient clinic, with broken furniture, erratic electricity, and no running water. In similar settings across India, a consulting physician might see more than one hundred patients per day, in minutes-long sessions with time only for prescribing and confirming diagnoses. Residents may see fifteen to twenty-five patients per day in sessions lasting anywhere from ten to forty-five minutes. Here, diagnosis takes a backseat to treatment and matters more in the training of doctors and in legal cases than in doctor-patient interactions. It is often considered to be less important that patients understand the name or cause of their illness, except in rare cases. They are more often reminded, "Just as you will have to wear your glasses for the rest of your life, so you will need to take these drugs," than they are instructed in the biological nature of their illness.

While such practicalities may be related to a lack of resources, they leave room for techniques that involve the family in reshaping the selfhood, desires, expectations, and social behaviors of patients. Doctors, nurses, and residents may encourage patients to return to established orders and hierarchies, seeing social performance as an indicator of wellness and a way of coping with things beyond one's control. Though potentially constraining, this approach demonstrates doctors' recognition of the limits of biomedicine for patients in straitened circumstances. It suggests they are aware that in challenging social worlds, learning to live with constraint may be the most accessible route to wellness. Many said as much to me. Even though doctors' efforts may be driven by practicality rather than ideology, restoration of the very social norms that generate distress for women in vulnerable kinship positions is one of the less forgiving effects of pragmatic medicine.

In north India, then, at the end of the asylum, psychiatry in all its avatars is a form of intimacy and of the mechanics of kinship. This is so whether it involves inpatient or outpatient care, drugs or behavioral modifications. Just as family involvement differs from setting to setting, the stakes of mental illness vary, as do crises. Diagnoses tend to cluster differently in varied settings, especially where women are concerned. With different diagnostic paradigms—different diseases and explanations and ideas about cure—come different ways of thinking about and involving families, ideas about love and its breakdowns. In the large government clinic many young women, married and unmarried, were diagnosed with dissociative disorder, an ailment clinicians casually referred to as "hysteria." These women were treated with pharmaceuticals and subjected to disciplinary techniques involving spouses, parents, and in-laws, who were instructed not to respond to their demands. Few such diagnoses were made in the private clinic. This presentation rarely appeared. More often, young women were diagnosed with depression and treated with medication and little advice about family involvement. At the same time, the long-term involuntary commitment that occurred in the private clinic was all but impossible in the government hospital. Patients in the latter were not separated from their families, including young children, many of whom visited or even stayed in the ward. Many expressed the desire to stay *longer* in the hospital.

Where, then, do we find the end of the asylum? Where do we find its traces? It may be in departures from, rather than linkages to, what we know to be true about the kind of power, social control, and system of care that the asylum represented that we find ourselves entangled in the instabilities of love, medicine, and narrative. Indeed, rather than the battening down of social mores that the nineteenth- and early twentieth-century European asylums offered, the complexities of contemporary psychiatry and family life show medicine's role in social lives to be multiple and contradictory—to offer possibilities as well as constraints. It may be the case that to begin to understand contemporary crises of caregiving we need to look beyond the asylum as a ground for critique, beyond the question of its persistence as a system of discipline, a model for knowledge practices, and an symbol of the regulating of norms. Or it may be that the history of the asylum in India and things particular to contemporary psychiatric practice in a pluralistic setting tell us something about madness other than that psychiatry is, first and foremost, a way of enforcing what society views to be "normal."

Beyond South Asia, women's madness holds a central place in the history of this question—that is, the question of psychiatry's place in systems of power. Medicine's attention to hysterics, psychotics, neurasthenics, and other "madwomen" has illuminated social anxieties about changes in family life and gender norms and the social and economic structures that buttress both. Seen as a bellwether of cultural change, women's madness has been explored by historians for what it reveals about sexual politics, gender ideals, concepts of biology, labor patterns, and notions of rationality (Showalter 1985; Lunbeck 1994; Gilman et al. 1993).

What this history shows is that scrutiny of intimacy is nothing new to psychiatry. Indeed, women's intimate lives have been focal in psychiatry's early history and its formation as a profession and scientific discipline. Love, sexual desire, and women's place in families have long been seen as the source and result of distress for female patients. This was, of course, true for Sigmund Freud and Josef Breuer's iconic hysterics as well as for women who, prior to Freud, entered Jean-Martin Charcot's Parisian clinic and were displayed and photographed in often erotic rigors and contortions. Matters of agency were also concerns for the less-renowned women diagnosed with hysteria in the early twentieth-century United States (Lunbeck 1994). Indeed, throughout the twentieth century, even after shifts from psychoanalytic to neurochemical models and treatments, psychopathology for women remains negotiated in terms of family life (Metzl 2003). This is so in spite of received wisdom to the contrary—that pharmacologically oriented psychiatry separates people from their social contexts and personal histories, rendering them biological bodies to be chemically tinkered with. As scholars have found, popular representations of mental illness, drug advertisements, and even clinical records show mental illness to be deeply gendered in precisely these terms, with women's ailments represented in terms of their effects on intimacy (Metzl 2003).

In India, a prominent critique of psychiatry's treatment of women echoes the formulas described above but in terms of Indian cultural realities. In this view, clinical structures share with families and religious systems the work of enforcing women's subordination. This is seen as accomplished within the household and via medical diagnoses and treatments as well as by separating women with mental illnesses from the "normal" society that they may be viewed as threatening. Such critiques see contemporary, outpatient-oriented and pharmacologically driven psychiatry as continuous with asylum-based systems, and medicine's newer disciplinary effects on female patients as continuous with the problem of "dumped women," though in new and perhaps less vivid incarnations. In this view, Indian psychiatry serves the interest of protecting families from the contagion of women's mental illness (seen as threatening the marriageability of a woman's sisters or offspring) and removing faulty or shameful elements from kinship networks. Seen as an extension of the triaging practices of global medicine in an era of profit-driven pharmaceutical production and medical care, psychiatry engages families in the work of making people discipline themselves, by way of the body and its biology and according to unspoken, or quietly spoken, ideas about what is moral or right.

Through drugs, management of inpatient stays, and family involvement in care, psychiatry becomes entangled in intimate life. The regulation of rules of intimacy is among its effects, amplifying existing domestic politics and making households "always on the verge of becoming the political" (Das and Addlakha 2007: 128). In this sense, what Paul Rabinow (1999) described as "biosociality"—new social configurations that emerge on the basis of a shared biological identity—extends citizenship into the home, "the sphere in which the family has to confront ways of disciplining and containing contagion and stigma" (Das and Addlakha 2007: 129). Such contagion and stigma are seen as particularly acute for women, requiring the family to discipline those who defeat the purposes of kinship, as women with mental illness often do.

Such disciplining is seen as putting Indian religious and kinship structures in collusion with medical systems, meaning that, in evaluating women's afflictions, psychiatry not only reduces familial or social control of women to individuated crises of loss and thwarted desire; it enforces systematic control of women in culturally familiar terms that align religion (often Brahmanical Hinduism), kinship, and biomedicine in the name of healing (Davar 1999). Thus, contemporary Indian psychiatry is seen as sharing with the family the task of separating out the "defective" (Addlakha 2008) in ways that bring kin structures and cultural ideals in line with more universal-seeming biomedical efforts to enforce normality (means that appear acultural but that represent a cultural system par excellence). This critique sees psychiatry as serving the interest of creating and disciplining ideal mothers, wives, and daughters, and involving families in the work of enforcing social norms by enforcing ideas about the self in biological terms.

This argument echoes Foucault's sense of the relationship of family to asylum in nineteenth-century medicine. In these terms, the crisis of dumped women is not unlike the domestic disciplining of gender through psychiatry in which women treated for mental illnesses become subjects of governance. Their situation can, in this reading, be compared with contemporary settings represented as epitomizing global economic and social conditions, private medical institutions that are sites for governing bodies, desires, and subjects. In these spaces, a public health logic oriented around population-based matters of contagion, one making use of neutral-seeming scientific language, intersects with pharmaceutical companies' ever-growing needs for profit, with the effect of producing "zones of social abandonment," spaces to which those deemed unfit for humanity are relegated to die (Biehl 2005). Through the weeding-out work of the family, certain medical institutions perform the work of biopower, a form of governance in which the lives of some will be fostered while the lives of others are disregarded to the point of death (Foucault 2003a; Biehl 2005).

While accounts in this book resonate with these arguments, on closer look they also show their limits, especially where women are concerned. The lives described here, in the way they hold together as "cases" and in the ways coherence comes undone, demand we look elsewhere than the history of the European asylum and contemporary appearances of the kinds of power and scrutiny it established. Many of these accounts involve clear crises—forms of suffering, constraint, and isolation that were generated as much by efforts to care for and treat as by illnesses themselves. But these crises are not (or not only) explained as the outcome of knowledge systems creating subjects to measure and regulate, or the exclusion and containment of lives deemed not worth living. They require other explanations and raise the question of whether the relationship of the family to psychiatry that Foucault identified for nineteenth-century France is adequate for understanding contemporary global psychiatry.

This question might seem overly embedded in disciplinary debates were it not for the fact that critical languages deriving from it have created ethical languages that appear to offer universal applicability. Trenchant critiques of global economies of care in late capitalism provide a means for unpacking tenets of liberal humanism and efforts to enforce medical ethics in their terms, exposing, for example, the way languages of consent produce new subjects for exploitation even as they claim to offer protection from harm (Petryna 2009). Explicating ethical languages as products of power arrangements is important work. But models emphasizing the normalizing and exclusionary effects of medicine and scientific knowledge, while they may illuminate some aspects of women's lives in India, and undo the inviolability of ethical languages, nonetheless do not fully account for the situations I found in Moksha and elsewhere. There, lives reckoned through clinical attentions and labors of kinship at once exceeded and failed to live up to the biopolitical paradigm and the idea that power structures work to regulate notions of humanity.

It may be the case that many clinical efforts reach for but ultimately evade disciplinary practice. Fields of power and authority, and people's habitations of them, are seldom complete or seamless. Psychiatry's disciplining effects, like those of families and the legal structures that enable them to form, unform, and reform, may be imperfect, partial, and limited. Their plurality may tell us something, too, about the different systems of authority with which people—doctors, patients and families—contend. In north India, psychiatry's "incommensurable and antagonistic vocabularies of the self" (Pandolfo 2008: 330) give stakes and shape to clinical practice; these grammars emerge in the convergence of legal and clinical structures, and they are found in different patterns of care. At a basic level, in seeking attention for affliction people in India move through multiple spaces. Just as the structure and feel of each setting may be different, the role of diagnosis may also vary or the family may have different responsibilities. Different clinical settings also involve different ideas about what it means to be a person, and different demands on being in the world. They demand different choreographies of social interaction, patterns of sensation, ways of moving a body. And they involve different systems of meaning and authority—legal structures related to marriage, policies that situate mental illness differently, for-profit medicine versus government health care, the practice of medicine yoked to or unyoked from doctor training.

Medical multiplicity is not only conditioned by different settings in a vastly pluralistic system of care, it is also evident in what Annemarie Mol (2002) refers to as "the body multiple," different visions of the body within a single clinical location. This places patients at the intersection of discourses, forms of authorization, and kinds of truth. In psychiatry, it has been observed, understandings of personhood are plural, divided between neurochemical and psychodynamic visions of illness and healing (Luhrmann 2000). In India, many elements override this basic duality, making psychiatry far from monolithic, making it instead a complex map of personhood, bodies, and brains; ideas about what it means to be a person, a citizen, a man, a woman, and what it means to love, to desire, or to care for. Different settings offer if not incommensurable visions of the self then ideas that diverge, especially around the ways truth, desire, sexuality, and madness are connected to each other. They especially do so when patients are women. As well as condensing and enforcing visions of normative subjects—what it means to be human, what it means to be a man or a woman—medicine is also part of the undoing of ideals and norms. Furthermore, the process is inevitably incomplete. Where clinical practices seem to encourage social norms, they often also fall short of accomplishing their enforcement, sometimes by design and other times by accident, leaving open matters that might be closed, rendering uncertain identities that could just as easily be stamped with a label. This is both to the benefit and detriment of patients. Medicine may create subjects, but it may not do so consistently or even fully. It may involve points at which subjects break down as well as those in which they are shored up; it may create gaps in legibility by way of which complicated cases fall out of attention. And it may involve the way awareness of the messiness of life does something quite different than pathologize, creating zones of quiet acceptance as well as new sites for the expression of power. Here, dissolutions of love are part of the shape of affliction and caregiving, especially in a setting where love and madness are seen as always a bit intertwined.

Following from these general observations, and finding a way through the differences, contradictions, and points of uncertainty, the following chapters settle at the points at which craziness is part of love, all relationships threaten to go to pieces, knowledge (of self and others) is incomplete, intimacy begets constraint, and freedom can be as much alienating as longed for. In so doing, they make two main points.

First, contemporary clinical practice in India may not so much manage "abnormality" or remove "defective" people from society as negotiate dissolutions and the inherent vulnerabilities of kinship. This happens in terms that have less to do with categories of knowledge—the grids of normality that underscore diagnostic labels—than with conditions intrinsic to intimate life. These conditions involve the everyday plasticity of love and the fact that suffering can, indeed will, come along with it. And they include an inevitable sense of constriction that comes with the kinds of care and exchanges of desire, labor, things, and affection that bind husbands to wives, parents to children, and siblings to each other. In all of this, kinship (and gender) is revealed as being less a stable ideal that medicine operates to uphold than something which, like the selves in its midst, always threatens to go to pieces.

In other words, Indian psychiatry's attention to women involves clinical practices that tend to land on the space at which kinship falls apart, and attends to, as well as creates, different ways of inhabiting that space. Divorce is important to this picture, conceptually and in practice. Rather than simply demarcating normative conjugality, divorce is important to understanding how psychiatry works as a social force, but not because it is deemed something aberrant or wrong (though those things are also true). Divorce is important for what it reveals about the ways the vulnerability of relationships accumulate for women, and the ways medicine's palliative work plays a role in mitigating or underscoring, even enhancing, those vulnerabilities. Involving "unclear [rather than 'nuclear'] families," divorce is a means by which kinship and the self in its midst become "recombinant"—something whose ongoing work is in the remaking (Strathern 2005: 26). In other words, when thinking about the way relationships enact or establish selves in cultural terms, thinking with divorce makes it difficult to put the family at the center of analysis: "the family dissolves but kinship remains" (Strathern 2005: 26, citing Bob Simpson 1994). Kinship is not synonymous with "family," and an understanding of how medicine, as one of many forms of relief, one of many kinds of power, shapes selves and relations, may allow us to find more ideology and less social complexity in thinking with "the family" than in thinking with bonds that are constantly unmade and remade. This work of kinship happens in and through science and medicine as much as in households, weddings, divorces, births, and deaths. In asking how science and kinship share ways of knowing based on relations (Strathern 2005), I see in north India that the work of exploring relations is part of both intimate and clinical technique, kinship and medicine, setting the extent and limits of love in terms that involve, but are never entirely encompassed by, the governing of subjects. Clinical techniques—including diagnosis, electroconvulsive therapy (ECT), pharmaceutical prescription, and behavior modification—navigate the always mutable quality of attachment. They position intimacy and kinship as malleable. Clinical practice moves through flows of desire that are never entirely abnormal.

My second argument suggests that in order to understand these processes—unmaking relationships, inhabiting dissolution, bearing vulnerability—as sites in which crises and new forms of suffering emerge and are addressed, we must revise the ethical terms typical of global psychiatry. This returns us to our initial paradox, and to the core of this set of (often conflicting) accounts. For one thing, Indian psychiatry (like psychiatry anywhere) involves entities other than the individuated, self-managing subjects of disciplined life imagined within the frame of biopower (Rose 2007).

These are persons whose rights must be examined in light of multiple ways of attending to suffering (Das 1996). Looking at the possible and impossible subjects that emerge when structures of power and intimacy overlap in settler colonies, Elizabeth Povinelli observes that subjects at the crux of different regimes engage in ongoing "experiments" in selfhood, determining "which forms of intimate dependency count as freedom and which count as undue social constraint" (2006: 88, 3). In this triangulation, the subject of governance is on a continuum between poles of freedom and confinement, and abandonment becomes an inevitable outcome of neoliberal systems of governance, those that demand individuation yet depend on logics of race, sexuality, and the measure of human worth. Likewise, languages of "voluntary consent" and "involuntary commitment" place individuals on a spectrum between freedom and constraint based on criteria such as risk and rationality, while evaluations of institutionalization imagine patients on a continuum between integration and abandonment.

What I found in my shadow life in India, both in my own unraveling heart and in the dissolution and remaking of lives around me, was something askew in this (nonetheless powerful) arrangement of ideals—freedom and confinement, abandonment and care. Women, families, clinicians, and I were involved in struggles that distorted the exhausted dichotomies by which ethical decisions are so often evaluated—pitting freedom against constraint and care against abandonment. Instead, abandonment was less an eventuality of the governance of intimacy or clinical knowledge operations than a blurry field of everyday acts of loving, caring, treating, and being. In vital work, we grappled with the inextricable nature of freedom and abandonment, as with collapsing differences between care (or integration, or belonging) and constraint. Such work consisted less of finding a place between opposed categories, good or bad, than inhabiting the times and spaces in which different possibilities converged. Decisions were made and crises small and large were created and dealt with at the points at which differences between care and constraint were indeterminate, freedom bled into abandonment, and vice versa. In some cases, the explanation of abandonment gave people liberty to enact inordinate control ("her family has abandoned her, therefore we must keep her here"); in others, an understanding of conditions of restriction justified the explicit reassertion of hierarchies as part of treatment ("we can't change cultural realities that affect women, so it is better they learn to live with them"). All of this—everyday practices among women and their lovers, kin, and clinicians—involved a shared choreography, the building of lives at the crux of blurred categories. This was work of both intimacy and clinic. It bore multiple and contradictory histories of governance in which female subjects might be established as independent or inherently related to others—families, religious bodies, groups—or their voices rendered capable or incapable of telling the truth about their own pasts. Just as lives came undone and were reknit, so certain conceptual boundaries were constantly remade. Indeed, this happened at points of dissolution, when relationships came undone and vulnerabilities compounded.

This was a deeply gendered equation. For women in north India, the borderlands between (and meeting places of) freedom and abandonment, care and constraint, are dense with vulnerability, rootedness, and meaning. Thinking about gender and about kinship, is, then, essential for thinking about the relationship of culture to medical ethics, even in a world connected by global medical paradigms and broad biopolitical arrangements.

In other words, in north India, psychiatric care may unfold less according to the dichotomies of evaluation that underpin global ethical models for, say, involuntary commitment or informed consent, than through practices attentive to the mutabilities of love, the stresses of being a self in relation to other selves, and the ways relationships depend on other relationships (a woman's relationship with her children, for example, hanging on her relationship with her husband and his family). These are choreographies that include clinical technique. They also involve long-recognizable matters of everyday life and love in households, particularly for women. This is something we know from the things women say, sing, and recite to each other in poetry, storytelling, songs, and jokes that cross religious and expressive traditions. Here women negotiate the relationship of love to constraint in conditions in which solo living is understood to constitute abandonment rather than independence, in spite of opportunity-expanding changes in lives and laws. Mental illness adds vulnerability to the already—and inherently—vulnerable condition of kinship. The vicissitudes of love come with high stakes.

Though it may seem to take us beyond kinship and medicine, another kind of instability—the instability of narrative—is important to consider on the path to finding, in all of this, shards of and possibilities for an ethic adequate to the events that appeared before me.

Up to now I have referred to women's stories. But to call them stories or to emphasize their coherence is to miss what may be among their most important messages to us—that stories can fail to hold together, and that there are things to be learned in the specific ways they fall apart. Stories can be changeable and unfinished, imperfect and power-laden; the truth they reference may be elusive. It is by now easy to recognize that medicine uses the power and performativity of its language to create truth as much as reference it, often in the interest of powerful agents and structures of meaning. Other features of language are perhaps less obvious but nonetheless essential to clinical life, involving patients' reflections, kin's reporting, doctors' narratives, and determinations with legal bearing.

In the chapters that follow, many people say many things about love and affliction, women, family, and mental illness, often reaching for a truth that is less than obvious. This includes patients, of course, but it also includes husbands, children, parents, in-laws, neighbors, doctors, ward attendants, social workers, psychologists, and an anthropologist—the troubled participant-observer busy telling her own stories. As I reflected on many of these moments of telling, coherence felt just out of reach and truth bafflingly elusive. Not only did content and meaning depend on the perspective and agendas of those who spoke—a *Rashomon* effect—but their finality was often temporary and pragmatic, a patchwork effort at best, or a figment acknowledged as such by those involved. Yet, narrative bore vital—at times unbearable—consequences. The stories people told offered source material for diagnosis, or gave heft to a legal claim, or determined freedom of movement in the world. Like all stories, they had cracks beneath—and occasionally on—their surfaces. This was true for the stories doctors told about patients, family members told about each other, women told about themselves, and I now tell about all of them. These lives, and the wary accounts I have tried to build around them, show us that narrative is unstable, stories are loaded, and often, if not always, insufficient, especially in the places where they mean so much.

Narrative has an important place in medical anthropology's understanding of clinical practice, experiences of suffering, and trajectories of healing, dying, and making peace with things as they are (Kleinman 1988; Mattingly 1998, 2008; Garro and Mattingly 1994; Good 1994). Following Paul Ricoeur's concept of emplotment, in which "the structure of human temporality itself, of life in time, is fundamentally related to the structure of narrative because both of these are tied to the structure of the plot" (cited in Mattingly 1998: 812), narrative is seen as ordering, providing meaning, stitching the contingencies and experiences of affliction to every-day life, and offering people who are suffering, as well as their caregivers, plans for proceeding into uncertain futures. Narrative's role in illness and healing relates to a more basic principle—"We make as well as tell stories of our lives and this is of fundamental importance in the clinical world" (Mattingly 1998: 811).

Accordingly, narratives apply structure to events, ordering the chaos of "one damned thing after another" into a meaningful trajectory (Kleinman 1988: 124), making those experiencing illness "archivists researching a dis-organized file of past experiences" (Kleinman 1988: 48). Such ordering cre-ates meanings. It makes things make sense. At the same time, it provides people with a sense of time and of cause and effect, a sense that there are beginnings and endings. For Arthur Kleinman, it is through narrative that "illness becomes embodied in a particular life trajectory" (1988: 31), and people—sufferers, doctors, and kin—enmesh experiences of suffering into the flow of lives. At the same time, narrative frames morality; it allows people to create and draw on the things most immediate to them to eluci-date the spaces, meanings, and life-worlds in which "what really matters" becomes clear (Kleinman 1988, 2006).

Where narrative can offer form, structure, plot, and meaning, it can also be open-ended and uncertain, extending the "subjunctive" quality of illness and healing into the everyday work of meaning making (Good and Good, 1994). Narrative can point to uncertainties as well as batten down the meaningful, it can be "suggestive rather than definitive of meaning," ever available for "new uses" and involving movements that need no "goal or denouement," a "back and forth, to and fro" movement that make even goal-oriented stories end in incompletion (Jackson 1989: 18). Storytelling is inherently interpretive, a hermeneutic process "organizing our desires and strategies teleologically" (Good 1994: 139) while depending on the con-text in which it unfolds. It can reflect misperceptions and misunderstand-ings as much as the approach to knowledge of self and others (Mattingly 2008).

Uncertainty and openness may be the nature of narration. But ambigu-ity and an asymptotic reach for truth can also be products of power ar-rangements. That is, both the knowable and unknowable are produced by the structures that make meaning possible, including knowledge structures, systems of scientific understanding, legal paradigms, and kinship structures. There is an urgency, even ethics, in accounting for these processes and spaces—the ambiguities stories play upon, the processes and structures that create *un*certainty, contradiction, and ambiguity, and the nature of that which lies at the edges of perception, which "no longer belongs to knowledge" (Derrida 1994: 5). There is certainly something of this in many of the accounts I encountered—stories that contain seeds of their own undoing, plays of shadow and light in which some things are rendered unknowable at the same time that a certain truth is produced. And in clinical settings devoted to dissolutions of minds, where so much about intimacy and emotion mattered so deeply, I sensed over and over that some things and some kinds of truth were not knowable in any given idiom. The basic unknowability of a situation signified different things. In some cases it indicated the clash of regimes of gender and ideas about suffering. This seemed especially true where sex—as sign of agency or victimhood—was part of the picture, but it touched on broader difficulties in traversing the quaking terrain between care and constraint. In other cases it signaled a basic elusiveness of the truth of intimacy. In others it was an effect of social arrangements and the physical spaces through which stories moved, or the unsteadiness of language. At times that unsteadiness was intentional on the part of doctors, who withheld information from patients, or of patients, who framed accounts with careful intention. At times it seemed to be an accident of settings. This was especially so in places where women were confined. At other times the unsteadiness of stories and storytelling had to do with the sheer unknowability of people, "subjects," who might only be accessed, like archival subjects, through others' accounts of them or the way their lives pressed contours into the lives of others. This was especially so in cases involving sustained florid psychosis. At yet other times I felt that doctors and patients shared an awareness of the performative nature of narrative, the ways people knew their stories to be overburdened with import and used departures from narrative conventions to make that fact clear. This seemed to me to be the case with diagnoses of hysteria or dissociative disorder, or in situations where abandonment may have also come with degrees of freedom.

While it might be tempting to call upon an analytic of "experience" here, it would take too much confidence to claim access to any such thing. Experience was not easily identified and was often overwhelmed by the messy matters of how one came to feel the things one felt or know the

things one knew (Desjarlais 1997). Across different kinds of narrative instability, stories both reached for and missed the "truth" about experience.
Their relationship to it was fragile. Experience, as a cultural category, emphasizes interior authenticity, obscuring the sensing aspects of being and
focusing on the singularity of truth, replacing epistemology with ontology
(Desjarlais1997: 12). The idea of experience coalesces into narrative
"through the rhythmic pacings of time," making stories the only means of
"grasp[ing] our lives" (Desjarlais 1997: 17). But often, language, with its
multiple patterns, agendas, and worlds of power and meaning, shows experience to be unstable and ways of being to fail to live up to the security of
narrative (Desjarlais 1997). As Robert Desjarlais observes, mental illness
does not lend itself to the sequences or plots of storytelling; it poses reality
in the "absence of narratives," through the inhabiting of "empty time,"
repetition of words and movement, and reflections "cued to episodic encounters" (1997: 23, 18).

This unease with narrative and my interest in its breakdown emerges
from the temporally elusive and sensorially crushing aspects of the spaces
in which I found myself. It surfaced in efforts to make out of scattered
memories, observations, and notes a lucid, connected account, in attempts
to find pattern in impressions that were unclear, uncertain, and contradictory. At each stage, I felt that stories failed me. Indeed, even questions failed
as accounts fell into irreconcilable pieces, neither/nor positions exposing
the limits of frameworks for understanding and limits to the knowability of
selves. Rather than resolving the failure of stories—my own and others'—or
finding a way to make things fit, I found it useful to settle into those points
of limitation, to ask what they exposed about breakdown and the rebuilding
of lives, about surviving love and loss.

For one thing, it is clear that there are some kinds of experience or
subject, some ways of moving through life and being a self that cannot be
accounted for in the languages at hand. For many women moving through
spaces of treatment, there was seldom a story to be told, particularly not
about experience or the creation of subject positions. Possible stories emphasized uncertainty. This book's meanderings at the edges of the lives of
others are intended to offer a sense of how and why certain ways of being
cannot be easily explained. In some ways, this has everything to do with
the sheer plurality of medicine, healing, and clinical possibilities, the "het-
erotopic" nature of medicine, that is, its "ensemble of spaces" and alle-
giance to different settings and movements through them (Foucault 1986:
22). At another level, difficulty accessing the truth about situations had to

do with the possibilities for narration allowed by love and its inherent violence; mental illness and its variations on speech, perception, and emotion; and clinical life and its brutal ambiguities.

A certain kind of truth, at once unstable and weighty, emerged in these kinds of language and attention. It became especially vivid when medical effort intersected with breakdowns in relationships. These were points of dissolution rather than consolidation. Psychiatry's attention to breakdowns created an epistemological situation that was also an ethical situation. This does not mean there was not something true contained in efforts to represent what happened. Rather, it was a truth in and of instability, in and of "distortion" (Devereux 1967). Clinical truths, legal truths, and kinship truths (as well as ethnographic truths) about women were produced on a ground in which the relationship of language to truth was especially unstable, and language was least stable at the points at which it mattered most— where diagnosis would determine the outcome of a court case, when an account of marriage informed diagnosis, in decisions about whether a person would be kept against their will in a locked ward for another week, or another month, or another year. There were clearly things that were true and knowable about these cases, but in practice they were less important, and less indicative of happenstance or crisis, than things that did not appear via direct gaze. These elements were less hiding in the depths than best viewed sidelong or at the interstices of accounts.

Medical languages and practices were as unstable as the words of the afflicted. Stories fell apart for doctors just as they did for patients and families. The unstable relationship of language to truth was there in the way doctors recognized the limits of their own diagnoses or the performativity of medicine, or in the way an inpatient might have only partial access to decisions about her release, or when decisions were based on inconsistent accounts. In these processes, what it meant to be a patient (and a woman, mother, wife, divorcée, daughter, etc.) was less established through scientific gazes than forever slipping out of view. There were some ways of being a person that were simply unseeable, people who were what philosopher Gilles Deleuze might call "invisible subjects" (1989: 8). The task then was not only to be attentive to their presence but to grasp the nature of their impossibility, the way invisibility was a product of social worlds, power arrangements, medical practices, and ideas about life and love.

So just as categories of understanding may line up differently in these instances (care versus abandonment, freedom versus constraint), a language is needed to characterize selves and stories other than one suggesting the ordering and orienting capacity of narrative. This language would be attentive to the catastrophic nature of discourse itself, not just of the things stories are meant to tell about; it would be attentive to the violence of narration—its ability to pin a person or events into place—as well as its open-ended possibilities for making selves. It would leave room for the disordering and disquieting capacity of speech, and expose words' ability to provide ballast as yet another source of vulnerability. But it would also be possible to take a moment of refuge in the words of Jacques Lacan (whose words seldom offer refuge), who corrects himself in an introduction to his work: "All I can do is tell the truth. No, that isn't so—I have missed it. There is no truth that, in passing through awareness, does not lie. But one runs after it all the same" (1978: vii).

For a long time I have been drawn to another, entirely different, story of catastrophe and dissolution, to a love story about entities (in this case, a woman) breaking apart. The goddess Sati, wife of Shiva, was insulted by her father's refusal to invite Shiva to his grand sacrifice and, in a fit of outrage, threw herself on her father's sacrificial fire. Shiva, disconsolate, took her body on his shoulders and carried her across the cosmos, leaving death and destruction in his path. The concerned gods sent Vishnu to follow him and slowly, piece by piece, slice Sati's body with his discus. Where the parts landed, temples blossomed. When Shiva was releived of his burden, he returned to meditation in his mountain abode and the cosmos returned to normal. The land became fertile again and was dotted with holy sites—a temple to the goddess's hand here, to her earring there, and, holiest of all, to her *yoni*, in a site in Assam where a vulvic cleft in stone runs red with sacred water at certain times of year.

Sati's later incarnation, Parvati, has also had a particular appeal for me. It may seem odd to find a patron for the lives in this book in a deity best known for being a good wife and devoted consort, a domesticating, if passionate, female force (Kinsley 1986). But in her wifely devotion, Parvati is also a godly embodiment of *viraha*, the agony of separation from one's beloved, a form of love that is intense suffering. She is often separated not only from Shiva (or his attentions) but also from her children, through her own rejections and by the decisions of others. She is abandoned and abandoning, embraced and embracing, fearful and fearsome, and her avatars can be both those who are mad, and those who cause madness (Kinsley 1986). But more to the point, Parvati, like Sati, appears in mythology and verse as a woman in pieces. Parvati's splitting is also generative, but it takes different forms from Sati's. She often breaks into her opposing parts, benevolent and devouring, demon and goddess, dark and light, beautiful and ugly. As a singular entity, she is pushed to wild and devastating acts by her love for Shiva, by suspicion and anger at his frequent betrayals and infidelities (Wendy Doniger calls Shiva a "goddessizer," rather than a womanizer; 2000: 17). In another kind of dissolution, Parvati is often not herself. She is constantly shape-shifting, becoming an altogether different kind of entity, or being impersonated by others seeking to dupe Shiva. Demons, gods, and temptresses impersonate her, and she them, becoming a hag here, a maiden there, often to reunite with Shiva, or deceive him. In these transformations, too, she moves across poles of sanity and stability, kindness and destruction. As Doniger puts it, Parvati is "a woman divided against herself, or rather a woman forced by her husband to divide herself into her polarized halves" (2000: 71).

It has been ambiguous to me whether these stories tell us of incompatible and imposed components of womanhood (the things women are and must—impossibly—be, according to cultural schema), or whether these are inevitable things about being human, or relating to others, wild transitions we all dabble in. Either way, Parvati is a set of divine conditions related to love and marriage, attachment and separation, the most notable of which, for me, has been her dissolution and reconstitution, her shape-shifting and constant encounter with misrecognition, her thwarted connections and efforts to connect, and her suffering in love, even the highest sort. This may be an unorthodox reading of Parvati, and perhaps I overly personify her to meet my own needs, but there is something recognizable here in these conditions of flux and their tumultuous results.

Parvati in no way represents madness or healing, insanity or sanity. Rather, it is in her capacity to fall to pieces, to become—wildly—one thing and then another, and to wreak havoc with cosmos-rattling love that I summon her. And it is the way she does these things her capacity as wife (or lover) and mother, because of the wildness and madness of love itself, that makes her a touchstone for me in forging through the lives represented here. That many of the women here are not Hindu matters little. I do not invoke Parvati to imply a religious identification or even, necessarily, a cultural thematic in *their* lives, but rather to suggest, as I might with a Shakespeare sonnet or a passage from Norse legend, a quality that resonates. What things might be learned about the specific circumstances of women with mental illness in India from an orientation toward this motion, this state of dissolution and the things that shape it?

And so, chasing what remains elusive about the lives of women I met, both when I was imagining myself a researcher and in the times when I was just Sarah, as well as in the moments when, in a hospital or on my rooftop balcony, I was lost to my own vertiginous groundlessness, I return to something more earthly and mundane, that is, to the main point of this book: that the care of women with various forms of mental affliction elicits shared labors and structured improvisations at the crux of categories that defy the liberal subject of conventional medical ethics. These improvisations and choreographies are of dire consequence. They demand an alternate ethical language and an alternate vision of the power dynamics underlying women's psychiatric care than one modeled on the asylum, that is, the one typically used to understand psychiatry as governance, discipline, and subject-making. This language involves an orientation toward dissolution and brokenness. Framing a critical and ethical language to account for the layered suffering involved in women's mental illness in India (and, I would imagine, anywhere) has been difficult precisely because that approach requires attention to the very instability of the language used to frame it. Yet it is essential that an account of women's psychiatric care—and perhaps all forms of care and cure—leaves room for these tremors.

This book, and the self-undoing stories within it, is about women and mental illness in India. It is also about what it is possible to know about mental illness, what it is possible to know about intimacy and persons, and what conditions for knowing are established and foreclosed by clinical arrangements. It is about the way these arrangements involve the work of undoing kinship even as they are informed by what are known to be the inherently undoing effects of love. And it is about what it is possible and impossible for language to tell us under these conditions of finding, knowing, and treating, what can be gleaned from those impossibilities of knowledge.

Chapter 1

Rehabilitating Ammi

Here is all forest. Mother said outside is all forest. Here [ears] is forest; here [nose] is forest. The hands are forest. When I look at my hands I see this one is a forest, one, two, three, this is also forest, four, five. I look at my hands and I see them but I do not know what this face looks like.

In October, on the eighth day of the festival Navratri, Mrs. M. called Eve to her dining room. Today was Kanya Puja, a day to worship young girls as the goddess, to feed them sweet things. Instead of taking from our hands the leftovers of deities' feasts, they would eat first and we would take what they left.

The children had strung doll-sized banners of mango leaves under the eaves of the knee-high temple next to the driveway. A red streak of vermilion dashed the stone cobra inside. That morning I put on accordion music and French songs, mixed eggs and the creamy top of milk with chapati flour, and poured the batter on the iron pan used to make rotis. Lime juice and sugar crystals were rolled into crepes that looked like dosas and tasted like Paris. I ate what Eve did not finish.

Breakfast was interrupted by girls spilling out of the stairwell and onto our veranda. They took Eve to the front garden to gather platefuls of night-queen petals that had fallen overnight, putting some in the temple and bringing the rest to Mrs. M. She had made channa and puris, goddess food, to offer the girls, whom she called in one by one.

Everyday life in our Annexie was seldom banal; even long inactive stretches were filled with small events. Through all of it, Mrs. M. was an austere but loving companion. She was not a grandmother, neither affectionate Nani nor matriarchal Dadi. Our relationship was too formal for that. But neither was she Ma-ji or Mata-ji, terms, at once too removed and too intimate, used by her staff. "Auntie" did not feel right, either, though it would be suitable for any acquaintance a bit older than me. To both Eve and me, she stayed as she was when I first knew her, Mrs. M.

We had met years earlier when I came to the city as a graduate student. I had arranged to stay in a neighborhood at what I did not realize was the edge of the city, a dust bowl of construction sites. I had never been to this city before and was invited to be a paying guest by the mother-in-law of a student who had been in my Hindi class the semester before, someone I barely knew. It was a strange arrival. I thought I knew north India well, but this growing suburb was neither Delhi nor Bihar, my two coordinates. I had not yet learned the system of shared autos, buses, and rickshaws that would get me in and out of the city, and finding my way to a shopping area was an accomplishment. My room was through a half-finished part of the house, stubbled with open wires and unfinished brickwork. I felt surreal and isolated. My host, a poet, was friendly in the first days, but grew anxious and severe. In my recollections, she yelled at me, ranting about small things. In all likelihood it had not been that bad, but I suppose I was experiencing the shock of the new and was naive about certain adjustments. I'm not proud to report that I phoned the man who had met me at the train station—also a friend of a friend—and said, "Auntie is going mad." My language was too direct. He pretended he hadn't heard but said he would come by. (I wish I had taken more time and care to get to know her.) I found a taxi company and hired a car for the morning, taking along a printout of an email from a scholar I had never met who mentioned a guesthouse run by "a Brahmin widow near the cantonment." It turned out that she had meant someone different, but that scrap of information got me to Mrs. M.'s house, to a guesthouse in her large home in a neighborhood of old bungalows that was to be a sanctuary for years.

On my first visit with Eve, as work was slowed by the necessities of life with a four-year-old, Mrs. M.'s daily routine and ours mingled. Every morning, hearing the ring of the brass bell, Eve ran down from our flat to the household temple, where she joined Mrs. M. in prayer and song. Mrs. M. often called us to her quarters for lunch, and for tea at 5:30, as the sun dropped into gold heaviness and Eve ran in and out, sandals flapping in the hallway. She invited us to meetings, lunches, dinners, weddings, even an antique car rally in which we rode through the city in her 1930s Morris Minor, and Eve became a mascot at weddings held on her lawn. We were brought into her family's passages, its rites and celebrations, and taken to events—ladies' club gatherings, poetry readings, meetings of women's organizations, celebrations of one holiday or another. Some she thought would be useful for my work, others were only generally related. Her widowhood was busy, and the constellation of friends who visited, took her out, and checked in by phone was expansive.

So, too, Mrs. M.'s household was active even when empty of the foreign scholars and Indian businessmen who rented rooms around the fading Art Deco courtyard. Her staff lived with their families behind the house in a near-village bustling with children, visitors, animals, festivities, arguments, and shared and bartered labors. The children knew not to venture far into Mrs. M.'s house, though our apartment was always open to them and the empty corners made wide frontiers for exploration. Eve made a career out of expeditions through gardens full of roses and papaya trees, porticos run riot with bougainvillea. Angular concrete and plaster relief work grasped archways, the brick of the main courtyard was smoothed by feet, and new staircases and doorways revealed themselves daily as Eve found her way to parts of the house I did not know were there. In my searches for her, rooms I had assumed to be unconnected proved to be linked up; rooftops gave way onto other rooftops; balconies and half-indoor veranda rooms led into and out of small corners forgotten by everyone but boys in search of lost kites. In my absence, the grove of mango and papaya trees—a small, shady jungle behind the servants' quarters—was being replaced by looming five-story "VIP" apartments. I forbade Eve from following her new friends (and her curiosity) into the half-finished building, so instead she watched from our balcony as children climbed through the open levels and took baths from a spigot on the roof.

I was rebuilding a social world after a five-year absence. This included an unintentional remapping of the city. I knew its government offices, archives, shopping areas, and NGOs. But now, with Eve in tow, I wandered into other places—settings where women found food and four walls when they had nowhere to go. We went to Sufi shrines and their residential halls, rooms occupied by single mothers, widows, and divorced women, those with unwelcoming natal families or no kin. Here, women with unsteady minds, without husbands or households, or with a combination of these characteristics, collected like rainwater in dips of pavement. They taught in the shrines' schools; they cooked for the men who were its caretakers and healers; they spent long days in stillness. I was filling in a map of estrangement, one that fit certain conceptual and critical expectations in which kinship meant the peopling of life and a household was a location of belonging, while solitude and institutionalized living were things of brokenness. I would soon rethink this map.

On our second visit, a year later, I tried to connect with the housewives in our neighborhood (those in the now completed high-rises). We had little in common. I had slightly better rapport with the mothers at Eve's school, a small, Christian, English-medium school across the street, chosen for its proximity rather than educational merit. (I once asked Eve what they did all day: "We stand in lines.") At school, Eve filled notebooks with repetitions of Devanagari letters and multiplication tables and participated in art competitions sponsored by glue companies and consisting of challenges to see who could affix grains into picture outlines in the tidiest rows.

While I had brief but pleasant interactions with the mothers of these children, the women in my own neighborhood could not make sense of my decisions—to send Eve to this school, to allow her to play with the children of Mrs. M.'s staff, to go out on my own without a car and driver. After many hellos yelled across balconies, I had a few visits into the mysterious promised land of the "VIP apartment building" where I was told I should not let Eve play with the children who had become her kin in a world of imaginary relations, places, spirits, and rites—they were "dirty," they would teach Eve "bad habits." I should instead send her into their homes, whose back balconies looked down on the line of one-room servants' quarters where Eve's friends lived. There, indoors, she could "be safe," "be clean," "watch TV," and "be inside." They did not understand why I would let her run wild outside in a tribe of children whose mothers cleaned their floors.

But Mrs. M. and her extended network of friends, kin, and fictive kin were welcoming, if also opinionated. Though Mrs. M. and I spent many hours in conversation, ritually revisiting our days, I never did share with her the truth about my marriage, that my husband and I had separated, that I anticipated divorce. Though she was sympathetic and supportive about many aberrant things in my life, I also heard the disapproval in her voice when she spoke of divorced women. I couldn't bear the idea that such views might be used against me. I loved her companionship and adored her too much to risk that judgment.

Especially during the first phase of my time there, in which Eve was always nearby building her own little worlds, I found myself moving in and out of homes and families, talking to friends and friends of friends, and relatives of friends of friends, about my work, talking in ways that both were and were not research. Indeed, research felt out of reach. Stories were mostly secondhand, what I came to call caregiver narratives, or accounts of caregiver narratives, and felt loaded and partial. To what extent was any of it true? Where was it incumbent to verify an account, when could a story function as just a story? When was it OK to write down someone else's story, even if it was offered by one who was part of it, even if it was also another person's story?

Directing me to friends who had "someone like that" in their family, Mrs. M. and her friends suggested I "take the case" if someone mentioned a relative's mental illness. People mentioned another person's difficulties, suggesting that I talk with them or, more often, with a relative, advising me to use not only caution but deception, by introducing myself as researching another topic and then winding the conversation toward their medical history.

One woman was described to me by her friend as diagnosed with schizophrenia, always with "the same thought going around and around in her head." She had been to a psychiatrist but did not want to take medication. I was told I should phone the sick woman's sister but warned I should be careful not to say my "real purpose," because "in India people will be offended." I should offer my help because of my experience with "these things." This was not cold calculation—there was concern in the advice, not just for me but for the sick woman and her sister, herself suffering under the burden of care. Asking questions might be therapeutic, offering a person a chance to tell her story, to talk about herself.

I thanked them and put the phone number in my wallet, wondering what my university's human subjects review board would say about this tactic, but thinking also about the way deception, in this instance, contained elements of concern—attention without exposure, listening without naming.

Early in our first visit, when Eve still thought that speaking heavily accented English amounted to speaking Hindi, Mrs. M. summoned us for lunch and introduced us to Tulsi, the daughter of Colonel D., an army man like Mrs. M.'s husband, who came over from time to time to check on Mrs. M., bringing sweets and toys for Eve, whom he called "the dolly." Tulsi and

Mrs. M.'s families were connected by marriage, and they recollected together, retelling outrageous stories they had heard about notorious incidents and characters. With shared army lives came common histories of movement. While married life had meant a secure material existence it also brought difficulties—frequent moves, long trips, and being left to manage households of children, animals, visitors, and servants. They shared a vocabulary of terms and places reminiscent of an earlier era—clubs, cantonments, postings, and bungalows.

Tulsi was strikingly beautiful. Perched between understatement and elegance, she was exquisitely put together, soft-voiced, soft-edged, generous, and respectfully opinionated. Though hardly ten years older than I, she was settled into the comfort, authority, and aches of middle age, the mother of a son about to begin university. By contrast, I felt in myself the instability of extended youth. I was barely beyond my own schooling, in a childlike state of singlehood (in my travels if not yet my marital status), and dragging my child on long journeys. In terms of a female life scheme, I got the impression from many women that all of this was a bit embarrassing. But Tulsi did not judge, though later my unsettledness and impending divorce would concern her. These would be things she would give me sisterly advice about, things we would argue about.

Mrs. M. told Tulsi I was in India studying "women with mental problems" and introduced Tulsi, dropping into silent euphemism: "Her mother-in-law was one of these . . ."

Tulsi explained the dangerous facts differently. "Yes, Sarah"—she often used my name—"She was in Agra for twenty-seven years."

"They took her out of there," Mrs. M. said, with evident pride. "They rehabilitated her entirely."

Tulsi was modest, but spoke with a tone of wonder as though the events had happened weeks, not years, ago. "Well, Auntie, it was not easy, but yes, we did take her out. Sarah, you would not believe the change. She was nothing, like a worm, when she was in that place. She is a whole person now."

Tulsi's mother-in-law, whom most called Ammi (mother), had spent much of her adult life in a mental hospital in India. In the 1960s, after the birth of her second child, Ammi's condition deteriorated into depression and ultimately psychosis. She was diagnosed first with depression, then schizophrenia, and after a decade of treatments, her husband, Keshav, placed her in the Agra Mental Hospital, an old and notorious former asylum, where she stayed for twenty-seven years. Keshav divorced her, turning guardianship over to their elder son, Nishchal, who was at the time beginning his own military career, and then moved to England. In the 1990s, when Nishchal, now married to Tulsi, could withdraw from military service, he and Tulsi brought Ammi out of the hospital and, in their words, "rehabilitated" her. They built a comfortable home in a small city some distance from Delhi and installed Ammi there with a servant to care for her. Seeing medication as part of a pattern of addiction developed in the hospital, they took her off it, which settled her into florid psychosis. For Tulsi and Nishchal, Ammi was not "like a worm" in Agra because of her mental illness; schizophrenia was something very human and full of thwarted efforts to "connect." Rather, Ammi was reduced to "nothing" by the institution. Her wholeness after "rehabilitation" was in the flares and slow burns of her illness, not in spite of them.

Soon, Ammi's ex-husband, now returned to India, began staying at the house. Her bedroom was moved into the servants' quarters, where, though separate from the family's living spaces, she had a view of the mountains. About a year after I met them, Nishchal took a job overseas, and he and Tulsi moved away. They visited Ammi when they could.

Over the next several years, I spent a lot of time with Tulsi, Nishchal, and Ammi, but especially with Tulsi. These were visits in motion, pins on a map of north India as we met in different cities with people from both Tulsi's and Nishchal's extended families, in households that made up a large and complicated family history. Before Tulsi moved, we saw each other frequently. When I passed through Delhi, we met in restaurants or went shopping, talking about Ammi in the car between destinations. On one of these visits, I realized what a small world Delhi society is when I met a friend for coffee and discovered that not only had she dated Ammi's grand-nephew—for years hearing about "the crazy auntie in Agra"—but we had both gone to college with a daughter of one of Nishchal's cousins.

In the midst of this scenery of memory, but all but absent from it, was Ammi. Her life and story held together spaces, persons, and stories, even as her madness and movements pushed people apart to different homes and cities, to different versions of the past. Ammi was hard to know, difficult to reach though always present in one way or another. She stayed in the house Nishchal built for her with its marble floors and high ceilings, never cross-ing its gate into the neighborhood beyond but going to the rooftop to look at the hills. Though members of her extended family knew she lived there, she was more vivid to them as a feature of the past. As part of the present, she seemed less a person than a piece of a story.

I visited Ammi's home on a number of occasions. Its quiet cool and pristine comfort were a refuge from the city in which I spent most of my time. Though Ammi's ways of being, speaking, and moving sometimes frightened Eve, I found in them exhilarating challenges to my habituated ways of knowing, narrating, and remembering, and in Ammi's remarkable ways of interacting I felt connections and disjunctures at once beautiful and elusive. Eve and I slept in a room with a doorway to the backyard. Ammi often passed through on her way into the main house, leaving small offerings. An old greeting card, a book, a scarf, or a stone would appear on the bed and then disappear. We ate meals with Ammi when Keshav, referred to as "Nishchal's father" or "the Brigadier," or by Eve and me as "Uncle," was not there, and we were present alongside her, though not necessarily *with* her, as she moved through a forest of entities, memories, and sounds to which we had no access. On her passages through the household, a routine of movements with evident but indiscernible purpose, she paused to speak to a large portrait of Sai Baba, or hear what he had to say. During meals, she scolded it, telling him to stop bothering her while she was eating. She sat with us silently or conversed, answering questions in phrases surging from one place, person, and language to the next, through levels of scrutability rich with possible meanings and possible ways of making meaning. She spoke in a warp and woof of multiple languages—dialects from her childhood, Hindi, Urdu, and the elegant English that was evidence of a privileged education. Toothless, wearing an ill-wrapped sari and, in winter, a worn Mickey Mouse sweatshirt, hair pulled into a gaunt braid and a sag of skin on her aristocratic bones, she looked decades older than her years. I was repeatedly surprised to hear passages of nineteenth-century English poetry from a person whose body and attire suggested that such things should be incongruous.

Ammi's life story is vibrant, complicated, and rich with drama and characters. At one point early on, when it was proving difficult to find people to talk to or institutions to work in, I thought Ammi's would be the only story I would tell. Condensing it into a few pages is difficult and unsatisfying. There are volumes to say and lifetimes, generations, and cities to explore. In all of it, I was troubled by the question of whether and how this is, or could or should be, "Ammi's story." Here were multiple stories about lives experienced through another, a life dispersed into the lives of others, outlines coming in and out of clarity less as pieces of a larger whole than as overlapping sheets that refuse to be bound. To use a different metaphor, these stories did not unfold over time so much as fold and refold, origami-like, into different shapes at different points. Through their permutations, what was "Ammi's story" slipped in and out of view, just as what it meant to be a whole person, or a whole family, came in and out of focus. At times, it seemed that as I knew pieces of Ammi's story better, other parts would sink into haze, becoming less true or knowable as new elements appeared. It felt difficult to know the whole thing at once, difficult to see the mountainside for the trees upon it.

There was an ethical question in this too, present in the demands on truth and action raised at points at which narrative fell apart, points that involved a woman's mental illness and the unknowability of the subject at the story's center. There is an obvious conceit to this representation of Ammi as a cipher, knowable only indirectly: Ammi spoke. She spoke a lot. But I have, for the most part, carved around her most recent actions and words, rendered them with ellipses and gaps in description. I have reproduced vague habits, and events from the past described to me by others. The decision to trace Ammi in the accounts of others involved many things, not least of which was an ethical concern. Tulsi, Nishchal, and others felt it worthwhile to document their own lives in relation to Ammi. We could call these caregiver narratives, as I have suggested. But I am both unable and unwilling to render the text of Ammi's life as she voiced it, choosing instead to focus on the way other lives became meaningful through hers.

I am confident that Ammi understood and welcomed my presence in her family's life. Because her language and self-knowledge were conditioned by psychosis—a state considered, legally and in formulas for research ethics, to be of compromised rationality—it was not possible to locate an expression of consent in conventional terms. Of course, consent was already at stake in her life, its foreclosures part of what her life exposed, as were the vagaries of attention and disregard. Variations on these matters involved expansions and contractions of agency, desire, movement, and identity, and these were important to document. My decision to limit reproducing Ammi's words may entail a paternalistic—or arrogant—cordoning off of forms of self-knowledge and self-expression that might not map into normative grids—these include the dense opacity of Ammi's speech, its labyrinthine moves, its bodiliness. Regardless, in spite of my notes and observations, and in spite of the desire to tell Ammi's story—a desire I shared with Tulsi and Nishchal—I realized early that my concern had to be less with Ammi's story as such.

My interest, then, fell on the way other people's lives, other people's histories were formed by way of Ammi's. The movements of Ammi's confinement and rehabilitation were also theirs. They were especially part of Tulsi's marriage—a pattern in her story about herself and what it meant to be a wife in a comfortable, cosmopolitan family in north India, to become, at nineteen, bound to a new web of kin. Ammi's life was woven into family life in the way kinship was, more than a collection of histories or perspectives on the past, a series of relations and interactions, in which storytelling about Ammi was an important part. Her illness and movements brought people together, pushed them apart, and made them reevaluate the nature of family, care, and love for decades, though for most of that time Ammi was physically absent, a void at the center of a vortex.

Turning these histories into an account has been fraught in many ways. There are questions of its ownership, of the veracity of its parts, and of the interests, desires, and fantasies that go into framing it. Indeed, there is the question of its "itness"—its singularity. There is also the matter of the unreachability of its center, its subject. Ammi's life is knowable only in relief, in the contours of other people's stories. In them is the outline of a subject but not its presence, a pointillist self dispersed across the selfhoods of others, as all subjects may be, but here only knowable as such.

Four days after their wedding, Nishchal took Tulsi to Agra to meet his mother. Ammi had been living for nearly fifteen years in what was then called the Agra Mental Hospital. Visitors were not allowed into the yard or living quarters of patients ("inmates," Tulsi called them). Instead, they waited in a large shed. Nurses were slow to bring Ammi out, taking time, Tulsi suspected, to clean her up.

Nishchal introduced Tulsi as "your daughter-in-law, my wife," but Ammi interacted only with her Chitu, her little ant, as she fondly called her son. They brought gifts—mangoes and the sweets Ammi loved, stacks of new clothes to replace worn ones. That morning they had gone to a sari shop that sold the previous year's stock at reduced prices. They selected ikat patterns, cloth that was Ammi's favorite and didn't tear easily. Ammi responded to the offerings, then slipped back into her own world, pacing, singing religious songs, performing devotional rites in the air.

On their first visit, Tulsi was moved by Nishchal's distress. "He was sitting there with tears down his eyes for all those numbers of hours. We were there practically all day, and when we came out, I said, 'You know, she's not even all there.'

"He said, 'No, but maybe she knows, she's quite reassured that somebody came to see her and someone's there.'"

It surprised Tulsi to see Nishchal cry. She barely knew him; their marriage was "practically arranged," and she was still getting to know his family. "I was the new bride. What did I know? I was so stupid at that time, so young. I didn't feel disturbed by the place, just that it was very intense. I didn't come to see that something was wrong until much later."

Tulsi and Nishchal told their stories together and separately as we sat in the elegant drawing room of the home Nishchal had built. Sometimes Ammi joined these conversations, coming in and out with recollections and non sequiturs. These narrations were intimate recollections, momentary creations of companionship through skeins of the past. Tulsi's speech, full of pauses and quick diversions, was difficult to follow. There seemed something important in this, not in what it said about her psychology, but in the kind of telling it amounted to, the way it represented kinship as tenuous, something to be held together and pulled apart with words.

After Tulsi's initial visit, they continued to visit Ammi at least twice a year, depending on where Nishchal was posted, visits that were mandatory, Tulsi said, as Nishchal was Ammi's legal guardian.

The hospital was on a large campus, with wards arranged around open courtyards and much of daily life lived outside. It did not surprise Tulsi that Ammi referred to it as "the ashram."

"The place is quite nice," she said. "It's quiet. It's very spread out. It's not bad. But that's just the look of it. It's just an old, quiet place on the outside, but then you get inside, into the sections where the men are and the women are, the inmates. It's quite terrible. They are just lying there, and you see the attendants there yelling at them, '*Chelo*' [move it], and they just treat them like cattle. And what happened in the dorm, I don't know. I don't even know if she had a bed, or. . . . She was always dirty, her hair . . . I used to see her and think, my god . . ."

The institution's openness shaped daily life into a series of movements—gardens and pathways allowed routes for pacing. "Mom was very fond of walking, pacing, walking up and down, which is typically one of the things that symptomatic, schizophrenic people do. So she would pace up the walk, and she could almost walk for three hours a day. And that's why she's in physically very good shape. . . . And typically she had this habit of feeding the . . . , making friends with the animals."

Tulsi cut in, "Birds. The *pallu* [endpiece] of her sari would get eaten by rats and cockroaches and all sorts of things, so we had to say don't [keep food for the birds], not 'don't' but we had to get her out of that habit. But over there, always in her sari a *laddu* [sweet], she put it out for the squirrels and the birds."

In the mid-1990s, Nishchal took a study leave from the military and began planning for retirement, for a life bound to a single place. The mobility of army life, even for officers, had not been compatible with a dependent like Ammi. Now living outside of Delhi, Nishchal got their household in order, vacating tenants and expanding the living space. He began to talk about bringing Ammi out of the hospital. K. C. Dube, the head of Agra at the time of Ammi's admission (and a family friend), had first advised that Ammi be admitted. Though retired, he had been urging Nishchal to take Ammi home. Not only had thinking about care changed, but Ammi's disease had "burned itself out." It was no longer aggressive, and her current state was unlikely to change. Nishchal recalled, "That is the time, [Dube] says, that it's a great opportunity to bring out the patient and try to rehabilitate them and put them in as much of a natural environment as you can. There is nothing happening for her benefit in the hospital any more. So we said, 'Let's do it.'"

Tulsi said, "He was all the time going over there and the doctors were hounding him, saying, 'Look, she's your mother, you have to take her out, or we'll send her with a police escort and all.' You know, the humiliation. . . . And we were just not in the situation because of the postings, and the doctor was telling him, 'She needs open space, you can't put a person like this in a closed space or she'll just have a breakdown again.' So we were just trying to figure out what to do."

The idea of bringing Ammi home was causing fights between Nishchal and his father and brother. Both wanted Ammi to stay in Agra. Ammi's existence, once a widely shared but closed secret, would now be an open one, and breaches that had formed around the matter of her institutionalization would be exacerbated. Nishchal's father felt Ammi's presence would disrupt family peace. Nishchal recalled, "My dad was very worried because during the very aggressive part of the disease he was unable to have any sort of control over her, so he was worried about that, back to those sorts of times. And we all had no training in handling a patient like that."

After two decades, Keshav had returned to Delhi. In a poor emotional state, he "needed rehabilitation himself," Nishchal said. His father sided with Nishchal's younger brother, whom Nishchal blamed, along with his father, for institutionalizing Ammi. Keshav felt that the fact that Ammi did not recognize her younger son was caustic to the family. Nishchal's brother's attitude was understandable, he felt. But Nishchal blamed his father and brother for failing to try to "connect" with Ammi. Fights between the brothers took on new gravity as the small conflicts of family life were loaded with histories of blame and conflicting senses of responsibility. The brothers soon stopped speaking. In these arguments, an ethos of "connection" and "recognition" took shape, formed around the peculiar combination of presence and absence that was Ammi. These terms meant different things about family life to Nishchal and his father, differences that prescribed different actions.

Tulsi was also uncertain, "scared out of [her] wits." "Nobody was ready for it," she said, "I mean honestly not even me. I was young, it was a fear of the unknown." Nishchal's father urged her to change Nishchal's mind, telling her she would be driven mad herself. "He almost brainwashed me, and I thought [of Nishchal], God, what a devil of a man. Where has my life gone?" This decision threatened to set the tone for the rest of Tulsi's life. Fearing for her future, she turned to her mother, who advised her to consider Nishchal's perspective. She asked, "Can you abandon your son? He can't abandon his mother, and there is no one to care for her, who's there to shoulder [the burden]?"

Tulsi recalled, "You're quite stupid at that age, you don't know, and it is a huge amount of restriction of freedom, you know, you have a kid and a family, and you don't think beyond that point, and suddenly you have a person . . . and the fear, you know. . . ." Though Ammi's freedom would mean the loss of the same for Tulsi, who would shoulder the labor of caring for her, kinship involved the same thing: loss of freedom was part of the securities of marriage.

Tulsi laughed as she recalled the day Ammi was brought home. "One time they were in the middle of all these fights, with his dad and his brother, and," turning to Nishchal, "Remember that car you came in?" She looked back at me. "He just took it one time and they drove to Agra and he came back with her."

Ammi's reentry into domestic life was difficult. There were angry and physical outbursts. She no longer knew how to bathe; she was lice-ridden and urinated wherever she wanted. Rehabilitation involved breaking such habits, rehabituating her to domestic life, and introducing her to a world she had never known—faster cars, busier streets, noisier cities. Tulsi and Nishchal began by trying to institute a routine, which meant figuring out how Ammi's days were patterned in the hospital—what time she woke, what time she ate, what time she expected to bathe—by watching her actions and observing the timing of her needs and desires.

This had an emotional effect. "I used to personally bathe her," Nishchal said, "And we got all the lice out of her hair, and all that sort of stuff. And slowly we conditioned her, and got her into her own place and she built up her confidence."

Tulsi said, "You know, the confidence breaks down. [Our goal was to] try and get her so that she feels she is part of the . . . you know, she is not an outcast. Because they know these things. They know."

Nishchal and Tulsi were concerned about addictions Ammi had developed, including addiction to *paan* [betel nut chewing tobacco] encouraged by the *ayas* [ward attendants], who, they suspected, had used it to bribe and coerce patients. Ammi's antipsychotic medications were part of this pattern, they felt, so they took her off them and tried to "treat [her] with love and try and connect as much as possible. And just be compassionate toward [her] . . . and she'll respond according to that."

According to Nishchal, Tulsi's efforts to connect enabled Ammi to become not only part of the family but "human" again, a status that deteriorated in Agra, where, as Tulsi said, conditions had turned Ammi into "a nothing, like a worm." Ammi's entry into home and humanity involved being treated as a person capable of connection. Nishchal recalled, "Tulsi made her into a whole by interacting with her a lot. You can see, she's still not very coherent, but she tries to connect. Earlier that wasn't the case. She would be very incoherent, but now she tries to strike up a conversation."

Tulsi laughed. "I did my best to be attentive, but Ammi was so aggressive at that time, she wouldn't connect with anyone, she wouldn't get out of her room. If you would tell her, 'Eat your food,' she'd get angry. And she'd say, 'Now get me parathas, get me this, and make this for me.' And you remember?" she said to Nishchal, "She was very jealous. She'd say, 'What are you doing in my front room? Get out.'"

"But then, because of a lot of interaction with her, now she says that you are God." He laughed. "So she is very comfortable with her now."

Ammi settled into a routine, retaining habits they could only guess began in "the ashram." Instead of feeding birds out of her *pallu*, she now offered food from her plate, insisting others take a bite of whatever she had. Fearing doctors of all kinds, she refused to see a dentist to get dentures fitted and so remained toothless.

Before long, the house began to feel too small. Nishchal bought a plot in an elite, quiet enclave of a small city some distance from Delhi. Servants were found to care for Ammi, who was shifted to the new house while Nishchal, Tulsi, and their son stayed in Delhi.

No one, it seemed, knew what to make of the black box that was Ammi's time in Agra. Though K. C. Dube was a family friend, Tulsi and Nishchal's portrayal of Agra as isolating and dehumanizing could not differ more from Dube's place in the historical record, or the Agra he represents in Indian psychiatry. In 1963, in a paper published in the *Indian Journal of Psychiatry*, Dube called for "unlocking the wards." His eloquent critique of the use of physical restraint in psychiatry recommended reinstating the "personal liberty" of patients by offering movement through hospitals and communities as part of therapy (1963: 2). Dube described the terrible conditions he found in Agra's locked wards and the lack of care attendants showed patients. Instead, hospitals should be "therapeutic communities" (1963: 2, 6), as clinical environment was vital to patient well-being. A healthy environment was formed through "healthy relationships," which were only possible if restraint on movement was removed (1963: 2). Ensuring a feeling of freedom was not just an ethical practice but part of treatment.

Dube contrasted this freedom with the Western approach, the attitude that wards might be opened only after patients adopted a better attitude to the hospital, "a feeling the hospital is theirs" (1963: 6). This seemed backward. Observing that a number of patients were permitted to sleep outside in the hot weather, Dube made a sudden decision to unlock the wards (1963: 4), much to the staffs' consternation. He documented the results, finding that patients showed less "hostility," were "relaxed and happier" and that "escapes were very few" (1963: 4).

Agra was, then, during Ammi's time, a place for experiments in freedom, for challenging received wisdom about the nature of the mental patient and the environment in which she must abide. And yet this was so not in spite of, but precisely because Agra had also long been, and remains, iconic of the constraining and corrupt nature of asylums, used in everyday speech as a teasing threat ("If you're not careful they'll send you to Agra"), and appearing in the news as a place of corruption, of doctors who issue false insanity certificates to facilitate government welfare, divorces, and inheritances.

Agra is one of the oldest of India's large mental institutions. Founded by the British in 1859 under the Indian Lunatic Asylum Act as part of the growth of new institutions in colonial India, it was, like most, founded to attend to British, not native, patients (Kumar and Kumar 2008), indeed, for the madness of one man—J. R. Colvin, the lieutenant governor of Agra. The fact that Agra was built to house British patients does not mean its conditions were good. From the start it was a notably wretched place. In its first year, of the thirty-nine "inmates" brought in, twenty-five died (Kumar and Kumar 2008).

Like other asylums, Agra was first administered by the Inspector General of Prisons as part of a system of confinement. In 1905 it was taken over by the Medical Superintendent, and by 1925, the shift of asylums from spaces of containment akin to prisons to sites of medical treatment (in principle, anyway) was embodied in the change of Agra's name to the Agra Mental Hospital. Agra's peak in terms of conditions, research, and population came under Dube's leadership (1950–1975), which overlapped with Ammi's residency (Kumar and Kumar 2008). A progressive physician and administrator, he not only unlocked the wards but also instituted occupational therapies to supplement and in some cases to replace restrictive practices. Dube was also an important figure in global research. His contributions to path-breaking epidemiological studies on schizophrenia in the 1970s were fundamental to the radical idea that schizophrenia outcomes could be better in developing countries.

In the 1990s, following negative publicity and reports of abuse, Agra Mental Hospital was directed by the Supreme Court to restructure its procedures and personnel, and to refashion itself as a research and teaching institution. A committee was formed to reshape other old asylums as well, leading to the end of the system of custodial care, the overhaul of institutions, and a changed relationship to the state as hospitals were disentangled from government control. In 1995, Agra and other former asylums were made into autonomous institutions, though they continued to receive government funding and to function in public capacities (Kumar and Kumar

2008). Like similar places, Agra became part of a health system emphasizing outpatient medicine and focusing on rehabilitation instead of residency, while doctors and heads of hospital attempted to locate the families of dumped patients. It could no longer be said that the state was participating in the abandonment of the mentally ill. Outpatient clinics rather than inpatient wards grew overcrowded as the new legislation had a social impact beyond its institutional effects. It changed the way people viewed mental illness, reduced its stigma, and placed emphasis on treatment rather than institutionalization.

In spite of what we know about Agra, Ammi's experience there—nearly three decades of her life—is all but unknowable. Shreds and guesses, imperfect recollection, opaque phrases, and things read between verses of official history are what can be gleaned of Ammi's Agra. Their truth is undermined by their contradictions as well as their sources, including, but not limited to the unreliability of schizophrenic speech, its paranoias and delusions. And it is limited by its own fragmentary nature—what Tulsi and Nishchal would witness from the visitors' shed on infrequent afternoons, or what Ammi decided to communicate in those encounters.

Stories of Dube's tenure offer one way of locating Agra in Ammi's life, and her life in its history. But much about that history contradicts Tulsi and Nishchal's description of Agra as dehumanizing and of Ammi as reduced to a state of wretched existence by its conditions. Thus, we might also know about Agra from the shadowy things they observed, by Ammi's state of mind and body when she was released, and from the shreds of things Ammi herself has said.

Tulsi describes Ammi's physical condition in strong terms. In Agra, she was underweight, ill groomed, lice-ridden, filthy, and incontinent. She had intestinal parasites, lost teeth, and aged rapidly. Agra's social—as well as physical—conditions transformed her, making her protective of herself, her body, and her belongings.

This was a national problem, Nishchal said. In India there are no therapies that socialize patients, "no getting them and trying to rehab them."

"There's no care," Sujata added. "They're just locked. What happens is there is no organized structure, [no] handling patients and educating them, treating them according to their capability and the level of that disease." Because Ammi's schizophrenia was not the most florid case, Nishchal felt she had "slipped out of attention" and was merely medicated and given electroshock therapy (ECT).

ECT is a large part of what Ammi seems to recall from Agra. This is no surprise, given that in India, electroconvulsive therapy is typically administered "directly," that is, without anesthetic. "When we got her out," Tulsi said, "I think it was the first day or the second day, she was sitting in the dark. I went into her room and I said, 'Ammi, put on the light.' She was so scared of any electric thing. And doctors. Even today she won't see a doctor. She's absolutely scared. She says, 'I'd rather be ill than see a doctor.' The minute you say the word doctor she is very upset."

Nishchal's father blames the ECT for Ammi's inability to connect, and Ammi has mentioned "shocks to [her] head" and "wires." She also talks about doctors and "sisters" (nurses) in Agra as menacing—"attacking" patients, "making the patients their brides." Tulsi and Nishchal had a strong impression that ward *ayas* took Ammi's new saris and made her massage their legs in exchange for *paan*. Ammi repeatedly talked about the way she used to massage the nurses' legs, and while Tulsi was not sure if this was "just a story," she was troubled by the upset hierarchies and past transgressions encoded in Ammi's offers to press *her* legs, when daughters-in-law should be massaging mothers-in-law, not the other way round.

It is not surprising that narratives of progress leave little room for lives and experiences that undermine their trajectories. Such myths are easily undone. At the same time, the disjuncture of Dube's reputation with Ammi's life may indicate the unevenness of medical practice in a single setting and the mismatch of everyday conditions with lofty visions of reform. In relation to conditions I witnessed in inpatient units, it was not difficult for me to imagine that Ammi's life was different from the progressive ideals of Agra's highest administration, though its policies may have afforded days of movement through relatively open spaces. Even if wards were unlocked and patients free to roam, nurses could still steal clothing and demand leg rubs, ECT could be administered to conscious patients, and physically healthy patients could get sick, grow skinny, and age rapidly.

In, not in spite of, this crisis around what is knowable about Ammi's experience, we learn something more about lives than that institutions can be dehumanizing. Ammi's time in Agra suggests that some lives—perhaps all—are accessible only in glimpses of pieces of the past, configurations that include the very circumstances in which things are recalled and told. These "sheets of the past" evade the knowledge work of memory, they cannot be "debased into recollection" (Deleuze 1989: 122). For Tulsi and Nishchal, and anyone else trying to know Ammi, this was inevitable. Agra did not allow for the fullness of recollection; its history could not be "debased" into memory.

Ammi's name, of course, is not Ammi. It is Neelam.

Neelam was born into a landowning Brahmin family in a city where most aristocratic zamindars were typically Muslim or Kayasth Hindu. In this setting, their family was unusual. Not only were powerful landowning Brahmins rare, theirs was a notorious line, infamous for things unpriestly and profane. Nishchal's great-grandfather, Ammi's grandfather, was a lawyer of sorts, a powerful wheeler-dealer. He was a "very affluent as well as a very competent person," Nishchal said, "a real colorful guy. He used to pretend to take on cases, but he wasn't a proper lawyer or anything." It was said that he had two wives, and his home, colorfully known as Mor Koti, Peacock House, had been given to him by a wealthy courtesan. His house was brisk with visitors, performers and, according to Nishchal, "even at one point an elephant in the yard."

Though the atmosphere sombered in the next generation, Neelam was raised in a busy household in a Muslim neighborhood in a city known for its poets, musicians, and dancers. She grew up with five sisters, two brothers, and a household of servants. While her father was strict and serious, a learned lawyer who quoted Shakespeare, Neelam's mother was quiet and simple, a country girl who spent much of her life surrounded by children—one at the breast, one in the lap, and one on the finger, Neelam's sister said.

Neelam's older sister, a woman Tulsi called Sita Mausi (Auntie), described Neelam as an outgoing child, "spirited" and full of jokes and wild stories, a lover of drama. She danced and acted in plays, winning awards and enjoying the audience. "She was a very romantic person," she said. "Used to love dance. She loved poetry. She was a very good dancer, extremely good."

Neelam occasionally went to the rooftop to pace and walk, and from time to time talked to herself, but those moments never lasted long—there were so many other children to draw her into games and play. Neelam's little sister Samhita was the apple of their mother's eye, and Neelam was fiercely jealous for her mother's attention. Her mother doted on the youngest daughter, who teased Neelam and accused her of misbehaving. Their mother would scold Neelam, and soon her siblings joined in, making the lively, imaginative girl the butt of family jokes.

The sisters were all trained in Kathak, a form of classical dance associated with courtesans and the artistic worlds of their city, but everyone said Neelam had a particular talent. Her guru, who gave lessons at the house, was a widely renowned teacher, the patriarch of the city's lineage. He trained his own son alongside Neelam and pronounced her the more promising dancer. He told Neelam's father he wanted to make Neelam his special student, to bind her in the ritual ties of discipleship.

Neelam had begun performing at programs and competitions, earning medals and being recognized for her talent. Sita Mausi recalled, "One day, someone said, '[the guru] is calling, there is a function going on, and they want her to perform.' And my father was there. And he said 'At this time of night? It's 7 o'clock, it's getting dark, she can't go.' And from that day onward it all stopped."

"Everything, even the lessons?" I asked.

"Yah, no dancing, no dancing. 'Not from my family, no one will go out and dance like that,' [my father said]. So that was it. . . . Our family background was such that my father didn't like it. He thought that if she goes out and performs here and there, it will bring a bad name. . . . He didn't want her to be like one of those dancing girls. It was very backward then. It's not like south India, where they think of [dance] as a good art. . . . Somehow I think the artist inside her got broke."

Nishchal had told me a similar story. "[My grandfather] said that she's a zamindar's daughter, a great family, so how dare you come and say that she'll be a dancer and a performer. So from that day he stopped it. He just restricted her to functions in her school and in her college, otherwise she would have been an outstanding dancer," Nishchal recounted. "So that was, you know, maybe something that was a creative need which got suppressed."

When the pronouncement was made, Neelam, who was not surprised by her father's prohibition, said nothing. But she began retreating to her room where, surrounded by mirrors, she danced for hours. Tulsi said, "She would shut her door and just dance around in front of the mirror. There was a whole wall of mirrors in her room, so that too maybe . . . maybe it started then."

Neelam's father placed great value in his children's education, including his daughters', and sent them to the best schools in the city, where they spoke English from the earliest grades and mastered English poetry, drama, and literature. Seeing that Neelam was studious and smart, if also outspoken and "full of fun," he thought perhaps she, too, would become a lawyer, in the family tradition.

At twenty-three, as Neelam finished her master's degree in Hindi literature, her family began marriage negotiations with Keshav's family. Though not well-off, their son showed promise in his army career. The two courted, taking afternoon outings with a sibling chaperone to a south Indian coffeehouse in the center of the city. Keshav quickly fell in love with Neelam. He wrote love letters and called her by pet names. Everyone could tell he was "enamoured."

The early years of the marriage were happy, in spite of family tragedies. Keshav was fond of taking Neelam on small trips on his motorcycle. One afternoon, when Neelam was pregnant with Nishchal, they visited a *mazar*, a Sufi shrine, arriving at dusk and climbing the hill to the empty shrine. Neelam was suddenly overcome with the urge to vomit, and Keshav had "a feeling that I have never had before in my life. All the hairs on my body stood up and I had this very strange feeling, that maybe we had disturbed some kind of spirit in that room." Keshav later reflected that perhaps this was the start of Neelam's illness.

The newlyweds lived with Keshav's family. Within a few months, Keshav's mother grew ill and died, a shock to the new bride. Though Keshav and Neelam were still very much in love, Neelam had begun to say things others found it difficult to believe—that her father was taunting her, that her family was saying cruel things.

Soon, Keshav's postings meant shifts from one city, town, or base to another. Neelam gave birth to one son and then another amid the hardships of army life. Frequent moves and her husband's long stays away from home were accompanied by financial struggles, and Neelam was often left to run the household on her own. She was responsible for many people. In addition to her sons, she was raising Keshav's young niece while the girl's widowed mother took a teacher-training course in a distant city.

When Keshav was sent to the front during the war with China, Neelam's quirky behaviors became something more worrying. Nishchal said, "She started to lose confidence, she was not able to handle the routine stuff of the house, she was always lost in herself in the sense that she would be pacing up and down. She just dropped out of the whole social scene at that point."

Neelam's depression worsened, she would cry, sleep for long stretches and then not at all, forget to bathe, and pace for hours in increasingly erratic moods. Nishchal—then a young teenager—and the servants became her caregivers, but the task was overwhelming. Tulsi said, "She'd walk out in her petticoat, not in her clothes. Once she hit the servant, she punched a woman, she broke her nose, and she'd go sit in the local chai stall in the corner." Embarrassed by his mother's behavior, Nishchal would go outside and beg her to come in. But his mother was oblivious. "She was in her own world."

When Keshav returned, he took Neelam to a series of doctors, first the army psychiatry department and later doctors in private practice, for what was diagnosed as depression. He thought Neelam might benefit from taking up dancing again, but lessons were difficult. Her body had changed; she could not concentrate. Neelam took a job as a teacher. This was also short-lived. She saw a European psychiatrist, beginning medication and what would become decades of electroshock therapy.

When Nishchal was in his late teens, Keshav retired from the military and entered the foreign service. He now needed to travel overseas for work and could neither take along nor care for his ailing wife. He had begun seeking the advice of Dr. Dube, and Neelam was now diagnosed with schizophrenia. During an extended trip to Europe, he sent Neelam back to Mor Koti.

Family differed not only on who was to blame for Ammi's decades in Agra but also on the source of her illness. According to her sisters, the constant movements of army life, financial struggles, overwhelming household labors, and a husband's long absences pushed a woman with a vivid emotional life into mental illness. For Keshav's family, Neelam brought illness into the marriage, coming from a family of wild personalities and generations of questionable moralities. Tulsi recalled Keshav telling her he had been tricked into marrying Neelam, that her family had withheld knowledge of her crooked fingers and toes ("These things some people think are signs of madness").

Tulsi took me to meet Ammi's sister-in-law, a woman she called Bhabhi-ji, brother's wife, during a week in which I was taken from one south Delhi colony to another to meet women from Ammi's family, elegant sisters and sisters-in-law who, though approximately Ammi's age, looked decades younger, evidence of Agra's effects on Ammi's body. On a breezy afternoon, we met in Bhabhi-ji's drawing room. While Eve played in the garden, Tulsi and Bhabhi-ji mapped the personages of kinship, the way facts of a family story might be seeded in alliances and jealousies, patterned by prescribed statuses, colored by the quirkiness of personality.

Tulsi and Nishchal often observed that few of Ammi's sisters visited her in Agra. Her older sister Sita, with whom she had stayed when Keshav was away, as her condition worsened, visited Agra only once. After that, she said, it was too difficult to "see her in such a place."

But Bhabhi-ji, an in-law, was immune from judgment and visited on a few occasions. Bhabhi-ji had known Neelam since she was six, when her own marriage arrangements began, but it was not until Neelam was twelve that Bhabhi-ji became a part of the household. As Bhabhi-ji was herself just a teenager, the two grew close. Bhabhi-ji was sympathetic to Neelam, who already seemed troubled.

"By the time I came there she had already retreated into herself. She did not talk much. When she did talk she talked very sweetly and sensibly. But she would prefer to be alone for long hours and she would dance for hours in her room all by herself. So, people would make fun of her, of her dancing, they would say, 'Stupid girl.' There was no psychology at all in large families at that time. Now of course people are aware.

"We had a three-story, and on the top story she would go and walk up and down for hours. She loved walking. A great deal. On the roof. All by herself. Everyone used to laugh at her. I don't know . . . she was a mixture. Sometimes she would retreat into herself, sometimes she would just talk.

"I was a student of English literature when she was studying Hindi, so I always used to ask her questions about Hindi, and she would tell me long and interesting stories. You couldn't say she was already not quite sensible or not quite logical. She was perfectly logical at that time."

I asked if she was a good student.

"She became quite backward in her studies as time went on, I think in her graduation she had to repeat some paper or something. That affected her quite a lot, but she passed after that and did very well in her postgraduate studies. I don't know, there were a lot of signs . . . but nobody paid much attention to it. . . . Nobody had any sympathy for her."

This was a period in which marriage negotiations were a constant reality in a household full of daughters close in age. Neelam, already jealous of her younger sister, was upset when Samhita's marriage was arranged before her own. The family had chosen a boy for Neelam, but when his people came to visit, the family asked for Samhita instead. "Neelam didn't even know them, but she considered it a personal insult when they decided to marry Samhita," Bhabhi-ji recalled.

Tulsi had noted that early in her marriage, Neelam was poorly looked after. When Keshav returned from his travels he was seldom home, working long hours, and unaware of what was happening with his children or his wife.

Bhabhi-ji disagreed. "No, child, he was always getting posted, and he went off, and he had to leave the children. But when he was at home he looked after the children, he would come from the office tired and he would make them do their homework, he would look after them. You know, there was no food because she would not allow any of the maids . . . she would throw the maids out, and she used to beat up the children also, so she was in a very bad state."

Bhabhi-ji not only witnessed Neelam's adolescence but was there during the period when Neelam returned to Mor Koti in the flux of illness. She had sympathy for Neelam's mother, who worried and tried to keep Neelam inside. Neelam had taken to sitting on the street dressed only in petticoat and blouse. Her concerned mother could not bear the responsibility. "Anything might have happened to her," Bhabhi-ji said. People began talking of putting her into an institution. "That was the thing," she said, "Not that they wanted to put her into Agra or anything like that."

Tulsi said she had heard that Neelam was teased by her brother Saikiran, who inflated Neelam's growing paranoia by saying that Keshav had gone to Europe to have an affair.

Bhabhi-ji disagreed. Neelam's inclination for outlandish storytelling had reached a new level at this point in her life, and she was susceptible to delusion. Her family had treated her poorly, she agreed, but stories about Saikiran's teasing were false. "God knows whether she [said] that, she was always making up things about people, she made up things about her own father. She might have told [Keshav] that, 'Bhaiya [brother] was telling me all of this.' They were false, but they were not lies. It was all quite untrue. But she believed it. It's not as though she was making it up."

When Keshav returned from Europe, he was devastated by his wife's condition. Neelam refused to come out of the house to meet him, perhaps believing that he was returning from a dalliance with another woman. Keshav took her home. Their younger son was still in school, and Nishchal, beginning his own army career, was away at the military academy.

Neelam's placement in Agra was a keystone in arcs of family history. Most held Keshav responsible for the decision. Tulsi said she heard it was Saikiran's idea to put Neelam in Agra. "No, [Keshav] was the one who took her," Bhabhi said gently, "I'm absolutely certain of that. They all said they didn't want her in Mor Koti. It was not just Saikiran."

Tulsi returned to Neelam's poor treatment during her marriage. "Her sisters say Papa [Keshav] used to go to work and was out all day, and what was happening to the children, what was happening to the wife, he didn't know because he was away. She was all by herself and there was no care, and her sister said, 'I have written to the parents myself to say please come and help her.' And no one came. No one from the in-law's side came, no one from the parents' side came."

"No, they didn't come. That is true."

"She said that while [Keshav] was in Germany they didn't have milk to drink in the house, she had to sell off a family plot, and [when she went to Mor Koti] they treated her so badly over there she didn't want to stay."

"Yes, they didn't bother about her, they didn't bother about anyone."

"Papa said, 'When I reached [Mor Koti] Saikiran told her she was not talking to me, and they took her to Agra and they put her there."

"He put her there?"

"Saikiran."

"That's not true. No, he never took her there at all."

"But then they said, '*Nikal ke lao*,' let's bring her out, 'Let's give her a second chance.'"

"My goodness, he's [Keshav] the one who planned it all! Because he was going to England and there was no way that he wanted to take her. Because by then she was quite out of her mind. . . . Keshav was the one who took her to Agra. No, I'm absolutely certain of that. We came down always to Delhi in the winter, he always came with her, so I know exactly what she was going through, what she was feeling, but the fact that this was all due to the people in her mother's house is perfectly untrue. Dhananjay [Nishchal's brother] took her in the car."

Tulsi agreed. "They told her they were going for an outing, and they took her there and left her. Nishchal came home from his studies. He asked, 'Where is Mummy?' [His brother] said, 'Mummy is not here.' He said, 'Where is Mummy?' He said, 'We put her in the mental asylum.' He said, 'Why didn't you tell me?' He said Papa and him . . . apparently she had to be given a pill so she was this thing, and they drove off in the car, this is what he got to know.' He said, 'I was stunned, where is she?'"

"Of course, that's true," Bhabhi-ji said gently, "I am also saying the same thing. But the fact that they [Neelam's brother] took her is wrong."

Much was at stake in the question of how Ammi came to be placed in Agra and how she came to be released. So, too, much was at stake in determining what it was, if anything, that drove her mad. Accountability moved across kin; so did the kinds of attention families pay to their members, the ways they guided a person through life, choosing their marriage partners, disallowing their passions, moving them from one city to the next. Versions of the story reflected affiliation with branches of the family but not chauvinism. The work of creating these accounts showed the different positions women might occupy not only as affinal (married into) or consanguineal (born into) kin, but also their different positions as in-marrying women whose lives were characterized by movement, multiple households, and refracted perspectives. They showed that women are outsiders to different degrees with different stakes and circumstances in their kin networks, in homes that are only ever partially theirs yet define their place in the world. These conversations mapped kinship through time and mapped time through love, sorrow, and desperation. They crafted the kind of truth—about a person, about relationships—it was possible to tell in moments of breakdown, and what threads might stitch struggles inherent to kinship to other dissolutions. They bartered in the kinds of story it might be possible to tell about an act that stung with abandonment but was always something more—and less—than the term would imply.

Not long after putting Ammi into Agra, Keshav moved to England. After several years, he returned with news that he had met a woman he wanted to marry. She was also an expatriate and, as Tulsi put it, he was smitten again, blinded to her faults by love. He explained to Nishchal, who was twenty-one, that for him to divorce Ammi, Nishchal would have to take over her legal guardianship. Nishchal agreed, lawyers were brought in, and, as Nishchal put it, "He got a divorce in one hour."

In Tulsi's words, "No terms at all, no consent, just his [Nishchal's] word that he would look after her."

Nishchal became his mother's caretaker again, visiting between postings and when on leave. Decades later, the decision to take Ammi out of Agra was complicated by his sense of responsibility to his father. After getting a divorce from his second wife, Keshav had taken a job in Kuwait. The start of the Gulf War meant he had to leave suddenly and under difficult circumstances. He came back to Delhi as though from exile—traumatized, depressed, and in poor health. It wasn't until he was stabilized that Nishchal felt he could turn his attention to Ammi.

It would be easy to vilify Keshav as the one who "dumped" Ammi in Agra and divorced her. But not only had he loved her deeply and felt her loss when schizophrenia set in, a moral code was present in his decisions as well, one that hinged on connection and recognition. Recognition came up frequently in people's accounts of the mental illnesses of others—the inability to recognize others was often a sign of madness, and many funny and uncanny accounts hinged on an interaction in which a sane person mistook for normal someone who was mad. Misrecognition was a trope of craziness, just as mistaking the crazy for the sane cut close enough to the boundaries of sanity to make a familiar plotline. For Nishchal and Keshav, recognition and misrecognition held great moral weight.

For some time after I met him, Nishchal said I should get his father's "side of the story." This happened spontaneously during one of my stays in Ammi's house, when members of Keshav's extended family gathered in a nearby home to celebrate Diwali. A number of Keshav's cousins had built retirement homes in the neighborhood. They met often but neither visited Ammi nor acknowledged or spoke about her. If they stopped in to see Keshav, Ammi would pass through the room, ghostlike, or sit in a chair at the edge of the gathering, murmuring quietly, but no one interacted with her. (According to Tulsi, one of the aunties had said, "in company," that, "people don't like to come to the house because that old woman is there.")

One night, at a table full of aunts and uncles, nieces and nephews, Keshav reflected on his life with Ammi. While it is difficult to decide what to reproduce and what to shroud from a wider gaze, his was an account—and defense—framed by the idea of research, of the need to establish "the facts." This, he said, was "science." It was also an account of care and futility.

"She was fine after Nishchal was born. But after the second child she went into a very deep depression. She began to have these symptoms and couldn't come out of the depression, so we took her to some psychiatrists and they did some tests and spoke with the family for the background, and they diagnosed her with depression and schizophrenia. . . . Sometimes it was very bad and I had to hospitalize her. I put her into the hospital once, and then she got a bit better and came out of the hospital, and then it got bad again and I had to put her in again. And then I got a posting in the UK and of course had to take that and went away for some time. Later, a few years back, we got her out of the hospital, and found this woman Rani and set up the home for her here."

Keshav claimed a part in Ammi's rehabilittion. "After some time we were able to get her out and rehabilitate her. Some people didn't think we could do it, and it was a great hardship to rehabilitate her, she behaved very abusively and very badly and was very difficult when we first got her out. But now she is on no medications at all. And Rani is like a saint. Because no matter how much [Ammi] yells, and she does yell a lot, she yells at me, she yells at [Rani], but no matter how much she yells, this woman [Rani] just becomes more and more cool."

Nishchal cut in, "That is because she has compassion. The most important thing is compassion—you must have compassion."

Keshav responded angrily. "I put up with all the things she says and does, the ways she abuses and yells. Compassion is easy for you to talk about, but you are not here."

Nishchal reminded his father, "This is an academic conversation, this is just for research, because she is a research scholar. She wants to see how it is different here from in the West, where in the West when there is a problem like this they will treat a person as a separate unit, they will drop them in the hospital. Here the whole treatment is integrated with the family, the family is around, not like in the West where they are treated individually, as a case, away from their family, but here they are right in the middle of it, the person will connect with and interact with and be looked after by the whole family, by this person, by that person, and there a person will lose all those connections, here the connections will stay."

Keshav agreed, things had changed in how families felt about each other, but he held Nishchal accountable for the same failing in refusing to connect with his younger brother. He described the way Ammi could not recognize people in her life.

Nishchal said, "She recognizes me, she recognizes Tulsi, she recognizes Shubhash [their son], she recognized Amba Bua's daughter [the niece Ammi raised], it is strange, it is hard to see the reason."

"She does not recognize her own son [Dhananjay]. She has no recognition. She cannot connect. . . . At the beginning she was given quite a lot of electric shocks, and that damaged her brain. Her memory from before that is fine, but from after that there is no recognition. . . . The issue is that one has to connect. The problem is that she does not connect. She cannot connect with her own son, she cannot connect with anyone. She sometimes recognizes but does not connect."

Nishchal smiled and hit the table with his hand. "Yes! This is exactly what I am talking about. You need to connect with her. You have to make an effort to connect, you have to talk to her kindly, you have to make an effort with her. The connection is the important thing."

For Keshav, Ammi's inability to "connect" was vitally important, a sign of incompatibility with family life and relations, of the inability to be incorporated into reciprocal bonds. His younger son's hurt was understandable, and in Ammi's inability to recognize others was an offense similar to Nishschal's broken bonds with him. For the family to remain coherent, Ammi must come second. Connection was a state of being, a precursor to relationships.

For Nishchal, recognition and connection were not given qualities but efforts. They had to be offered to be received. Though Ammi's inabilities to recognize others caused pain, connection was a goal, not a quality, and reaching out in spite of its absence was necessary for rehabilitiation, a form of intimacy Ammi had been denied. For Nishchal, connection was not a condition but an action, one that could reinstate the humanity lost in institutional life. It was the work of being human, of making human again.

Responding to Nishchal's plea for an "academic discussion," his father replied, "Yes, I know about science. I am a scientist too. I was in the army, but before that I also studied physics. I have a B.A. in physics . . . , so I understand about scientific research. A scientist wants the truth. A scientist wants the facts, so I am giving her the facts. This is frank. I am being honest. This is the truth. I was her [Ammi's] husband. I had rights and needs as a man. She does not even recognize her own son. She is the mother and she does not know her own son. My son lost his mother. He had many other people who were his mother because she was not there, because he lost his mother. She [points at his sister] was there, he [Tulsi's dad] was his mother, I was his mother and his father. The son has suffered, and I am the victim here too. And now she yells and screams and can you imagine how I feel with her acting like that when the neighbors are right there peeping around the fence. Now she is my mother. I call her Mata-ji. She calls me Bhagwan [God] and I call her Mata-ji. She was my wife and now she is my mother. But I also had to stay sane, and look at me, I have stayed sane. That was not easy, putting up with all of it; so many people said I should have gone mad too. But I am eighty-two and I am an integrated personality. I am sane, I am OK. I am at peace. If death comes to shake hands with me tonight I will be able to say, 'Hello death.' I will be able to shake hands with death. I am peaceful. There is your research."

For Keshav, connection was not opposed to disconnection. Lack of connection did not produce disconnection; instead, it reordered relations. Without recognition and connection, kinship was disorganized, reorganized into maddening, but somehow livable, configurations. To be kin is to know kin. By not recognizing, new conditions were made. A husband can be the son of his wife and he can also be her god. Ammi reordered kinship just as kin reordered themselves around her. This might defy sanity and wholeness, but it was possible to persist in spite of it, to find some kind of peace.

A year after we met, and about a decade after bringing Ammi out of Agra, Nishchal took a job overseas, in the same city where he and Tulsi's son was in university. Though they worried that the rest of their family would say they had "abandoned that woman," Tulsi and Nishchal left, returning a few times a year to visit.

Ammi's home was comfortable and spacious. It had views of mountains and stayed cool through the summer. Unmedicated, she developed precise, if less than explicable daily routines, moving through house, driveway, and gardens in circuits. She continued to call Nishchal "Chitu," and Tulsi "Bahu" (daughter-in-law); she called Keshav "Bhagwan" and me "Mother Rose" at Tulsi's suggestion after she thought Ammi might be calling me by the name of a childhood schoolteacher. And she called Eve "Blue Eyes." Occasionally Tulsi brought out Ammi's *ghungroo*, her dancing bells, and gave them to Ammi to wear. Sometimes Ammi took a few tentative steps. Tulsi showed Ammi her mother's bangles and old photographs, which she kept in a trunk in the bedroom.

When Keshav was not there, Ammi ate at the dining room table. When he was in the house, she took her plate to her room or to a chair at the edge of the dining room. Every morning, she visited his room, which she called "the library," and received from "the librarian" a book or pamphlet. Ammi took the offering from Keshav's hands, pressed it to her forehead, and went away.

At once embedded in kin and separated from them, Ammi's world came to involve two spatial arrangements, two possibilities for movement. When Tulsi, Nishchal, or the Brigadier were there, the house was open: bedroom doors and windows (and the telephone) were unlocked, and doors onto the garden were opened. Possible circuits of movements multiplied. When they were gone, bedrooms were locked, and only the kitchen and the living and dining rooms were accessible. Like many elite families, they felt it necessary to take precautions against thefts by household servants. Tulsi realized this could breed resentment but believed she had little choice.

Different routes channeled Ammi's movements into a routine for the passage of time. Of course, what Ammi's life was like when no one was around was difficult to know, especially within a worldview that mistrusted servants' words and recognized the interdependence of household staff and employers. Rani described Ammi's days as following a strict routine in which Ammi found comfort and regularity. But she also said she often went to her room and screamed. There were disputes about her care—how much milk Ammi would receive; whether she truly preferred, as Rani insisted, cold buckets of water for bathing; whether the cleanliness of Ammi's quarters was Ammi's responsibility or Rani's. Rani resented the mistrust embodied in the locks on the doors and phone. Tulsi, Nishchal, and Keshav argued over how much to interfere in the routine Rani established, at what point to risk angering the woman they depended on, and when to stand back and leave well enough alone.

"There is no care, Sarah, only survival," Tulsi said once, with sadness about Ammi's life with Rani, and the limits of what Tulsi could ensure. It was hard for me to evaluate if this feeling was justified by Ammi's life with Rani. It would be easy to assign value to the contrast between the open busyness of the house when family were present and its quiet, closed emptiness when they were not, on the assumption that more movement and people are better. But Ammi's perspective is hard to know.

I interacted with Ammi often, usually in the company of Tulsi and Nishchal, but sometimes alone with her. I tried to keep notes of those interactions. This was difficult. Ammi's speech was at once obstructing and illuminating. It demanded reflection on means of perception, how I came to know what Ammi meant or said. Traces of Ammi in my narrations were more often accounts of my experience than documentation of hers. They include the following:

> It is such a strange feeling to listen to [Ammi talk], a pleasure really, provided I stop trying to remember what she is saying, stop trying to understand the leaps. In Hindi it is very difficult—I understand the pieces, but lose the plot because in a sense there is none, or rather the plot is entirely unpredictable, and I realize how much predictability is a part of comprehension—the story, the narrative, the line of language goes, at least in shape and structure if not content, where one expects it to. Without this element, though, recall is all but impossible, and comprehension is more atomic, in a sense, piecemeal—I understand this phrase and then must move on and let it go entirely in order to grasp the next while the mind (mine) is struggling with what has just been said, reaching back a few seconds

in time to try to make the connection that is not there—or that is there but that I cannot grasp. But the experience of hearing it, if I can let myself engage time and language in a different way, following the forward push of language rather than the retrospective pull of constant analysis and understanding, the experience is lovely, like floating in a stream that curves and sometimes becomes turbulent, that may hold turns and eddies and even rocks, but ultimately soothes and carries one along. Listening to Ammi requires giving oneself over. My own efforts to enter into her discourse, to respond in small inconsequential mirroring kinds of ways as one does with a normal person, always seem to bring a sudden halt, a sudden splash, an interruption to this flow, this process—they engage the language, the meaning, the process of signification in entirely the wrong way. I ask about something she has just said, as though she were going to go on in this vein anyway but did not, as though that thing still exists as an object, but it does not. It is gone, it is no longer there to be held and reexamined. A bird has become a cooking pot; a book has become a person once loved or at least known; a song has become a movie star; Kalidasa is now Lord Byron; a forest has become numbers. I used to think of schizophrenic speech as akin to poetry, but now I think not, though poetry also engages the mind in a way different than that of other kinds of speech/discourse/writing. Schizophrenic speech requires not that one hold the pieces together and marvel at their togetherness, at the way surprising things fall one after the other in a meaningful if unexpected (but never entirely) way, as one does with a poem, but that one constantly discard what has just been uttered, that one let go of the need not only for linearity—that is the obvious part—but the need for the togetherness of the pieces. It involves a new relationship to time and meaning that is altogether different from that of hearing poetry. For these reasons, it is so difficult to recreate what she has said, to capture it not only in my mind, but then in words—it is not unlike trying to recall and retell a dream whose intense sensations cannot be captured in anything so foreign as words. But some flashes, like moments of near lucidity in dreaming, come through.

Other fragments of Ammi reside in my notes. What strikes me most, and the reason I quote from them rather than rewriting them as narration or leaving them to the privacy of Ammi's world, is how much they are accounts of daily household intimacies, of interactions around Ammi. Ammi appears as a shadow cast by other people's lives. In what follows I have cut out descriptions of Ammi's actions and replaced them with ellipses.

> Tulsi was taking a picture of Ammi and I [sic] with her phone and showing the pictures to us on the screen. . . . It occurred to me that even though there are mirrors all around [the house], [Ammi] may not really see herself, and that seeing oneself like this—as an object, an image to be consumed or held separate from oneself—could be upsetting, suddenly resonates as "self." There were pictures of Ammi as a young woman floating around. Two. One that Tulsi found in a pile of photos, I wasn't there when she showed Ammi, but she kept saying, later, "Ammi, remember when I showed you the picture of you as a young woman? Everyone used to say, 'Neelam is so beautiful.'" . . . Looking at the pictures, what is most striking to me is how full, how round, how plump her face is. She is instantly recognizable, but it is not as though the old woman's face—as a mask of wrinkles and sunken cheeks where teeth should hold them taut—conceals the girl behind or inside, it is the opposite, as though in the picture there is the ghost of Ammi, the shiver or shadow of the old woman. She looks so smooth and filled out.
>
> Later, while we are sitting in the drawing room, T. and I, N.'s father comes out with a folder of things. The folder has the name of a hospital or nursing home on it, and I wonder if he is about to show us the literature about some place he wants to put Ammi, but he doesn't. He opens it and takes out a picture from his wedding. "This is a picture from my marriage. A day before my marriage. My wedding to Neelam." Again, the strange disorienting effect of seeing Ammi as a young woman, rounded out, eyes looking alert and straight ahead. It is also remarkable that Nishchal's father brings this out, I think.
>
> When I leave, the car comes while I am still inside. Tulsi is sitting on the porch, and Rani has brought my things out. I come out last, and the front gate is open. Ammi is going out and standing in front of the gate. Tulsi says, "She is looking for you." I go out. . . . I say I have to leave now, but I will come and visit again. . . . I thank her

for letting me stay in the house and visit her and ask if I can come
again. . . . I say that I enjoyed staying with her and will miss her. . . .
Rani tells her to go back inside.

Telling Ammi's stories and stories about Ammi, including my own,
comes with two challenges. One involves representing kinship demands in
relation to women's mental illness, and the other involves failures of language to produce coherent accounts of families, love, and madness. These
challenges require choices, including those made amid bureaucratic procedures like human subjects reviews and consent forms. These are represented in my decision to preserve some of the opacity of Ammi's language
in these paragraphs.

Some of these challenges are particular to schizophrenia. Raising uncertainties about the relationship of personhood to expression, schizophrenia's
forms of speech are "characterized by hesitations and contradictions"
(Corin, Thara, and Padmavati 2004: 113), challenging efforts to locate a
coherent person in language (Jenkins 2004b: 33). Such uncertainties pertain
not only to schizophrenic speech but also to the speech of those who would
aim to know a person, or themselves, through the schizophrenic speech of
another. Uncertainty involves shared efforts to know and understand, to
connect and recognize. At the same time, recognition and representation
can contain assumption and overwriting. The weight of imposed meanings
in knowing a person in psychosis is particularly acute: "How do we speak
about others' suffering without redoubling the lived violence by an interpretive violence anchored in the position of the 'well-informed' researcher?" (Corin, Thara, and Padmavati 2004: 110). This is a dilemma
shared by anthropologist, kin, and clinicians, for whom the needs to interpret, represent, and recount are part of a daily work associated with care
but not devoid of the confining architecture of imposed meanings.

The negative spaces in schizophrenic speech and speech about schizophrenia are like the unsteady spaces of violence and hopefulness inherent
to interpretation more broadly. And they are akin to the negative spaces
created and filled in by kinship at its moments of breakdown. Uncertainties
and anxieties about knowing in fraught moments of family life extend beyond the relationship of knowing to narration, described above, and into
the ways knowing is a feature of relations, weaving together social action,
knowledge of others, and self-knowledge.

While some suggest that schizophrenia poses the "erasure of the subject," others observe that it highlights the way all subject-making is intersubjective, subjects constituted by other subjects (Jenkins 2004b). In Ammi's case, I add to this the observation that intersubjectivity is never completely accomplished. The word "rehabilitate" means to make whole again, to bring together what has come apart. But the "whole" of rehabilitated kinship is as deferred as the whole of the rehabilitated self. Efforts to connect or recognize, in action, memory, or language, are asymptotes, goals rather than points of arrival.

The same may be true of the "whole," rehabilitated or not, of the family, a unit that is composite, partial, moveable, and ambiguous. In dissolving and reassembling selves and stories surrounding Ammi, relations on a smaller scale than the family come into perspective, what we might call kinship nodes. The emotions they involve may be evaluated in terms of their disruption of household harmony and, in particular, social hierarchies, if not necessarily "the breakdown of the family" as such. What they show is not that the family is breaking down now [or there, or here] but that the family is always in a state of breakdown.

Asking in what ways time might be portrayed beyond the usual sequential formulations of plot and causation, Deleuze observed that in the condensed visual and sonic sequences of New Wave film, time was portrayed as multiple, characters as things-in-relation, and causality uncertain. Time in such films was "forked," comprised not of movement toward a (closer) present but of simultaneous "sheets of the past" (1989: 50, 99). Here was recognition not just of the past in the present (by way of its reproduction, social or otherwise), but the simultaneity of multiple pasts in any one moment, a configuration that constituted, rather than undermined, the present.

This aesthetic of time suggests possibilities for knowing and representing entities in a field of "distortion," in the words of a very different thinker, George Devereux (1967: 42), in which the distortion of the picture—in our case, of a person—contains, rather than masks, the truth of its existence. For Devereux, applying the psychoanalytic principle of transference to scientific methods, this distortion exists in the way knowledge of an other is an encounter between complicated and desiring subjects. This is not unlike what Deleuze finds, in the films of Orson Welles, to be a "theory of shadows" (1989: 167), in which bodies are portrayed in relief, distorted by the means of viewing them, but thereby representing those means and, at the same time, their subject. Here, the subject is elusive as a stable entity, and " 'I is an other' has replaced 'Ego = Ego' " (1989: 133).

In schizophrenia, we may see this distortion carried into other domains: interactions among multiple people, the shape and content of conversation, the things people argue about. Or we may see that it has been there all along. Notions of distortion offer a way of understanding not only that access to Ammi's life lies in its points of compression against other lives, but what that fact may reveal about relationships between speaking of others, knowing others, and being with others. Importantly, for both Devereux and Deleuze, this is not accident but method, something useful not only in finding Ammi in others' lives but in telling a story about her, deciding what to leave in and what to cut out.

My point in summoning Deleuze and Devereux is that the challenges I faced in finding Ammi, in rehabilitating her to narrative, conditioned as they were by multiple forces, may tell us less about schizophrenia and less, even, about narrative than about kinship. In the tumble of stories surrounding Ammi, as families, subjects, and stories constantly dissolved, kinship was enacted as a compilation of pasts. These pasts existed not so much as multiple versions of memory than as ongoing relations in the present. Kinship was a form of time. Ammi's life involved movements through time defined by stoppages in space. Time flowed, but movement through space welled and was dammed. At the same time, these flows and pauses in and through space were also the rushes and tide pools of intimacy and dissolution. In film, subjects might be located and described less by recollection than by its impossibilities, "disturbances of memory" (Deleuze 1989: 52). In life, this may be so amid intersubjective efforts to remember. Stories and encounters may show the work of kinship—a work that was like rehabilitation—to be an effort to pull together what had come undone. At the same time, there is in them evidence of the way kinship can involve an effort to undo, to allow dissolution, as well as to re-form and bring together. Bonds must be unmade as well as made.

These challenges in making an account of Ammi also pertain to that map of the city, and of kinship and abandonment, that I plotted in my return, in which kinship and institutions seemed opposed along a spectrum of care and abandonment, with kin enacting either the casting out or the integrating. The stories Tulsi and others shared undid this picture. Which family would we turn to in order to find the family that abandoned Ammi, or the one that rehabilitated her? Where would we look for the completion of either act?

Extending the sense we get from Ammi's life that multiple pasts condition the present and that the work of kinship involves dissolution and remaking all the time, not just in the face of mental illness, we achieve an understanding to the side of one that might pose Ammi as either dumped or embraced. Rather than representing either the banishment of women from kinship or their return to it, Ammi's situation involved the rehabilitation of a woman never entirely dumped, but also, in her return home, dislocated from kin by kin, in some moments made into a sign of connection and recognition and in others their opposite. It is hard to find in this picture a coherent relationship between the family and the asylum, hard, indeed, to find the family, though the idea of it looms large. Thus, rather than producing the truth of the family and its processes through clinical management of defective subjects, possibilities for the truth about relationships were undone, rather than made, by the unstable place of the asylum in family life, indeed by the ever-changing nature of family life. Here, the asylum was a thing of guilt, accusation, anger, authority, and, surprisingly, connection, care, freedom, and even friendship (embodied in Dr. Dube). In relation to it, kinship and the truth about it, like selves, clinical subjects, and stories, was not so much shored up on the ground of women's madness as it was exposed in its sheer vulnerability. The work of self-making, like the work of kin-making, involved pulses of dissolution and rehabilitation.

In Ammi's case, as in all "recombinant" families, the family as such disappears, while kinship continues (Strathern 2005, citing Simpson 1994). That is, Ammi's confinements, freedoms, and rehabilitations; breaks and disavowals; are the ligaments of kinship, even as the family they constitute becomes difficult to locate. Specific relationships bear the intensified negotiations her illness demanded. These relationships—between husbands and wives, mothers and sons, mothers-in-law and daughters-in-law, fathers and sons, and sisters—were both patterned, following rules of north Indian kinship, and improvisatory. To disappear these microrelations, these binaries and triads into the gloss of "the family" would mean losing a sense of how the details unfolded, losing the *normative* contradictions within the family. Were we to think about Ammi in terms of the family rather than in a multiplicity of relations, we could not account for the complexities of both patterned and improvisatory kin life and the various pulls it exerts on efforts to address a family member's illness. And we would be unable to account for the sheer contingency of love and its dissolution.

In Ammi's movements is evidence less of her casting out from kinship to institutions, or by kinship for institutions, than of the ongoing abandonments and constrictions of and within kinship, of and within, that is, freedom and integration—which Tulsi, Bhabhi-ji, and Keshav all seemed to recognize. Ammi is "at home" but, for the most part, "alone," though how we evaluate each—"home" and "alone"—is a matter requiring careful reflection. She is often in the unwilling company of the husband who set her adrift decades ago, physically and legally (and who now rejects her in order to foster an ethic of respect and connection), but a sea away from the son and daughter-in-law whose initial willingness to connect rendered her human and integrated into a world of recognition. She is lost to psychosis but free from the constraining possibilities of medication, though again, each characterization involves heavy moral judgment. We can feel both discomfort and relief with the present situation.

Ethics of representation are not far from those of kinship and medicine; all involve dynamics of constraint and capture. This is perhaps most vivid in the kinds of narration that tell us what is wrong. But it is also the case with stories people tell about their mothers, sisters, wives, and daughters as ways of telling stories about themselves. And it is also true of the stories anthropologists tell about others or ourselves (also forms of diagnosis). To return to the uncomfortable matter of "writing" Ammi, rehabilitating her to narrative, and its ethical dimensions, we might ask, if a subject is defined by her ability to consent (rather than, say, to connect) what would constitute consent in this frame? What would constitute refusal? Is there a way that the partialness of connection and recognition offer an alternate frame of ethical understanding? Or do those terms, too, take us to a similar dilemma? It is not possible to answer these questions in conventional terms, in which freedom stands in dialogue only with its other, constraint, or care in dialogue with its other, abandonment, or truth in dialogue with its other, invention. There is a subject as well, in the more indeterminate space where freedom, care, and abandonment may be more alike than the twinned crises of abandonment and constraint. It remains necessary, as it also remains impossible according to certain rules, to account for the subject who evades consent as such, neither fully consents nor fully refuses. This is a space of ethical crisis, to be sure, but it may also be a space of aspects of subjectivity typically shrouded from consideration. Here there is room for one who neither fully agrees to nor fully refuses kinship (and its breakdown—as in Ammi's divorce); neither agrees to nor refuses care and the forms it takes (in the case of Ammi's confinement in the asylum and her isolated freedom in the home), or connection and representation (in the lives and stories of others and the accounts reproduced for the sake of understanding or, worse, scholarship). This, too, is a state of being that requires consideration.

This uncomfortable location is best described in Ammi's words, which, breaking my own rules (as I have in the epigraph to this chapter), I turn to for their simultaneous refusal and self-identification.

Ammi says, "I will not talk tomorrow. I have no stories. The mother, she makes a circle, like a zero, she makes a circle. I am inside. It is like this. And [pointing to her ears] there is a circle like this."

These words offer, perhaps, a sense of structure and authority as maternal, encircling, and indeterminate, rather than paternal, phallic, and direct. If it is recalled that Ammi refers to me as "Mother" (though she may not be referring to me here) they may also attach to the production of knowledge and the kinds of subjects it demands and creates. Either way, the sense of the powers that direct desire, time, and stories is circular, encompassing in an embrace that might also be containment, confining at the same time as defining and protective. This is an indeterminate space. It is not entirely acceptance or refusal. It is beyond stories but also beyond time—in the far-off land of the near future.

Chapter 2

On Dissolution

"I keep thinking that soon it will be over—the life expectancy of a
cloud is supposed to be only twelve hours—and then I realize
something has occurred that can never be over."
—Lorrie Moore, "People Like That Are the Only People Here" (1998)

Moksha is the name I have given to a small, private psychiatric clinic on the
edge of the city. *Moksha* means liberation, with a touch of transcendence,
depending on your soteriology. The name's irony is my effort to capture
the unkindness of the clinic's real name, in which the idea of surpassing
freedom abutted the most basic fact of life in the wards—immanent containment. Moksha was established in the early 1990s by a psychiatrist with
an interest in providing mental health care in a nonhospital setting, and a
vision of incorporating religion into therapeutics. Patients would be encouraged to take up practices like yoga and prayer. Chants would be played
over the loudspeakers in the early morning to offer a soothing environment
of contemplation.

Moksha opened when psychiatric care in India was in a state of flux.
Former asylums were being transformed into research institutions, courts
and media reported scandals of abuse, ideologies had rejected custodial care
in favor of "community-based" psychiatry, and economic liberalization resulted in increasing privatization of medicine. Settings like Moksha appeared—clinics treating psychiatric ailments, serving mostly outpatient
clientele, with small inpatient units where families could pay for care they
were not equipped to provide.

Though many of Moksha's patients came for addiction treatment, staff said growing awareness of mental illness brought more and more patients seeking treatment for ailments like depression, anxiety, and "tension." In spite of its director's interest in nonmedical therapies, treatment was dominated by drugs. Interactions were directed toward prescribing and facilitated by a range of practitioners—psychiatrists, general practitioners, social workers, and psychologists.

Moksha had several inpatient units: a private ward with separate rooms (for men and women), three public locked wards for men, and one locked inpatient unit for women. On any day up to fifteen women occupied the locked ward, a setting for both acute care and long-term residence (though staff downplayed the latter). While male patients were housed in facilities tiered by amenities—rooms with or without air-conditioning and television, alone or shared, in the basement, the ground floor, or a higher level ("private ward," "A/C ward," "general ward," "welfare ward," and "family ward"), women all stayed together in one female ward. In a dazzling range of states of mind, body, emotion, and spirit, they shared a long hall without air-conditioning or televisions, with several rows of beds, a large table, and a line of toilets, sinks, and showers.

It was because there were fewer female patients, one doctor said, that there was only one ward for them. For the same reason, women did not receive the group therapies, newspaper-reading sessions, and other activities offered to men. Instead they were sent baskets of vegetables to cut, spices to grind, and rice to clean for the kitchen. Occasionally social workers led rounds of the singing game Antakshiri. In the outpatient clinic, social workers and psychologists conducted therapy sessions. But not in the ward. Yet something therapeutic happened along the way, when clinicians on rounds checked on patients and offered pieces of advice, words of assurance, and admonitions about how to be and behave.

I found Moksha by accident during an early visit, my first trip to India with Eve, one that was also a homecoming—to a household I knew well in a changed neighborhood. This venture was exploratory; I was investigating the possibility for researching community mental health efforts in slums. I spent two months following tenuous leads among NGOs, doctors, social workers, psychologists, and others who might have an interest in the sufferings of the poor. These efforts existed, but linking myself to them in any meaningful way seemed less interesting than exploring mental health care as it happened already, beyond the scope of newness, as traces of a longer history. This meant seeking out the hospitals, shrines, and doctors' offices to which people brought themselves (or, more often, were brought). I went as well to the few government institutions that might be considered rehabilitation homes or halfway houses, visited a women's prison, and spoke with matrons who oversaw homes for the destitute.

Mrs. M. was involved in such enterprises, having a long involvement with an organization that provided female prisoners with legal services. She directed me to her friend Mrs. P., who was familiar with "a new hospital for people with mental problems." As her aunt had spent time in Moksha, Mrs. P. had interacted with its doctors and director. The place was "good medically," she said, but "shifty, full of thieves and quacks."

Mrs. P. gave me the name of Dr. K., a physician who had been helpful. I tried for weeks to reach him. Whenever I called, the receptionist said he was on rounds, or not available. Try later. Finally, making an evening attempt, I was put through to a woman who said *she* was Dr. K. I said I had been trying to reach a different Dr. K. (the handwritten first name was male and not hers) and was told there was no such doctor at Moksha, and never had been. *This* Dr. K., however, would talk with me, though she was reluctant to let me join trips to the rural areas where Moksha had outreach programs (in spite of my insistence that I had lived for a year in a small village). The villages would be "too difficult for someone like you." I ended up shadowing her at Moksha, trailing her on rounds and sitting in the back of her office.

I learned little about Dr. K., only that she had trained at Nehru Hospital, was married and had one child, and that her daughter, a few years younger than my own, was cared for by her mother-in-law not only because there were few other options but because even if such options existed, people would think poorly of women who made use of them. Where in the United States some might consider a woman who put her child in day care in order to work selfish or a bad mother, here, she said, no one would worry about that. They would wonder instead why she had no family—no in-laws, that is—to care for her children. We discussed this after she commented that it must be difficult for me to do this work with my daughter here but no family.

Dr. K. maintained a Buddha-like calm in what were at times hectic spaces. Her dispassion seemed to border on dissociation, a quiet, inward-turned affect I would come to recognize in the doctors at Nehru as well. In one of my first visits, during rounds through the private ward, the costly facilities occupied almost exclusively by men in for "de-addiction," two

men—one wearing a shirt that said "I'm nuts. Someone give me a screw"—
got into a fistfight in the room where Dr. K. was seeing patients. As one of
the men grabbed the other by the throat, a partition wall was knocked over.
I tried to calm my flight urges. There was nowhere to flee—behind me was
a locked door, there were walls on two sides, and I was supporting the
partition with my shoulder. Dr. K. sat calmly behind her desk, hands
folded, and said quietly, "These patients can be very difficult."

I met the head of hospital, Dr. M., to get permission to visit the wards.
His office was in the deep interior of the building, a windowless room
behind a windowless foyer. In our first meeting, I sat awkwardly in its air-
conditioned, carpeted emptiness and was told there was no human subjects
review as such, only Dr. M.'s personal permission, which he gave with a
wave of his hand. While most psychiatrists spoke English with me, Dr. M.
insisted we conduct our meeting in Hindi, perhaps to assess my ability to
communicate with patients. This would be our only interaction. Though I
tried to make appointments, I could wait only so long and he came too late
(hours, often), so I stopped making the effort. I came to view him as
women in the ward did—a near-mystical being, all but absent, present as
though on a whim, but with absolute authority. The only other time I saw
him, he was pulling one of the female patients—a woman with develop-
mental and intellectual disabilities—off the floor by her ear. She was on
new medication and could not stay awake but was not moving quickly
enough for Dr. M. He did not notice me sitting there.

Dr. K.'s daily rounds were brief and patients came to her office in erratic
intervals. There was too much waiting around—hours in the egg-shaped
plastic chairs that circled the large, dark waiting room—so Dr. K. suggested
I spend time in the female ward, where my presence would be a welcome
distraction. After a while, as it became clear from her quizzical looks that
she no longer wanted me to pop in to tell her I had arrived, I started going
directly to the ward, spending long, quiet hours that felt like waiting even
if what I was doing was "working." I brought magazines and decks of cards,
played games with the women, and participated in preparing food for the
kitchen. Dr. K. remained inscrutable to me, and Dr. M. as mythical as the
Wizard of Oz, the man behind the curtain. The women in the ward, with
diverse backgrounds and mental states, were more welcoming, interested,
and knowable.

That was my first summer in Moksha. A year later, I returned with the
idea—planted by Dr. K.—that Moksha had moved to another part of the

city. I had a neighborhood in mind, where Dr. K. had said a new hospital was being built, but no address. I asked around—did anyone know where I might find Moksha, the psychiatric hospital that had once been on the edge of the city? Many asked if I meant the big institution in the middle of the city, where "Lunatic Asylum" had graced the wall just a decade earlier. (That hospital, founded in the nineteenth century as a colonial asylum, was later transferred to missionary hands and eventually to an international Christian foundation. It catered to a more elite clientele, though like Moksha its clients came from many places.) No, I meant Moksha. Had they heard of it? Few had, and asking about mental hospitals elicited strange looks. When I phoned Moksha, the endless ringing made me assume the number had been changed. After weeks of trying to "find Moksha" (the phrase, of course, means "find liberation"), I hired a rickshaw to take me to the edge of the city where I would ask around to see if anyone knew the hospital's new location. On a muddy monsoon morning, skirting puddles of unknowable depth, I arrived, rain-splattered, at the old site. The hospital had a new sign, its gate was open, the gate guard at his post, and a ward attendant I had met the previous summer was waving with a surprised smile. Perhaps Dr. K. had been mistaken, or the move had been postponed or fell through. But Moksha was where it had always been.

This was the beginning of a second, longer span of visits to the female ward, a space that often left me feeling drained and devastated, especially by the observation that many of the women there for the long term were divorced or divorcing. Many were desperately unhappy with their placement in Moksha. A sense of crisis was pervasive, conditioned by a web of muted sensation—stillness, quiet, stoppage of movement. As I sat with the women I was acutely aware of the empty measure of their days, the exaggerated impact of small movements in expanses of inaction. I was aware of their emotions, their delusions in some cases, as well as their "paranoid" access to something real. I felt it incumbent to keep these aspects present in my notes, though in doing so I became something other than an anthropologist with a research agenda among research subjects. Turning to things more sensory and atmospheric awakened in me feelings more human, outraged, and empathetic. In Moksha's locked female ward I suppose I did some research, but mostly I filled pockets of space and time and then went home to write about it, documenting something I could not easily name, impressions I could never verify.

In ways that included a hint of illegitimacy and wrongdoing, Moksha was a material outcome of India's history of deinstitutionalization, a patchy affair that took place during the 1980s and 1990s through changes to the structure of existing institutions and invigorated visions of oversight. Though, globally, shifts from long-term custodial care to (often private) outpatient clinics seemed to be something new, in India medical care has long had a spirit of privatization. A babel of small and large private hospitals, nursing homes, and clinics has been the background to an expansive (if also unfinished and unfulfilled) state system. At the edges of that system, filling in its many gaps, is a vast cadre of unqualified, semiqualified, or self-qualified practitioners with legitimacy shored up in extrainstitutional ways—through practice and performance, confidence and showmanship (Pinto 2008). Indeed, one almost wonders if something not entirely unlike "community care" has long been accomplished, if unevenly, by such practitioners and the more and less official small clinics that dot the landscape.

If the missionary and entrepreneurial zeal of settings like Moksha are long familiar features of Indian health care, so are their failings and abuses. The earliest mental health policy in India, the Indian Lunacy Act of 1912, devotes a considerable amount of verbiage to regulating such clinics, as does the Mental Health Act of 1987. Where globally, structures of oversight often assumed the state to be the purveyor of the worst excesses, in India, upstart private clinics are equal players in cases of abuse. Yet the National Mental Health Programme, which emphasizes multilevel care and specialized support from centralized health services to the district level, is derived from a logic of scarcity, according to critics. That is, it is modeled to provide care where it is absent rather than to change philosophies; its legal structures remain focused on admission to institutions rather than the conditions of care within them (Dhanda 2000).

In private settings like Moksha, relationships between patients and kin also confound distinctions between old and new, intersecting with a jumble of new and old conditions in family life, things that not only represent modernity and cultural change but materialize an ever-changing legal structure related to marriage and a social structure that depends in large part on women being located—physically as well as conceptually—in relation to families. While much has been made, and rightly so, of the way laws related to marriage in India treat women as emblems of community rather than individual agents, of at least equal importance is the way legal structures that would protect women's ability to sever family ties nonetheless assume and assert women's status as bound to kin. Laws that regulate postdivorce maintenance, inheritance, and custody, and the many legal and medical decisions that inform them, are part of the conditions that bring women into (and, ideally, out of) clinics. They intersect with different approaches to the role of families in inpatient care. While government hospitals rely on families for care in the wards and move patients in and out quickly, private hospitals may become settings for long-term custodial care (and, as a result, for an old kind of abuse) for patients with families who can pay and make do without women's loving and laboring presence. This is so even as the private status of such clinics, their focus on pharmaceuticals, and their orientation toward outpatient care stand for newer, postinstitutionalization philosophies. Such circumstances were part of what filled Moksha's female ward with women at the "margins of marriage" (the phrase is from Harlan and Courtwright 1995).

But the skeins of this relationship—between the kind of institution Moksha was and the practices, quirks, and social structures that made it a space of estrangement—remained to be unraveled. In getting to know women there I began to feel that in spite of the way the notion of "dumped women" hung cloudlike over Moksha, women there did not appear to be seen as defective or abnormal (as unmarried or mentally ill) and abandoned on those terms by families, societies, or global economic structures. Rather, their confinement was part of something different, the layering of dissolutions and efforts in the midst of those dissolutions. Tense and troubled family histories produced desperation and confinement less in shoring up ideals or policing the human than at the never entirely abnormal points at which relations broke down. No one, I am convinced, considered these women subhuman, animal-like, or incapable of social life. Clinical practices were full of uncertainty and disintegration. Women with dissolutions of mind as well as kinship fell into these cracks. Moksha caught them.

While I was visiting Moksha, I too, was falling to pieces. Returning to India after six panic-filled months making a temporary home of a new, small apartment around the corner from the home I had left, I was still too soon on the heels of separation, too enmeshed in the damages of a new (also temporary) relationship, and too adrift in the uncertainty of it all to be picking up the pieces. I thought I had begun to reknit, but I was still too deep in a state of undoing to become articulate again as elements of myself, my life, my words came back into jointedness, though that's what I thought I was doing. After moving back into the Annexie, I began filling in our spaces for a longer stay, a turn of seasons rather than a summer, beginning with the kitchen—a black-market gas cylinder, borrowed stove, new pots and pans, tools for making rotis and grinding spices, scrub brushes and buckets—and progressing to things to soften the edges: carpet, plants, a winnowing basket for the wall, a clay pot by the door. Eve and I spent a day running around the city selecting a refrigerator, entertaining the idea of a new pink one, a piece of shiny middle-class candy for our living room. I settled, to her bewilderment, on a battered gray one that arrived lashed with twine to the back of a rickshaw.

Just as the lovely back arbor had been replaced by an apartment block, the land around the next-door bungalow was being dug fathoms deep to make way for a ring of apartments. Eve and I watched the rise of buildings out of these pits. We mourned lost sleep as trucks moved earth and flood-lights irradiated the night. We listened to workers sing after they finished their midnight shifts, and watched during a festival as they occupied a room four floors up in the half-finished building, offering a dollhouse view onto their temple floating in darkness. For six days they sang with drums and hoarse throats to gods they brought from their home to the east. I did not know this ritual or its patterns of sound and light. More familiar was the way our days were carved into watches by calls to prayer rising from nearby mosques. On very still days we could hear calls alighting from further away, overlapping summons in stunningly beautiful dissonance.

As Eve learned how to be a north Indian schoolgirl in the mornings and mapped the staircases, gardens, courtyards, and rooftops of Mrs. M.'s house in the afternoons, I was caught up in efforts to reconstitute us as a family, to build a temporary but secure and populated home. Some evenings were especially difficult. At the waning end of afternoon, I watched eagles lift from the TV antenna on the roof of the new high-rise. While I waited for Eve to return from her adventures, I watched their wings stoke the wind and listened for the whistle of trains in patient call and response, waiting for the signal to enter the station a mile or so down the line. These things should have been comforting but they terrified me, reminding me of things that matter but are unseen. One night a friend stopped by after Eve had gone to sleep. A robust gal from northern England who was in town for a language course, she saw my condition and said, "Get some whisky down tha' throat, lass," pouring an offering of hazy respite.

In the midst of all of this and at the peak of my time at Moksha, my husband came to visit for three mournful weeks. He did so against my wishes but bearing gentleness. I pretended to those around us that we were a happily reunited family in the midst of temporary, necessary parting. I was angry with him and hated myself for enjoying parts of the performance. I went to Moksha not noticing the channels of dried tears in the road dust on my cheeks. I made a Christmas for us out of pieces of glitz from the bazaar across the railway line. We went away for the New Year, to a city where Eve made daily offerings of marigolds to the Ganges. On the return, we jumped out of the train when it stopped a short way from my neighborhood for its indeterminate wait for the station signal. Hurriedly, we passed daughter and bags down to the platformless tracks like novice bandits. Those short, cold days were a mess of desperately conflicting emotions.

And then he left. Our house was empty; my English friend and others had gone home; Mrs. M. was in Delhi; most of the people we knew were away; life was a desert. When I could not help shed tears at her father's absence, Eve hit me with a balled-up hand. The city had become cold, and activity stopped. In the winter haze, it felt as though the sun never quite came out, people never quite started the day. Eve came home dirty as a chimney sweep. The cold made bathing her a full evening's effort and sapped my energy to face the world, especially the conversations about who we were and why we were here, the constant negotiation of traffic and gazes. I went back to picking up pieces, to coping with loss and to sitting alone on my balcony after Eve went to bed, where I leaned into the sagging weave of an old chair as bats swooped above me, testing the boundaries of my rationality between knowledge that they wouldn't hit me and panic at their wing-breeze on my face. I forced myself to be still.

Throughout this period the locked, confining, and oddly protective space of Moksha did something for me, though I could not articulate the effect at the time. (I can barely do so now.) So did the Sufi shrines I visited with intense focus and regularity, by way of contrast. The two settings offered different means of inhabiting my own grief and dissolution, even as they exposed vital emotional work that happens for many north Indian women, dancing at the margins of kinship and in the spaces of love's vulnerabilities. It would be silly to think that my efforts to understand those elusive choreographies were not also attempts to locate patterns in my own entropies. These included the dissolution of the idea of research as well as my own more personal going to pieces and the dissolutions of those around me. In Moksha, I too was grappling with things falling apart and doing the urgent work of trying to bring it all into a new kind of togetherness.

Throughout, and even now, the purpose of my writing slipped in and out of focus. I felt the uncertainty of accounts of "what happened," the loss of a sense of reality in and about relationships and their undoing. In my uncertainty about what my words about Moksha might be *for* (research? a publishing record? tenure?) I was reminded of the self-reproach in Lorrie Moore's story, "People Like That Are the Only People Here," about, among other things, a parent's loss of faith in language during her child's treatment for cancer. In the final words of the story, language is reduced to barter, a thing to be sold to pay for treatments. I recalled, as I wrote about Moksha, her bitter, confessional words: "Here are the notes, now where is the money?" (1998: 250).

Self-doubt coincided with a sense of both the practical effects of language and its instability. This became an ethical equation, much as described by Maurice Blanchot, for whom the dissolution of language's hold on what is real has less to do with perspective, or with subjective or situated truth—stalwarts of revisionist anthropological epistemology—than with language's inherently undoing capacity, its negating effects and functions. In my own undoing, I came to side with Moore and Blanchot. In the absence of final, concluding facts, I found refuge in the conversational ways language dabbled with its own ends. I did so not to settle on the *fact* of disorientation but to seek in it something specific, pragmatic, and ethnographic; something about what was happening there (rather than "what happened"); something that, at the same time, I felt was impossible to pin down. "To converse," Blanchot writes, "is not only to turn away from saying what, thanks to language, *is*—the present of a presence. To converse is also to turn language away from itself, maintaining it outside of all unity, outside even the unity of that which is. To converse is to divert language from itself by letting it differ and defer, answering it with an always already to a never yet" (1995: 35).

And so, I had conversations.

The woman I conversed with most came to Moksha not long before I began my second stint of work there. There were similarities in our lives. We were the same age—thirty-four. Our marriages were over. Our young children were three years apart. Her life was, as she put it, "falling to pieces." Mine was not so different, though my disintegrations had evaded the long arms of psychiatry and the padlocked doors of inpatient care. I had fieldwork to hold on to; I had freedom of movement; I had my child.

Ten years earlier, just out of graduate school, Sanjana fell in love. Her parents objected to her union with a Muslim man and never accepted the marriage. In the thick of family tensions, Sanjana converted to Islam and built a new life as interactions with her natal family faded. She bore a son and lived a comfortable life in a middle-class neighborhood.

When her son was eight, the marriage became strained. "We began to fight, and it just fell apart, the way these things do," she said. Her husband spoke the triple *talak*, the verbal declaration of divorce, and, though unsure whether these pronouncements were official, Sanjana returned to her family, leaving her son behind. Laws relating to custody vary by community but tend to regard the place of the young child as with the mother and of the older child (especially boys) as with the father. For women, marital breakdown often comes with loss of children, particularly when mental illness is involved.

Sanjana's brother was not pleased, but he took her in. Animosity was the residue of "love marriage," and Sanjana's brother forbade her to go back to her husband's house. Her husband, insisting she stay away, threatened to file a police report when she tried to visit her son. Among natal kin who, she felt, saw her as a burden, and coping with the losses of son, home, husband, and religious identity, Sanjana grew depressed. Just before her brother brought her to Moksha, Sanjana had an episode. "I was bathing," she said, "I heard children playing on the street below the window. I felt strongly in my stomach that I wanted to take my son back inside me. I fell unconscious then."

In Moksha, she and her brother met with Dr. K. According to her chart and Dr. K.'s recollections, her brother described Sanjana as angry and out of control. Seeing her state and hearing her accusations that she was brought by force, Dr. K. thought the issue might be paranoid schizophrenia and committed Sanjana to the inpatient unit for observation. Though Sanjana did not want to stay, she signed the form consenting to admission.

Sanjana's diagnosis shifted over time. Changing evaluations returned to schizophrenia. But, rather than being muted by medication, her suffering grew worse. She insisted she was "fine," upset about her divorce but with nothing "medically wrong." She was here "by force," she said, a refrain common on the ward. Though her husband had divorced her, also by force, she was ready to make a new life.

One of the ward attendants, a woman in her mid-thirties named Pooja, was on the margins of marriage, like many of the patients. The widowed mother of two small children, Pooja took the job at Moksha, with its twelve-hour shifts and frequent night duty, because it was the only one available. She filled a daily log with notes about patients, describing behavior, what they ate, and how much they slept. She chided Sanjana about her love marriage and eating habits. Though giving up *paan*, chewing tobacco, became a condition for Sanjana's release, Pooja slipped Sanjana the silver foil packets when she arrived for her shift.

Every two weeks, all the women on the ward were taken to Dr. M.'s office, where they sat together opposite his desk, answering questions and awaiting his pronouncement on their release. Given the apparent weight of these sessions, Sanjana was suspicious. Dr. M. didn't ask how they were, she said, only about "little things." He didn't converse with them separately, but as a group. She recalled, "This is not the right way to do this."

What happened to Sanjana in her seven months in Moksha became a touchstone for me, appearing in most of the things I wrote along the way to this book. If my tone in these paragraphs is more strident than elsewhere, it is because her situation drew me quickly to outrage; in it I felt I could name what was wrong. Yet, juxtaposed with other situations, even those similar to hers, certainties frayed. That Sanjana's doctors struggled to name what was wrong—but found something unmistakably so—was important to her suffering. Even more important, Sanjana's confinement in Moksha and her entrenched agony were at least in part results of clinicians' explanation for her situation: abandonment. That Sanjana had been "forgotten" by family who did not "care for her" meant she would have to be "kept" in Moksha indefinitely. That such an explanation failed to live up to the conflicting facts of her circumstance mattered little.

A woman named Amina had been on the ward for a year when Sanjana was brought in. Their backgrounds were so similar that staff tended to talk as though they were a single unit, as Sanjana-Amina, or Amina-Sanjana. In her forties, Amina was the mother of two teenage daughters who had moved to Bombay with their father when they were children, after he and Amina divorced. Like Sanjana, Amina was taken to Moksha by a brother, and like Sanjana she said her family was "against her." She had been brought forcibly; she wanted to leave. When social workers suggested that Pooja take the women outside to "eat sunshine" during winter afternoons, they warned her to keep an eye on "people like Sanjana-Amina," people likely to run away.

Whereas Sanjana's diagnosis was uncertain, Amina's psychosis was easily confirmed. Before coming to Moksha, she was treated for schizophrenia in the older psychiatric hospital in the heart of the city. Unable to bear its cost, her family brought her home. When she relapsed, they found Moksha. After she had spent a year in Moksha on antipsychotic medication, her account of marriage did not stretch the limits of believability, but her affect and exclamations were easily recognizable as schizophrenic. Antipsychotic medications dampened these expressions, and over time, clinical scrutinies related less to diagnosis than to her body's response to medication, her passage toward lucidity, progress Amina steadily made, though not without long stretches of sadness about her exile in Moksha.

When we first met, Amina told the story of her marriage: "My brother has become my enemy. Nine years ago, my husband made another marriage. There was a court case, and my brother was involved. My husband and my sister had an affair [lit. married] and had a daughter. From that this animosity started. My brother took the payments for that sister. A *mehr* [bride price] was given. There was no divorce; their affair [marriage] was just like that."

Sitting at Amina's side, a ward attendant named Bubli (Pooja's counterpart), reiterated the details she thought I had misunderstood. "Her husband and her own younger sister had a child together, and after that the divorce happened. Since that time she has been living with her brother. There is a lot of tension between her husband's family and her own family because he took a divorce by force. They remarried their daughter somewhere else, and he went to Bombay and married someone else. Now he no longer comes and goes from [here]."

After separating from her husband, Amina had taught Urdu and Arabic, living in the ladies' hostel of a madrassa. "I want to phone my brother," she said, "I want to tell my family that I will get a job, I will support myself. Those people will not let me live at home, but I will get a job," she said. She hadn't seen her daughters in two years, and her ability to leave depended on her brother, who had become her guardian after the divorce. Even so, she said, "The doctors want the patients to stay so they keep getting money."

While doctors on rounds asked patients questions that focused on eating, sleeping, and the passage of time (what day is it?), social workers who came through later in the morning pursued more subjective states of being. Their questions focused on some patients more than others, those whose delusions were uncertain, whose psychoses involved lost love and broken unions. Questions about relationships, and about feelings about relationships showed the degree of psychosis for patients whose lucidity might be deceptive. A quality of feeling I have elsewhere called "rational love" (Pinto 2011) was sought in queries about struggles and losses—divorce, loss of children, conditions of life amid new family arrangements. These inquiries seemed to reveal suggestions of wellness, not only the ability to care for oneself and understand one's location in space and time, which the doctors asked about, but the capacity to be among others.

The social workers were mostly women in their early twenties, unmarried, and just out of graduate school. Their time at Moksha was often a matter of months before they moved on to other jobs, marriages, and further education. Making rounds after Dr. K., they were on friendly terms with patients. In the men's wards, their demeanor was fond and joking, with hints of flirtation but firm and sisterly. With the women they were more cautious and less inclined to joke, though they were conversational and often amused. Occasionally they lingered to play a round of Antakshiri, but more often they went from patient to patient, asking detailed questions of those whose stays were likely to be temporary.

Like many in the ward, Sanjana bracketed her responses by asserting, "I am not crazy; I was brought here by force." Many learned to introduce their speech this way, though for clinicians such statements announced lack of insight and the persistence of illness. While such interactions clearly exposed the maddening nature of inpatient psychiatry, I suspect they also reflected ironies of human interaction more broadly—of life with others, especially in the midst of broken intimacy. It is not just in psychiatry wards that "I am not crazy" comes to mean "I am no longer sane." I had heard myself say it, and heard how crazy it sounded, in my own life, when arguments were at their most heated and words at their least sane, when we bartered in accusations of insanity.

In Moksha it was not just the claim, "I am not crazy," that signified its opposite; "my family is against me" was a similar statement, as well as "I have been put here by force." Though not necessarily untrue, these words accomplished something at a remove from stating the fact of a family dispute, say, or forcible commitment. For doctors, they were symptoms. Yet for the women, the need to voice such things grew more intense in relation to the extent to which they were read as symptoms of delusion. True or not, these were feelings a person must disavow to show they were well enough to leave. In the same way, true or not, the sense of being wronged can be something a person must disavow in order to prove oneself sane in the crazy flux of broken love.

For Sanjana, questions probed marriage, divorce, and her relationship with her family. Was she accusatory? Did she say her brother was "against her" or her husband "had another woman"? While facts were unclear to clinicians, much hinged on her responses, whether she claimed her husband divorced her without consent or that her natal family brought her to Moksha by force. Clinicians made much of Sanjana's cross-community marriage. It was a natural cause of distress and, at the same time, a sign of inherent recklessness. A person must be held accountable for their choices in love.

When Sanjana was upset, Pooja chided, "Maybe you should think about why that is, what your *galti* [wrongdoing, blame] is here."

"Don't say that," I said, and told Sanjana I didn't think she had done anything wrong.

"No," Pooja said, "When a person is feeling like this it is a chance for them to stop and think at least once about what they did. That kind of marriage. . . . You have a love marriage, right? Cross-caste?" Sanjana walked away.

Sanjana was distressed about her divorce. She was concerned about its validity and her claims to her son and property. These were not questions I could readily answer. She asked me if the triple *talak* was valid. I spent the next week researching this—asking lawyers, visiting a legal bookstore, and photocopying articles, ending my short searches without a clear answer. The matter was unclear, I told her; its validity had been both challenged and upheld by those taking the perspective and side of wronged wives. More at issue were her legal claims on goods, spaces, and relations, the extent to which she would be expected to rebuild a life separate from her son, and the extent to which she would be financially dependent on natal kin or could seek maintenance from her husband, eking out a life independent of those households. Sanjana described feeling unmoored from spaces where "no one wanted her, no one will have her." To be sure, this city was not one where establishing a home and means to live were easy for divorced women, even those with graduate degrees. Even so, she spoke about getting a job and "supporting herself," describing call center jobs in the large complexes materializing at the edges of Delhi. But to say such a thing in Moksha could as easily sound like delusion as hope.

Though emotions related to marital life figured in medical questioning, these were matters with greater legal than clinical weight, establishing women's vulnerability within and without kinship. Legal paradigms surely influenced Sanjana's state of mind, just as they shaped her life in ways beyond her awareness. A history of disputes pitted women's right to self-determination against that of religious groups in a pluralistic legal system in which the private lives of Muslims, Hindus, Christians, and Parsis—matters related to family, marriage, inheritance, custody, and divorce—are governed under separate bodies of law. Court battles over divorce, inheritance, and maintenance—matters of survival for many women—involved the extent to which women might be permitted to make claims permitted in one body of law but denied in another. The watershed Shah Bano case of the 1980s had set the interests of women (claims for legal status separate from kin and community) against the sovereignty of minority communities feeling encroached upon by a majority-ruled government. At issue was Muslim women's ability to seek maintenance from husbands versus their need to depend on *mehr*, the customary bride-price that by the late twentieth century had been reduced to a token in much of India. Though the government's Muslim Women's (Protection of Rights on Divorce) Act of 1986 was quickly overturned, and with it the Supreme Court ruling that divorced women married under Muslim law were to be maintained by natal kin, the social fractures and female legal subject it produced were more lasting. For divorced women, claims in and against kinship and their stake and security in the world remained uncertain and involved identities larger than their individual status, highlighting the way women's independence might be framed as a social threat. This context made of Sanjana and Amina figments of law whose agency had ever-shifting parameters and whose state of dependence was assumed.

After the holidays, Amina's daughters took the train from Bombay. It was the first time they had seen their mother in two and a half years. Combining their visit with a family wedding, they arrived a week earlier. The marriage hall was a short walk from Moksha, so during the celebration, Khadija, the elder daughter, slipped out and stood outside, trying to get a sense of "what this place was." After the week of celebration, the sisters asked if they could stay on the ward. Dr. M. balked, allowing them only a twenty-minute visit. But the next evening he relented, and Khadija and Ruksar pushed together two empty beds and spent the night at their mother's side.

The girls' uncle was doubtful of their ability to stay on the ward, saying they would learn what they needed to from a visit. But Khadija insisted. "Usually you don't understand," she said. "The doctors give you a very jolly picture of how it is, 'Oh we take care, we take them out.'" But in order to really see her mother's life she had to stay "maximum *jitna* [as much as] we can."

At twenty-two, Khadija had finished university and held a promising job in a bank. Her sister Ruksar, fifteen, was still completing secondary education. Their lives were happy; they loved school and work and enjoyed creative pursuits like stitching, drawing, and writing, skills they said they inherited from their mother. They got along well with their stepmother, whom their father had married several years after the divorce. "She's a lovely lady," Khadija said, "She's very just. She says, 'I can't be your mother but I can be your guardian. So treat me like one.' Thankfully we're in the right hands. We're living a happy life. We've got a small brother now. Things are very peaceful."

Their parents divorced when Khadija was twelve. Though indications of their mother's illness had been gradual, symptoms had likely been present from the start of the marriage. "She used to always doubt my father. From the beginning, and these things never stopped, it just got worse, the stories got more dramatic over time."

"Would she tell these things to you?" I asked.

"She would tell these things to me, she would tell these things to the world. . . . Her mind [was] full of things that were all made up, that my brother is against me, my mother wants to kill me, my husband betrayed me, everyone around me is my enemy, this is what she always used to keep thinking, keep feeling, keep saying."

Khadija's father, "a learned man with a Ph.D.," understood the nature of his wife's illness, but "somewhere down the line, in sixteen, seventeen years," Khadija said, "he lost the patience to really push it." Realizing that Amina would not seek help, he suggested they both go for counseling. "He tried from his end, but after all, he was losing himself all the time, losing his respect, everything. A wife accusing you is the last thing you want, and it's very believable by the whole world."

After the separation, Amina returned to her parents' home. Discussions between her husband and natal family resulted in the decision that the girls should live with their father. Khadija struggled with this. "Somewhere I feel the decision was right, somewhere I feel it was wrong, but I think that for considering our future it was right." Their mother could care for herself, but she could not also care for others. "At that point," Khadija said, "We would be nothing but a burden."

Amina's family denied she had an illness and supported the notion that her husband had an affair. Khadija felt that this was due to their lack of understanding of mental illness. "If you're hurt on your foot, or on your leg, you can see it. But if your physical hurt is in your mind, no one can see." Their inability to recognize her mother's schizophrenia was part of its tenacity, she said. "The disease just went in, rooting, creeping in her mind."

After the divorce, their father was posted to Bombay. After a year and a half of caring for his daughters, "cooking and everything," he began looking at matrimonial ads.

The divorce had been harder for Ruksar to understand than for Khadija, who, though she had witnessed her parents' fights, was still "struck dumb" by their decision to separate. For several years she was angry at her father, finding it hard to forgive him and blaming him for "the fact that [she] didn't have her mother." But as she grew up and saw the nature of her mother's illness, her attitude changed. Through phone calls and visits, she became convinced her mother's world was one of fantasy and paranoia. Instead of arguing, Khadija began to placate her.

With adulthood came an ability to evaluate things rationally, to disentangle herself from her mother and dissolve conflicted feelings about her father. "I started objectively viewing her ideas and my father's, and I said, 'No, something's wrong, it looks like something's cooked.' So I started listening to her and not believing her. Just you know, 'OK, fine, OK, OK.' I said, 'Just let me soothe her and say fine.'" With new ways of thinking came new connections. Khadija and her stepmother grew close. "She's been quite a force in bringing objectivity in me. She never advocated [for] my father, she never defended him, she just said, 'You logically think. Don't think from one side. Stand in the middle, see how it is.'"

Khadija and Ruksar's departure for Bombay was a terrible blow to Amina. "She couldn't take that for a fact," Khadija said. "She loves us, she really does, and the fact that we left, that was the last straw in whatever was happening in her mind. She would blame every possible person for what happened in her life."

Khadija and Ruksar visited yearly. Each time, Amina's condition was worse. "When we would leave, the kind of behavior she would present was scary. I would shudder to think that I would want to come again." Khadija wondered if her visits were doing more harm than good, especially for her grandmother, who was left with the work of restoring Amina's shattered emotions. "We'd come for three days, but it would be an issue for them for ten months."

These visits deepened Khadija's sense of the blurry moral parameters created by mental illness and the complexity of her mother's lack of control. "I saw her worsen, [in] her letters, her phone calls, and I realized, 'No, you know what? My father was right.' But, then again, some things you really can't tell, because whatever she was, it wasn't out of her own will, she wasn't doing it purposely. Any right in the mind, sane in the mind person wouldn't do it, so it was something that was making her do all that, so I wouldn't blame her, I wouldn't say it was all her fault. And that was the conflict where I just came to a dead end, and said, 'Hey where to go from here?' Because I can't blame him, I can't blame her. I'm losing either way."

A poster hung on the wall behind the reception desk, offering images of superstitious and modern approaches to mental illness. In the middle, a sketch of a bride and groom, neither looking particularly happy, read, "Marriage is not a cure for mental illness." But down the hall in the female ward, signs of illness were constantly negotiated in terms of marriage—at its fringes, through memories, and in dim hopefulness about it—while treatment and prognosis seemed to hinge on emotions related to love. Women's talk of suffering focused on love and heartbreak, and marriage was both intertwined with suffering and part of healing. The fallout of its breakdowns curtained the locked ward. Yet, it was also clear that the truth of any story about love and its dissolution, about marriage or kinship, affection or mistreatment, might be shaky and changeable, a matter of perspective.

Though doctors in Moksha had little interest in the social insecurities of divorced women, they put marriage to use in other ways. What was the state of Sanjana's desire? Had anger turned into grief, or did she insist she was wronged? Had she come to accept things? What could be found in the way she spoke about her husband, son, and brother, in the fact that she used *paan*, or hid the peanuts her mother brought her? Though initially it seemed that answers to these questions might establish the truth of accounts of marriage, over time I began to wonder if the truth about "what happened" really mattered. Emotion was under assessment regardless of the truth or falsehood of accounts.

Kajol, a young social worker, at times reiterated what doctors said and at times was sympathetically agnostic. "How are you today, Sanjana?"

"I am fine. There is nothing wrong with me. I should get out of here."

"I think your mother came recently?"

"Yes, she came a few days ago."

"Did you meet with Dr. M.?"

Though the meeting had been put off for several weeks, Dr. M. had finally met with the women.

"What did he say?" Kajol asked.

"He said after Holi." Sanjana's face changed, collapsing into itself in a prelude to tears that made her look leonine and sleepy.

"Oh ho. After Holi. . . . That is a very long time." Kajol counted the months on her fingers. "If he said that then that is what we have to listen to. I heard your mother came recently? She must have spoken to Dr. M. too."

"I don't know," Sanjana said, "But he said I can't get out until after Holi. After that, my mother will take me back to Delhi. I will get settled there."

"You need to get out first, let's focus on getting you out first. You will need to establish yourself on your own."

"Maybe my husband can take me back," Sanjana said almost inaudibly.

"This is something we will have to think about. But yes, maybe that will be so. You must have a lot of attachment to your husband and children." I noticed that she used the plural.

"Yes, I am more attached to them than to anyone."

"It is better to not be so attached to anyone. So much attachment is not good. You are sick, right? You are sick, and if you are so attached and you are sick then who will take care of them? You should not be so attached but should depend on yourself. You seem very normal. You talk to all the other patients here. I also think you are fine; I also think you are OK. But what has to happen will happen. Just depend on yourself, stay active. Do yoga, do meditation, read magazines, watch some TV, keep busy."

"I am active at home."

"No, you must stay active here. Keep yourself busy. I get your report from Pooja and it says you bathed and then slept under your quilt all day."

"No, I get up, I walk around, I pray, I read."

"It says you are not active, and you need to stay active. Stay active here, and I will come back and see that you are active and I will tell Dr. M."

"I do stay active."

"You should talk to the other patients, get their histories, chat with them. What are their histories? What is Amina's story?"

"Amina's husband left her and married someone else, and her brother brought her here."

"Good. You'll go from here when you are completely fine. Stay active and talk to the other patients, keep them active and keep them talking too, and I will come and check on you. Is there any work or activity here for you?"

"I can read books in the library if I can go there. Can I go to the library?"

"It is closed now because of the cold, but it will reopen when it gets warmer."

These conversations were mediated by (and a way of mediating) biology, signs that drugs were taking effect. As Sanjana was questioned by a staff of practitioners who were never certain about her state or how to label it, she was put on shifting medications—antipsychotics, antidepressants, antianxiety drugs—whose names and effects she was not told. Her expressions were read for signs of changing biology. Such scrutiny was paradoxical. In a locked ward with little to fill time, it produced the very emotions it sought to mitigate, generating expressions that were signs of pathology. In it, clinicians demanded something more than acceptance of ill fate but short of denial of injustice.

Though expressions were reduced to biological signs, the possibility of truth was never entirely eclipsed. A sense of it remained in deliberations of "delusion," lingering in the term itself, imagined things granted undue measures of reality. Clinicians and staff agreed that Sanjana's account— "what she said"—was likely to be true, but this did not change the fact that her statements were legible only as symptoms, as fantasy by degree.

By all accounts, including her own, Sanjana's state of mind deteriorated. But Amina began to improve. Khadija was "totally zapped" to see her mother calm and lucid. Our conversation was charged with possibility, by Khadija's sense of her mother's reintegration as a person with a sense of herself in the world, with more strength and objectivity and an ability to "stand up and say 'Hello, I need to take control of my life.'"

Many "small, small things" were signs of change. Amina's emotions were more controlled; she was not inconsolable; she no longer threw things or become violent. The day before, Khadija explained to Amina that she and Ruksar would leave in the early afternoon to reach the station for their evening train. Their mother observed that on that schedule they would not have time to bathe before the journey. "She said, 'You won't be able to take a bath [if you leave at 1:00] because you've not got clothes, so you'll have to go and take a bath [at your grandmother's house]. So she said, 'You know what? I think you should leave a little early, I think you should leave by 10.'

"I said, 'I will be here until 1:00,' so she doesn't feel I am trying to run away, but she herself said, 'No, you go at 10, take a bath nicely, properly, eat food, pack bags, don't leave in a hurry, don't miss anything.' This is logical thinking which never happened before."

Amina could let her daughters leave. For Khadija and Ruksar, their mother's ability to cope with time's intrusions on intimacy was a sign of rationality, and her ability to recognize the needs of others indicated healthy detachment. Words breaking up, Khadija said, "Yesterday, when I left she just was . . . she felt bad that I was leaving, but the fact that she let me go . . . , and she said, just come back tomorrow, and I trust that you will. . . . She has an understanding, and she has trust now."

Though before, her mother had not recognized her own divorce, now she could acknowledge it, Khadija said. Khadija felt that this peaceable un-making of connections was the result of Amina's period of separation in Moksha. "One and a half years, no one has come down to meet her, except me now, and I think that has changed her because she now she talks like a normal person, normal, you know, mentally wise."

If wellness was visible in the dissolution of bonds, so it was in gestures toward the future; as Amina learned to separate, she could imagine new connections. Amina had begun to speak of marrying. For many in the ward, the future was synonymous with marriage, and marriage was less an index of dependence than a way of making an independent life. "She's looking forward now. She realizes, 'no, I need company. And I need to start my own life.'" Amina's ability to imagine her future intimacies was an indication that her inner world was settling into thoughtful awareness. This recalibration of loss and renewal was a revelation for Khadija, who began to cry as she said, "She used to always say things like, 'He's really not wanting me to be living, he wants me dead.' *These* are the things that she would discuss with me, not her life, not her future. Today I see her talking about 'I want to get out of this place and work and be independent.' . . . She's talking about settling down, she's willing to get married, she understands that today she needs financial and emotional support." Independence and support were intertwined as signs of a healthy future.

Several years ago, Khadija's uncle received a marriage proposal for Amina from the principal of a college, a widower with grown children who was in search of a companion. The man's daughter-in-law had visited, a sign the family was solid and caring, and the man was in good health and understood Amina's condition. "I can't expect my kids to take care of her when I'm gone," he had said, according to Khadija, "So I will take care of her financial security." He pledged ten lakh for Amina and a house in her name if he should predecease her. But Amina needed more strength before entering a new family and turned down the proposal. The family stopped looking for matches, hoping that when she recovered other offers would arrive.

Khadija's optimism was in part due to Amina's innate independence, her daughter felt, which was a sign of her ability to live with others. "She is a person who has never been dependent on anyone, she has always worked, she has always earned for herself, she has always actually supported people around her. She's not like that, that if she stays at our Nani's she will be a burden. She'd rather help out, she'll contribute in the family." That Amina now voluntarily took her medicine, rather than needing to be forced to do so ("a Herculean task") showed a new level of self-sufficiency, and her talk of returning to teaching showed self-concern. "When she talks like [this] I realize she's making a change, that, listen, someone's thinking about themself finally." Such thinking shaped Khadija's own perspective as well. "I'm really happy now, so whatever happened is history for me today. It's past, really. I'm looking forward for her to really take it up from here. I mean, life isn't lost, it's just the way you look at it."

Whereas Amina's life was charged with hope, in that moment, Sanjana's was slipping toward despondency. Through months of the same kinds of interactions with doctors and social workers, her pleas came to sound more, not less, paranoid. Her desperate requests—to get out, to speak with Dr. M., to use the phone—increased as she seemed more depressed, more obsessed with her marriage and more frustrated with conditions in Moksha and deliberations she had no access to. Her speech flooded with emotion, her movement slowed, her face sagged into heavier folds of sadness.

As Sanjana's mood declined, what doctors referred to as her religiosity increased. Sanjana had always enjoyed reading from the Koran, but to do so here she would have to borrow the holy book from other patients, who did not have one in a script she could read. There was a Koran in Devanagari in the library, but she was not permitted to take it out. So between calls to prayer, she used what was available to her—her hands, feet, and voice—walking and praying across the width of the ward, head bent, beads in hand.

Sanjana's feelings about her husband were conflicted. Often, she spoke of him with anger and a sense of injustice, saying he had destroyed her life by divorcing her without consent. But as her prayer increased, she asked me to pray that he take her back. She said once that all she thought about was this—her husband accepting her back into their home. Where marriage had been for Amina a sign of health and independence, for Sanjana it was something else. She spoke to another patient, "It is remarkable the way a single person can ruin another person's life, almost as though they have been put on this earth just for that. My whole life is in pieces."

I asked Kajol if Sanjana was getting psychodynamic therapy. "No, but she needs it. None of the female ward patients are." Sanjana's attachment to her husband and children worried her. ("Child," I said, "Sanjana has one son." Kajol looked surprised.)

Adding to her distress was the repeated deferral of release and of sessions with Dr. M. Kajol said she often told Sanjana her release was imminent, but that such statements were just to "make the patient happy." Her impossible advice that Sanjana "keep busy" did not, in fact, have high stakes, though it felt desperately so to Sanjana. Sanjana's latest meeting with Dr. M., Kajol said, had been a matter of routine, not a special meeting addressing her release. If Dr. M. had said Sanjana could not be released until after Holi, he must feel she was not ready to get out.

I asked what Kajol felt about Sanjana's husband, noting she sometimes seemed to agree it was possible they could be reunited. "Sometimes we tell the patients things just to ease their minds, but she made a love marriage fifteen years ago, an intercaste marriage, and then her husband divorced her and remarried someone else, and we don't know what that situation is."

While truth about love, marriage, and their ends did not matter but appeared to (with a sting of moral evaluation), truth about doctors' adjudications also did not matter in what was communicated to patients. Indeed, how it mattered was uncertain all around. In other words, Sanjana's expressions were scrutinized as indicators of wellness, and advice was given that suggested if she behave a certain way she would get out, but it would be too much to say her release depended on these things, or even that her release depended on wellness at all. Being "fine" and "normal" was not the same as being suitable for release, at least in what patients were told. What such suitability might entail was vague—"some signs," "what has to happen." But paradoxically, patients' acceptance of the confusing conditions of release was presented as a condition of release. It was as important as their acceptance of conditions of family breakdown and loss, among the things that exacerbated their dependence and made more vivid their vulnerability. Accepting the unacceptable was a condition of release from it. Or it seemed to be, when in fact it had little bearing.

The more time I spent in the female ward, the more I came to feel awash in its peculiar and hazy versions of truth. My notes reflected dislocation and dissipated facts, as well as a sense that anything of impact happened at a remove, away from those to whom it mattered most. I began to feel that in spite of the appearance of surveillance and moral judgment, clinical scrutiny of patients' normality or abnormality mattered little in the end. It had little impact on who would be permitted to leave and when, though clinician's inquiries seemed momentous, as did their (often false) pronouncements. More important than diagnosis or surveillance were interactions not involving patients at all, machinations that exceeded "clinical knowing"—things involving the hospital head and doctors, conversations women had no access to, meetings that did not happen.

These communications were full of slippery truths, incomplete exchanges, negligence, and exploitation, as well as accidents of time and forgetfulness. One afternoon, I stopped by Dr. K.'s office and asked about Sanjana. "People from her family" came in a few days back, she said, but it was not yet "time" for Sanjana to go home. I took this to mean that the decision was in the doctors' hands.

No, she said. Facts about the case were unclear to the doctors too, but, "If the family is willing to pay so much to keep her here, then surely something must be wrong."

I asked about the diagnosis. Dr. K. looked at me as though I should know this. "She is a case of paranoid schizophrenia."

Approaching the end of her stay, Sanjana asked Kajol if she had spoken with her mother about the date of her discharge.

"She phoned, but not on hospital timing," Kajol said.

"What's the difference?" Sanjana asked.

"If she calls at another time we can't talk to her. The hospital timing for phone calls is 2:00 to 5:00 P.M. But she did call and *bat hui* [a conversation was had]."

"So you did talk to her?"

"Yes, I talked to her. She should come see you soon. We call every Tuesday. But she needs to call on proper timings. If she doesn't, there is nothing we can say to her."

Another patient cut in to ask about own release. She would get out the next week, Kajol told her.

"Did you talk to Dr. M. about me also?" Sanjana asked.

"Yes."

"When will I get out?"

"That hasn't been decided yet."

Another patient spoke. "Look at her," she said to Kajol, pointing to Sanjana. "She is so depressed. She has so much tension. You can see it in her face. She is more depressed than anyone here. Is anyone going to pay attention to this? She should be in good surroundings, she should be able to sit among three, four people, she should be able to be out in the world, to get a job, to start a new life, then she will get better. But what happens here? She sits here, she gets up, she eats, she takes medicine, she sleeps. What kind of treatment is this?"

Kajol nodded. The woman went on. "Look at her face. She has the saddest face here. She will only get better if she gets out, gets a job, sits among people." There was a pause. Kajol took in this patient advocacy, then looked around to check on the others.

Amina's daughters struggled with the physical conditions of Moksha but resolved that this was "bitter medicine." "I can understand how hard it is for her to stay," Khadija said. "Because, I mean, eight hours, ten hours, eleven hours, twenty-four hours when you have nothing to do, trust me, it's not funny. It's not the best place to live in, but when you keep your emotions aside, you see, OK. . . . Because this kind of care, as hard as you try, it can't happen at home."

Khadija and Ruksar described the way their paternal grandmother, living with family, was treated: "She's got eleven kids, OK? There are five boys, five families staying in her house. And now she's on the bed, she can't move for anything. She's totally dependent. And there's no one. No one. None of the sons look after her, but my father, he comes down once in one year, once in two years. He's the one who is taking care of his mother, even though he's so far away."

Ruksar cut in, "So it's not about staying together . . ."

Her sister continued, "It's not about proximity, it's not about how close you stay, in the same house, sometimes those things don't matter."

Ruksar continued, "And even those four people who are looking after her are her daughters-in-law and grandchildren. Her own daughters don't, you know . . ." Kin through marriage were more caring than those one bore oneself. (In spite of the typically negative place of mothers-in-law in the Indian popular imagination, I often encountered the sentiment, in this and earlier work, that affinal kin—those who are at least in part "other"— are the backbone of care.)

"What is their problem, do you think?" I asked.

"Oh, come on . . . what can it be?" Khadija said, "Just lack of concern, lack of love. You know, they're so busy in their own lives and their own families, and entertainment, and, you know, the best of life, and she lies right in the middle of the house."

They told their mother about this situation, drawing it into a message about her circumstances. Khadija had said to her mother, "You are saying, 'My children are not with me, my children are not close by.' But how many Dadi has, and no one does a thing! They don't even turn to look." She reminded her mother, "Don't think because we are not with you we are not *with* you. It can be [that] we are away but we are with you. That is possible."

Getting Amina out of Moksha was complicated; independence required as much of caregivers as those receiving care. Though Amina was nearly ready, Khadija's abilities were limited by age and circumstance. "In my view, I would take her out the day she's fine. But then, I need to look at myself. Today I've started earning, yes, but I'm not earning where I can keep her as well as I can maintain myself. . . . I'm not so independent where I can stand up and say, 'Hey, I can support you.' And unless I can do that, I will not make the mistake of doing something abruptly, out of emotions, out of sheer impulsiveness and then end up saying, 'Oops . . . .' If she's totally fine I would not let her be here for one day."

Even their uncle would support bringing Amina home. "This is more like an obligation. Not an obligation, it's a pressure on them, financially, because they are not that well off. They just have him earning now, and he's got to marry [off] his sister, he's got to take care of his family, maintain his house, everything. [Institutionalizing his sister] is an added pressure; he wouldn't want to do that. He doesn't have the means for it. It is sheerly out of need that she's here; otherwise no one wants her [here], not her family, not me. Once she's fine we'll put her out of this place. Everyone wants her home, in comfort."

One afternoon, I asked Sanjana what she was thinking of. Her son, Sanjana said, whom she hadn't seen in months. His ninth birthday was coming up. She asked what day she came to Moksha. I couldn't remember, and we tried to work it out together, accounting for passages of time in a place that offered no way of marking it. "I started coming in mid-October," I said, "And at that time you had only been here two weeks, so you must have come in early October."

"No," she said, "It must have been earlier, at least September." We tried to figure out if she had come before or after Id. Neither of us could recall.

"This time when you go to the *mazar*, pray that my mummy will get me discharged from here." This was the first time she asked me to pray for her release and not for her husband to take her back.

I asked what her mother said about her discharge, understanding what Sanjana meant when she had said of getting out, "It is the only thing we talk about."

"My mummy says that when Dr. M. says it's OK I will be discharged."

Later, I asked Dr. K. about Sanjana's mother's visit. She said her mother had met with Sanjana but not with doctors. "The family is not keen to take responsibility. They don't even come and tell the history, they only talk to the patient and not the doctors. They want to be tension free. They are not bothered and do not care about the prognosis." According to Dr. K., Sanjana was a "dumped woman." The concept offered a social explanation for Sanjana's crisis. But its plot was disconnected from the details of Sanjana's life and the ever-extending duration of her stay in Moksha. The *idea* of abandonment had great consequence for her confinement, justifying doctors' decision to keep her on the ward. But it was unclear whether Sanjana's brother and mother's actions constituted abandonment, or even what those actions were. My impression was that her mother cared deeply about bringing her home, but was waiting for Dr. M.'s pronouncement and was confused by the hospital's unclear rules and expectations. It was hard to tell if this was an example of miscommunication or exploitation, or some mix of the two.

As I tried to trace decisions about Sanjana's release through hallways and offices, files and the things people said, the only consistent element was confusion. It was impossible to know who had spoken to whom or what was said, and it was impossible to know whether there was any durability to what one person or another said, whether a statement remained true beyond the conversation in which it was spoken. But it was easy to trace clinicians' language of crisis: "Sanjana had a love marriage, her husband divorced her, and now her own family will not care for her." Calling Sanjana abandoned, and emphasizing her love marriage over other elements in her life, created a series of double binds. First, it obscured the conditions and causes of her confinement even as it formed the grounds for keeping her in the locked ward. Second, it created an impossible script about release, one that emphasized social dependence while demanding self-determination, even as conditions in Moksha made displays of self-determination all but impossible. In a third double bind, such contradictory conditions created the very feelings and symptoms clinicians said Sanjana must show that she no longer suffered. In other words, they made her more depressed while demanding she no longer feel depressed.

Sanjana said her mother was waiting for Dr. M.'s sanction to take her out of Moksha. She spoke often about getting a job, supporting herself and making a new life.

But as Dr. K. said, "We care for her because her family won't." In Moksha, neither admission nor release involved language of risk or harm, concepts dominating passages in and out of locked wards elsewhere. Here, a social critique justified involuntary confinement. Regardless of the facts of Sanjana's mother's position, the complex deliberations of kinship, or whether Sanjana might be capable of caring for herself, the notion of abandonment glossed her situation. As a discourse, it obscured the possibility that a person could, and might want to, live a life on her own, underplaying women's efforts and imagination in this domain, their actions and desires to establish an independent life. In it, there was no consideration of whether a person might manage on her own.

Sanjana was released from Moksha seven months after she had been placed behind the padlocked door for "observation." She was received by her mother and taken to Delhi (far from her son, but close to new job possibilities) while I was in Boston for a month. When I returned and found her gone I asked how the release had finally happened. Everyone repeated a version of what Pooja told me: "Dr. M. must have decided she was fine to go home."

Against Sanjana's and Amina's tales of marriages come undone, against Moksha's use of familiar tropes, against Khadija's hope for their mother's future, against all of these plays of light and shadow, of interdependence and self-sufficiency, were movements of other women in and out of Moksha, other shapes of kinship and estrangement, dependence and vulnerability. Women came in, some for days, some for decades. Moksha was, among other things, a frisson of passages, a place of movement and stasis, puddle and flow.

A nineteen-year-old named Riti told me, "In three days I will have been here a month." She counted, reminding herself of the date of her arrival. "Yes, almost one month here in this jail." She was, now, very calm. She did not yell. She did not pace. She sat down to tell me how she fell in love with a boy from her neighborhood, someone her parents had not chosen for her. "We ran away and got married." (This I took to mean that they had had sex, not that they had an official marriage.) The boy rejected her after several weeks and, devastated, she "got sick." She was returned to her parents by the police. They were angry but took her in. Other things Riti told me made less sense. "I have two babies; they were born out of a pot of *kheer* [rice pudding]," she said. She named her parents as two powerful politicians (in a highly unlikely pairing) and bemoaned the way they were portrayed in the media.

For months a plump older woman sat quietly on the edges of my conversations. One afternoon, in a voice deep and clear, she said, "I have been here fifteen years." Isma was born into a middle-class family, her childhood spent in a large house surrounded by extended kin and at one of the city's most elite private schools. She was "fine" in childhood, she said; she did well in school, was close to her mother, and had many friends. But her father often beat her. Learning from him, her brother began beating her when she was a teenager. In her early twenties, after Isma's mother, her protector and comfort, died, Isma "got sick." She began to "feel bad," to sense everything around her was dirty, that there were lizards on her body and insects under her skin. Her family took her to a hospital where she received electroconvulsive therapy. Later, her father found a doctor who made house calls, bringing the equipment for shock therapy with him.

As she got older it became clear that Isma was not marriageable. Her younger sister had married and moved away. Though she visited and promised Isma she could live with her, as yet there was no space in her husband's house. Their brother found Moksha and brought Isma in. Isma was happy to have never married. But because of this, she said, her father's inheritance was in question. Unless she was married or deemed mentally unfit, she stood to inherit a portion of his estate, reducing her brother's inheritance.

A year ago, a woman was admitted to the ward and put in the bed next to Isma's. She and Isma discovered they were from the same neighborhood. The woman was a lawyer and, several weeks later, when released from Moksha, she filed a suit on Isma's behalf, charging Moksha with keeping her involuntarily and her brother with defrauding her of inheritance. Police officers had come in to talk to the doctors and, Isma said, "to write everything down." But since then she heard nothing about the case.

Many of the staff were aware of Isma's situation. Kajol told me she no longer had access to Isma's file, which was now kept in a locked drawer in Dr. M.'s office. I asked Meena, one of the psychologists, about the lawyer who had been on the ward. She laughed and said, "That was the woman who ran away!" I must have registered surprise, because she went on, "Yes, she ran away after three weeks and was later readmitted. It must have been after the second admission that she filed the case."

I asked if there were often situations like this. No, Meena said. "People with paranoia tend to take out more [legal] cases. They don't understand that they are sick; they think everyone is against them, so they submit more cases. There haven't been many like this here, though."

On arriving at Moksha, Ruksar waited outside while Dr. M. told Khadija it was not possible to stay the night. Sixty thousand rupees in payment was outstanding.

Khadija was suddenly "paranoid." She had promised her mother that she would stay and worried she would feel betrayed or think she was "just cooking up stories." She phoned her father and uncle, who together put in forty-five thousand rupees, which she withdrew from an ATM. Dr. M. said they could pay the remainder over the next two weeks.

About a month after their visit, I went to Amina's bed one afternoon and asked if she would join us for singing. She said, "No, I have been lying down since the eighteenth." Where Sanjana struggled to account for days she claimed were busy, Amina had no difficulty counting days of inaction.

This surprised me until she explained that since her daughters had left, she had not heard from them. Her sisters had called; relatives visited for Id, but "no one has come to take me out." I held her hand.

Later I asked Dr. K. about the situation. She said Amina's daughters had visited. I said yes, I had met them. There was no one in the family who was in a position to take her now, Dr. K. said. "Her daughters have come to see the place and are convinced that the conditions are OK so she will stay here for a while." I was not sure how to reconcile this with our conversation, with their hopefulness about settling their mother into a new life, or their sense of the scope of Amina's future outside Moksha. But perhaps things looked different from afar, in the settling of recollection and from a distance of time and train journeys.

Later, Amina and I had what I described in my notes as a "sad, quiet conversation." She had risen from bed and was at the table reading the Koran. She had been trying to ask "the doctors" when she would get out, but "you people are very busy."

"I have been here for one and a half years," she said. "It is time to get out, but I do not get to talk to the doctors. Since my daughters left no one has come to get me."

Kajol, who was standing by the table, said, "Yes, this is a bad thing, but this is a matter of the family, it is their wrongdoing [galat bat]. Did you speak with Dr. M.?"

It had taken Amina some time to accomplish an appointment with Dr. M., and when she finally met with him, he said she would stay in Moksha "for a while." After this, Amina took to sitting at the ward door, in the one window that received direct sunlight, where she read from the Koran. "I'm not well," she told me one afternoon. "I was crying earlier." Khadija had phoned with the news that her mother-in-law had died. "She was always left to lie in a bed in a corner," she told me. But no matter how poorly she was treated, her mother-in-law had always been kind to her.

Conversations in Moksha had a strange relationship to time. Language was momentary. Sanjana's expressions of sorrow, Khadija's account of hope, Amina's resignation, tales of wrongdoing, and everything clinicians said— these were just passing things. Removed from more linear causalities, they pulled against each other, one expression undoing the certainty another achieved, as Khadija's memories did for her mother's story or as Isma's and Sanjana's accounts did for Dr. K.'s understanding of their lives, or as social workers' narratives did for Isma's. They pulled against my own hold on outrage and understanding, showing inconsistent ways of drawing ethics out of dissolution, representing language at its most momentary and uncertain.

Stories tided toward resolution but receded from conclusion, their emptiness marking the limits of certainty. The wall between the women's ward and the rest of the hospital was a barrier, but it was not impermeable. Words took strange and inconsistent routes, their meanings uncertain and mismatched. Words whispered and stuttered; they were incomplete and burdened with consequence. Perhaps it was my perspective from "this side of the wall," but it seemed that the slipperiest speech was not that of women in psychosis—insisting the government had kidnapped them, babies were born out of food, or husbands had affairs with sisters. Rather, the most difficult speech to hold in place came from doctors, whose words were supposed to be effective, who could make things happen in the world.

In Moksha not only did words and ideas mean different things at different times, they *meant* differently. Where scholarly concern with language practices in medicine typically focuses on *what* things mean, what understandings might be unearthed or interpreted, Moksha made me question *how* things mean. It drew my attention to what meaning does, to the way shifts in modes of meaning are powerful social actions. Was a patient or doctor's statement meaningful because it showed their ability to tell the truth, because it offered explanation for suffering, because it performed emotion, or because it pacified a patient? All were possible, none consistently.

Tacks in meaning-making were a condition of Moksha. They characterized wider things—desperation, sorrow, and fear, the way partial transmissions happen between people every day, especially when intimacies are under strain, when what is said is unreliable just as it becomes impactful, or when therapeutics collide with life's catastrophes. Lest too much ethical or epistemological value be granted to uncertainty—the anthropological "it's complicated" to which authoritative generalizations cannot live up—it is important to recall that lack of clarity can also be formative of crises.

Something similar is explored in Moore's short story about a baby's terminal illness, in which a character called the Mother fails to find solace in philosophy or hopefulness (1998). Her child's illness highlights tricks of time. She "has trouble with basic concepts, such as the one that says events move in one direction only and do not jump up, turn around and take themselves back" (1998: 219). A moral voice called the Manager chides her efforts to barter for her child's safety. Don't you know, the Manager asks, that the surprise of the future is our only hope for "redemption"? To "know the narrative is not human," it says. "The mystery is all." The idea of "the story," of knowing how it all turns out is just a trick, a "piece of laughable metaphysical colonialism." This soteriology of uncertainty is "bogus" for the Mother, who wants assurance her son will live. But she is surrounded by those who live it—parents in the oncology ward, the "people like that" of the story's title, who make from uncertainty something hopeful. The Mother is a writer and her stock-in-trade is the filled-in passage of time, the telling of one thing and then another. This crisis is beyond narration, not just in its complexity or unbearable possibilities but in its chaos of elements, its "Hieronymous Bosch of facts and figures and blood and graphs," a "nightmare of narrative slop" (1998: 223).

Moore's story is pressured with the unknowable, with the way events at their most unbearable carry its weight, the way the unknown taunts those whose lives hang in the exploded time of catastrophe. In the Mother's "notes" we experience the undoing of story and time. We witness clinical countermoves in which explanation solidifies into technique and the unbearable is approached with a semblance of pacing and strategy. And we are part of a larger countermove—the story, the effort to string together undoing into something that will, in spite of itself, be coherent. At every turn, there are gestures to things that loom beyond the here and now. There is, to use terms of Gilles Deleuze and Félix Guattari, a futural element, a horizon (1983). Such horizons can emphasize containment and futility just as easily as hope and release.

The locked ward, similarly, was delineated by what it was not. The padlock on the metal door and the noisy rituals of its undoing were scene breaks around intense interiority; they showed the ward to be defined by its outside, what was remembered, unknown, imagined, or denied. Here was a constant re-creation of immanences and transcendences, interiorities and exteriorities, distributions by which immanence was distinguished from things beyond (Deleuze and Guattari 1983). Immanent states of dissolution were loaded with the future, a consequential other place. Indeed, they were loaded with layers of futures as well as pasts; competing possibilities hovered beyond the ward, creating its space and enhancing its boundedness. The future's transcendence dominated their days, but seldom through the certainty of narrative, only in "narrative slop," with occasional pauses for reach, for hiccuping repetition: "Getting out is the only thing we talk about."

There were horizons, too, of relations, haunting possibilities and impossibilities. As new relations required an "out" from old ones, women's lives showed the possibility of something outside of kinship that was neither abandonment nor independence but a horizon whose expanse might be threatening or promising. At the terrifying edge of relations, Sanjana, Amina, and others grappled to tell, know, and recognize themselves in the shadow of a future that might involve undoing as much as pulling together. There was an externality to what was said, an outside to women's claims and expressions, to the notes I took, to any language, all language. Alternative possibilities pressed on conversation and at the same time undid them. Every utterance seemed to negate itself with everything it was not. The ghosts of language were, as Blanchot has written, not just differentiation from what was said but the negation of what was said in the moment it was named, even in the security of naming and telling, in the "rigor of taut patience" (1995: 47). All of these "outsides"—of kinship, places, words— converged to make Moksha a kind of satellite. Exteriorities of time, space, and relations enfolded the ward: the horizon at the other end of the phone, the "somewhere" Khadija spoke of when she said "somewhere, she knew" the decision that she be raised by her father made sense. This time and language of catastrophe exposed the way medicine traffics in horizons in ways that can undo as well as shore up, the ways its own language is always in imminent dissolution. In blunt repetitions of otherness ("getting out"), certainties of clinical telling were exposed for their violence, and delusions were revealed to be something true and desperate.

Similarly, in Lorrie Moore's story, the horizon of invention—of story—is like the horizon of crisis. Fiction, she writes, is the same "kind of thing" as the trauma of a child's cancer: "It's the unlivable life, the strange room tacked onto the house, the extra moon that is circling the earth unbeknownst to science" (1995: 235). Delusion—so carefully stitched to traumas, real or imagined—is another "extra moon." In the locked ward, *all* speech might be delusion, statements true only by degree. Here, the truth about "what happened" was negotiable and contested, and yet as real as a vivid dream that directs the day's emotions. Connections between true and false were less ontological than social. In other words, in Moksha (as in the horizons of kinship), actions, demands, conditions, and negotiations put the "or" in "true or false." At times they replaced "or" with "and."

The difference between truth and falsehood was especially contested for the kind of delusion that stood well to the side of distinctions between invention and reality, the idea about which we are never certain if it is real or a delusion. Different (by degree) from the livid disconnects of floridly psychotic speech, these were things we might call maybe-delusions, the false but understandable, the possible but not (in this case) real, the real but still pathological. Maybe-delusions are also "strange room[s] tacked onto a house," especially, it would seem, when they involve love, marriage, and divorce, things that may demand, as well as create, delusion. The maybe-delusion crosses from sickness to health, clinic to home, diagnoses to relationships. If the hospital is, in Moore's words, "merely an intensification of life's cruel obstacle course" (Moore 1988: 240), then Moksha's confinements shared with kinship unstable relationships between language and truth, a layering of what meaning is and does. In both clinic and kinship, seeds of dissolution waited in the soils of stability, and life was full of maybe-delusions.

Rather than separating faulty women from "the family" or defective beings to shore up a vision of "the human," Moksha and kinship shared efforts involving a different force—dissolutions from within and inherent vulnerability, the constant threat of going to pieces. Through instabilities of clinical life (missed and mixed messages, lies, and evasions), medicine did not protect normative visions (of desire, family, gender . . .) but attended to the fungibility of love and kinship, parts of life that are risky less because they are hegemonically oppressive than for the way they threaten to go to pieces. Moksha participated in the gendered fallout of kinship, and, though there were rebukes and other signs of disapproval along the way, it was not the case that abnormal subjects (even those at the margins of marriage) were managed but that breakdowns of kinship were mediated. Language bore the same vulnerability. Its relationship to truth was unsettled, as was the inviolability of experience. This was in part because of the way intimacy itself destabilizes language and involves risk. Madness was on a spectrum of recognizable responses to love.

Paranoia was a primary effect in these dissolutions of kinship and meaning. At a certain point, all passages in and out of Moksha seemed to be marked by it—not only paranoias of psychosis, but Khadija's paranoia about what her mother would think if doctors did not let her stay, my paranoia about the effects of my interactions and presence. These were also maybe-delusions. There was truth to them, even if they were not, or not always, true. In such an atmosphere, it was less the case that social realities were converted into biological abnormality, made over into disease, than that biology was used to dissolve bonds. Social explanations obfuscated actual proceedings in which life was a symphony of catastrophes large and small, a concert of wildly diverse states of mind and ways of making and deferring meaning, ways of telling, inventing, and struggling. In the process, rationality and relationality—sanity and intimacy—were mutually constituted through close attention to women's paranoia, attention that also enhanced that paranoia (Pinto 2011). These tremors were catastrophic just as they played upon catastrophe, but they were also continuous with the idea that madness and love travel together, that love can be self-destroying and rationality is unsettled by intimacy. Relations were unmade, and catastrophes of that undoing were clinical practice—"mak[ing] human life work as social life, the grand project of creating society" (Strathern, citing Wagner, 2005: 11).

Clinical attention to maybe-delusions pitted dissolutions of minds against dissolutions of relations, judging the status of one on the ground of the other, even as the truth about relations was seldom in question (women in Moksha really were divorced). These attentions were part of the undoing of bonds and the way relations are at stake in relations, involving struggles—shared by patients, families, and clinicians—to inhabit damaged worlds. So while women were confined and estranged, Moksha was not a space of "social abandonment" for people whose lives challenged ideas about the boundaries of the human or other social norms (Biehl 2005). It was, rather, a space where relations were unmade, a zone of heartbreak for those bearing the brunt of compounded dissolutions. As an effect, clinical choreographies of contradiction and deferral reconstituted anger as loss while producing (as much as reading) the very emotion that was a sign of illness—the paranoid feelings patients were required to disavow.

And so, here is what I find myself saying in my more strident moments: Moksha capitalized on horizons of uncertainty, including hope; it made use of inherent instabilities in intimate life, kinship, and narration; and it destabilized truths, making facts more fungible in the supposed interest of making things more certain. The effect of this was long-term involuntary commitment for women who had mental illnesses but may have fared well enough in the world, looking after themselves and using clinical care as outpatients.

While I struggled with whatever role I might be playing in the tragicom-edy of promises and deferrals that held Sanjana in Moksha, it became clear that Moksha was part of her desperation, shaping not only the fact of her estrangement but also the devastating conditions of existence. Sanjana was made sick by Moksha. Among its maddening conditions was the way the doctors posited abandonment as cause, using it as a reason for confining her. Where Isma was concerned, things may have been even more stark. After months of visiting, I never regained whatever faith I may have had in Dr. M.'s intentions.

But here is what I find myself saying on second thought: doctors (many of them, anyway), social workers, psychologists, and ward workers strug-gled with the same things I did, the same things patients did—uncertainties produced in times of crisis, disconnects in ideas about people's responsibil-ity to each other, and points at which sensible people reach the limits of what is possible in caring for others. They were challenged in efforts to name afflictions and chart treatment, and by the question (when they asked it) of whether a woman could care for herself in a difficult world. Though attentions were uneven, they were part of processes involving the unmaking of relations and selves; the space of Moksha and the dissolution of kinship were part of each other's scenery. This would always be uncertain work. For Sanjana, effects of life in a maddening space could be differentiated from more uncertain efforts to grapple with dissolutions.

Both views, I think, are true.

Scholarship on gender and mental health in India holds, quite reason-ably, that divorced women with mental illnesses bear a double burden (Thara, Kamath, and Kumar 2003). Movements in and out of marriages and in and out of Moksha—the fact that so many women in Moksha were divorced—may show that burdens are not so easily separated as to be con-sidered double. What might be disarticulated as overlapping stigma, or linked as cause and effect, may be multiple movements toward and away from dissolution. Those lines can intersect or be parsed; one undoing can relate to another differently at different moments. Through differently freighted ways of telling, divorce and madness orbit each other like twin stars. The pull of uncertainty—between Sanjana's reality and Amina's, Amina's and her daughters', doctors' and patients'—left little ground for consistent explanation or easy separation of delusion from its contents, fact from fiction, fiction from hope, hope from insanity, insanity from truth.

It offered the possibility for ethics less in categories like integration and abandonment, or hope or its denial, than in something to the side of them, in and of points of momentary reality, in and of their constant dissolution.

Moore writes,

> The trip and the story of the trip are always two different things. The narrator is the one who has stayed home, but then, afterward, presses her mouth upon the traveler's mouth, in order to make the mouth work, to make the mouth say, say, say. One cannot go to a place and speak of it; one cannot both see and say, not really. One can go, and upon returning make a lot of hand motions and indications with the arms. The mouth itself is necessarily struck still; so fast, so much to report, it hangs open and dumb as a gutted bell. All that unsayable life! That's where the narrator comes in. The narrator comes with her kisses and mimicry and tidying up. The narrator comes in and makes a slow fake song of the mouth's eager devastation.

I struggle still with my kisses and tidying up, like those of others who narrate here—doctors and social workers, of course, but also daughters, sisters, other patients, ward attendants, and patients themselves, telling their own and each other's stories, sometimes to find meaning and sometimes just to show they are "active on the ward." I struggle with the slow, fake song we make, together and at odds, of other people's lives and other people's slow fake songs, with the long kiss of narration that may be, in fact, a suffocating kind of ventriloquism.

But something solid remains when words and stories fall silent: accumulations of sensation, the solidity of walls, beds, floors, windows, and doors, and the concreteness, if such a thing can be said, of time. I turn now to those things.

Chapter 3

Moksha and Mishappenings

> [It is] an action transposed into a world, into a kind of space-time, which is no longer quite the same as everyday life. [This involves] . . . the mystery of a body which suddenly as though by the effect of an internal shock, enters into a kind of life that is at once strangely unstable and strangely regulated, strangely spontaneous, but at the same time strangely contrived and, assuredly, planned.
> —Paul Valéry, "Philosophy of the Dance" (1983 [1936])

Some days in the ward we pick stones out of rice, a task so common to Indian women's kitchen worlds that it has its own verb. I sit on the floor with Pooja, Sanjana, Riti, and Isma. The rice arrives from the kitchen in a plastic bag. Pooja pours it onto plates, one for each person. The sound of grains on metal is like a shower of tiny bells, loud in the sleepy hush. We lean over, bodies reaching earthward, fingers walking through shifting dunes. Our eyes fall on flashes of gray. Our fingertips catch something sharp. A husk. A bad seed. A stone. A density that could break a tooth. The sustaining element of the next meal—what makes it food—moves through our hands and we became absorbed in our white microcosms.

It is not easy to tell stories this way, eyes down, fingers in motion. There are long pauses, drifting minutes between comments. Through this void, words rush by like meteorites. They connect to nothing. They burn out quickly. This is "time-pass." It is also waiting. It is therapy. And work. And it is hunger, the slow rise of emptiness in the stomach, the intensity of stillness, the pulse of purposeful concentration. It has meaning, but only just.

In Moksha, as with Ammi's family, I constantly felt the limits of research. As I spent time in a mode best described as punctuated habitation, at points it was clear that my activities could no longer be labeled research, though it was not easy to say what they were or identify the aim of talking, sitting around, and just being there, aside from talking, sitting around, and just being there. I spoke with women who passed through, and I got to know those who stayed longer. Many were eager to have their situations recorded, acknowledged, and shared. Many were quite lucid, though I was aware that even in lucidity some things were recognizable as "the things crazy people say," equal parts symptom and testimony. Others were far from lucid. As the notion of lucidity became a matter of impression, I became acutely aware of the ability of psychotic speech to express uncomfortable truths.

More important than these plays of consciousness were the immediate conditions of affliction, the way suffering had to do with the place itself. Many women whom I would neither treat nor regard as research subjects were nonetheless inhabitants of a place in which they felt contained. This did not change the fact that feelings of persecution can be part of schizophrenic feelings and terrors. Parsing ways of perceiving constraint seemed less important than documenting flows of time and feeling across the real (but slippery) divide between psychotic speech and lucidity.

Then there was the matter of understanding practices common to Indian psychiatry with what we might call cultural sensitivity, that is, in a way that attended to the realities of life and medicine in India and gave due note to doctors' own ethical considerations, their sensitivity to social conditions, and their struggles to practice good medicine under difficult conditions. I was often in the presence of behaviors that in other places might be questionable but that here were quite normal. Knowing when to be outraged and when understanding of doctors' struggles was a challenge. Some things I was uneasy labeling as crises. Some I wavered on. Some I was comfortably appalled by. For example, untruths told to "protect" patients from their circumstances fit into a consistent logic of care that extended from clinics to schools to households. So did the use of physical aggression, threatened swats to the face, real slaps. But neither untruths nor slaps were things I could relegate to a relativist sense of ethics or see entirely from doctors' perspectives. This is largely so because it was clear that patients wanted to be told the truth about their circumstances and did not want to be hit. They wanted to know the names of medications they were on; they wanted honest assessments of the duration of their stay and conditions of their release; they wanted to know why their blood was drawn. Clinicians felt that telling patients "the truth" would increase their suffering, or that patients could not understand, or that these were necessary protections. I think the clinicians were wrong. Patients' suffering was increased, I am sure, by lies they were told about their conditions, treatment, and prognosis. Other practices were more obviously troubling—things like being hit, or being locked to a window grating with metal chains.

That these things happened, systematically in some cases, to people who could not, given their states of consciousness, give "informed consent" to participating in my "research" did not mitigate the need to document them. It also did not disallow the possibility that, as many of them said to me, they wanted their lives and conditions in Moksha to be accounted for. Likewise, the fact that most women in long-term commitment had signed forms consenting to their admission was part of this paradoxical picture. Typically those forms were presented to people in states of deep distress, in the presence of staff and family members whose subtle and not so subtle encouragements made their signature an empty performance. On consent forms, buried in a list of items patients agreed to was "any research the hospital may be conducting." By entering the ward, women were put in a position of "consenting" to a range of possible researches—typically drug testing. This, too, was part of what made it important to document lives in ways that broke through the idea of research, even as it was a conditioning factor that brought us together, bracketing my own endeavors and the very forms of suffering I felt it increasingly necessary to document.

Consent, here, as an ethical practice, was integral to confinement and coercion, a situation that troubled me greatly and made it harder and harder to name (to myself) what I was up to, for so many reasons, not least my unwillingness to make these women into research subjects. My effort shifted to a different kind of accounting, one that commingled with my own life as I took note of people—and the abuses they experienced—who would otherwise disappear in the very enterprise that constituted ethical anthropological inquiry. In other words, if I wrote and observed strictly according to such rules, I would no longer be able to account for the gravest injustices or circumstances, or practices that furthered the suffering of women not in a condition to consent to my research. Their lives could not fall within the scope of my description. Ethics, paradoxically, would disappear into its own aims. If I were to document such things in the spirit of both ethical inquiry and inquiry into the practice of ethics, I would violate the terms of my field's paradigm of engagement.

It is a paradox I still struggle with.

But I continued to write things down.

In turning notes into chapters, it became clear that I would have to make decisions about what to include and what to leave out, especially where the speech and actions of those in the depths and flights of mania and psychosis were concerned. Ironically, but not surprisingly, women in florid psychosis, those conventionally considered unable to provide informed consent, were often the most resistant, the most likely to refuse to speak with me or object to my presence. Their suspicious and angry language often contained germs of truth ("you take our words for your own use") and touched my deepest insecurities ("this isn't real research"), even as their defiantly self-protective refusals undermined boundaries between the rational and irrational, as much in psychiatry does. Often, those in lucid states (sometimes the same women, after a week or two on medication) were happy to talk with me.

My strategy has been to leave out much of what was said by women in florid psychosis, those whose "irrational" speech would, for some ethics reviewers, render them incapable of consent, though I am certain that many (not all, of course) women in such states understood quite well why I was there and what I wanted in speaking with others on the ward. But how could I know the difference, or the boundaries between lucidity and illness? What about the passage of time? I asked myself the same questions over and over: would a woman in a lucid state (with whom I may have lost contact) want me to share things she said and did in a different state of mind, even when names were changed, locations hidden, details omitted? Aside from questions of identifiability, would a person want their story, their self-in-illness, to become part of my story? At the same time, to what extent were other women's conditions of floridity part of the atmosphere, of conditions that exacerbated crises of involuntary commitment for women like Sanjana? To what extent was it necessary to document details of delusion and psychosis in making sense of it all? To what extent did they became part of my struggle, something I could tell as my own? As with Ammi, in negotiating these in-between spaces in Moksha, I have tried to err on the far side of caution, aware of the fact that those efforts exaggerate qualities like lucidity, floridity, delusion, and psychosis and render abnormal and inaccessible ways of being that exist on their own terms, defy conventions, and offer new possibilities for being and expressing.

My approach in Moksha, as with Ammi, follows Deleuze: "Sometimes it is necessary to restore the lost parts, to rediscover everything that cannot be seen in the image. . . . But sometimes, on the contrary, it is necessary to make holes, to introduce voids and white spaces, to rarify the image, by suppressing many things that have been added to make us believe that we are seeing everything" (1989: 21). "Making holes" rather than accounting for silences or using inventive glosses, is an explicit strategy of representation. It tells about conditions for telling (the double-bind logics of consent, the paradoxes of institutional review board procedures, the clinical misuse of notions of "voluntary") by taking some things out of frame, telling about power by creating omissions. At times, this has meant leaving aside things that are beautiful and illuminating, or disturbing and telling, words and actions that are the little gems anthropologists love to make use of. At times, I have, here too, broken my own rules and filled in voids I perhaps should have left agape. This purposeful effort is another way stories come undone in these pages, where coherence fails for structural, moral, and bureaucratic reasons, reasons that expose, among other things, contradictions, impossibilities, and ironies of research ethics.

In the locked ward, just as the consenting subject of global ethical paradigms dissolved into microinteractions of generated consent, so the idea of research dissolved as a means of accounting for such a place. Here, everyday life demanded attention in proportion to the degree that a coherent subject of research faded. The latter happened as the former became more necessary. If there was an ethics to be found here, it was in the end of research as such and in the everydayness of life amid movements, stillness, feeling, and dulling. It is equally impossible to isolate from webs of sensation a person to call a research subject, or leave to the haze of background those unable to be subjects, even though summoning them requires breaking certain bureaucratic-cum-ethical rules. I suspect I am not alone in writing to the side of consent about things anthropologists have always written about—people involved in plays of bodily habitation, ways of being in space and time. Here, movements are at once institutional and interrupt the institution. They are shaped, but never wholly, by the social arrangements that come into being around affliction.

In looking for such systematic arrangements, the obvious places to turn were matters like diagnosis, prescribing, case writing, commitment proceedings, family histories, and mental health policy, practices establishing people as objects of knowledge and regulation. But what left the strongest impression on me, what filled the most expansive territory of thought and reflection were the sheer conditions of the place, the *sense* of inhabiting Moksha's locked ward, the ways women filled the time Moksha burdened them with. This involved things as elemental as picking stones from rice, windows painted over in blue, the presence of a telephone that never rang, the weight of a quilt. It involved the ways people interacted with each other, cared for each other, and abused each other in these borderlands. Each of these elements, and their purchase on movement and sensation, located women as bodies in space and time at the same time as they established them within conditions of confinement. These were also the stuff of "clinical practice," leaving craters in women's lives deeper and wider than the subject-making, surveilling, and knowledge-producing work of things more readily identified as clinical. They involved the slipperiness of feeling and the crux of voluntary and involuntary movement, intensities of bodies in motion and stasis, the flow and drip of time. Movements (if not "action")—like pacing, sitting, lying, repetitive trips through small spaces—hung together in something not quite coherent, evading narrative and interpretation (Desjarlais 1997: 23, 18). Choreographing days, weeks, and months, these habitations were part of arrangements in which people participated, willingly or not, ways of being that invited interpretation but also defied it. The question became less "what kind of subjects are these?" and, instead, "what kind of presence is this?"

A pillar in the middle of the room rises from a chest-high barrier. On it hangs a yellowing piece of paper inscribed with colored pencil.

Wake at 6:00 a.m.
Bathe.
Prayer or yoga at 6:30.
Breakfast at 7:30.

More possibilities—group meetings, classes, library time.

Lunch, nap, exercise, prayer.

Movement in and out happens by way of a key tied to the end of Pooja's sari, a key to a padlock on the inside of the hollow metal door. First a hand raps, a shivery boom. Someone calls out, "Who is it?" The person might identify herself by name, or might say, "It's me," a teasing, if unintended, assumption of familiarity. One forgets, through a solid wall, that they cannot be seen.

Inside, a pause of anticipation. Someone may say, "It is the doctor," "It's Kajol," "It's the food." Heads may look up. Or they may be undisturbed in their stillness—resting on a pillow, eyes closed or focused on the wall or locked on a holy book, part of a body in motion across the length of the room.

Pooja or one of the long-term residents unlocks the padlock. The door opens; the ecology changes. There is a bit more light. The door shuts. Now there is a bit less light. Now we are us plus one.

There is not much to do. The list on the paper schedule is often the extent to which activities materialize, aside from the basic needs of getting a body through a day. The morning, begun by the administration of drugs and breakfast, is punctuated by brief visits. Dr. K. comes through. "There usually isn't much going on there," she says of the female ward, so she doesn't stay for long. She stands at each bed and watches. Briefly, quietly, she asks about a skeleton of activities, life sustaining and necessary. To some she asks for the day of the week. Awareness of time's passage, like "keeping busy," is a sign of wellness, though there is little to distinguish one day from another. Responses show degrees of lucidity and drugs' effects on patients' presence in the world. The ability to account for time, to observe and demarcate its passing, and to show it is filled with activity indicate well-being and an awareness of the realities of being.

Patients ask questions and make complaints. Mostly they ask, "When will I be released?" Some have stomach ailments or a sore throat. Some ask whether there has been word from their families. Dr. K. gives brief answers. "When you are better you will be released." "We will send the doctor." "We will give you different medication." Her voice is quiet. She gazes silently and makes notes. Then she is gone. A social worker may or may not come later, one of a shifting array of young women with stylish haircuts. They stay a bit longer, they chat casually, or lead a round or two of singing. They do not interact with everyone, especially those in more acute states of distress, but often they talk to patients about their pasts, about their families. They offer advice about "keeping a positive attitude," "staying busy," "keeping your mind active."

A stationary bike against the wall greets one upon entering the ward. One day, I am standing next to it with Riti. "It's hard to be here. We get so bored," she says. "It feels awful inside here. It is closed up; it is dark; you can't see out the windows; it is so boring. There is nothing to do." Isma and Sanjana are standing around too. They agree with Riti. I ask about the library. Riti says, "They let us go for an hour. I have never gone, but I hear there is one."

I sit on the bike and say I should exercise but I don't like to. I try to pedal. The pedals turn but are disarticulated from the wheel. There is no resistance. Such effortless movement brings a sense of unease. Without the feel of purposeful action, a bike that doesn't push back feels strange and unsettling.

I ask if they use it. Someone says, "Yes, I use it sometimes." I express surprise. Sanjana says, "I do some yoga."

Someone else says, "She doesn't actually do it, it's just in name."

I say, "I'm like that too, I always say, 'Yes, I think I'll exercise today,' but when it comes time to do it I think, 'Nah, not today.'"

Sanjana smiles, a rare occurrence. It is like a light going on.

I often think of the ward as doldrums, a middle latitude, a preternaturally still sea. Mostly people lie down, drugged into sleepiness by medication, heat, the white roar of fans, and the absence of activity. Some sit on their beds reading the Koran or another holy text. Others pray with beads as they pace the room. Others wander, sit for a time, get up, and move on, to the windows, to the sink, to sit with someone else, to their bed, to sit, stand, and wander again through the bracketed partitions of the room.

When new patients come in, their movements are often a stark interruption of this languid timelessness. Their angle and contrast are not unexpected, however. They do not surprise, though they stir the air. Long-term residents seem resigned, if also annoyed, by these intrusions of erratic movement and loud sound, by the way they change the scenery. Plastic chairs are light enough to be hoisted above the head, shoes and magazines to be thrown. Pressured motion is different from the measured tide of ward wandering. It consumes space like flame. But, familiar with the impermanence of these states, women know the timing of drugs, the pace at which ways of moving, talking, and being change.

A young woman is brought in and put in a bed in the corner. She thrashes and weeps as she is carried by two men. Initially tied down with torn sheets, she is soon taken out of restraints. She sits immobile, frozen in terror in the middle of her bed, her voice a high wail. She is newly married, the daughter-in-law of one of the kitchen workers. They are from a village, and, the staff says to each other, it is only because the mother-in-law works here that they knew to bring her to the hospital.

Visitors, mostly young and middle-aged women, come in and out all day. They sit across from her, sharing the space of an abutting bed; they bring water and damp towels. Pooja comes by. A visitor rises. Pooja begins to sit at the edge of the patient's bed.

The woman screams, "The snakes, the snakes, there are so many snakes! Don't sit on the snakes!"

Pooja raises her arm at an angle to the girl's cheek, as though to hit her, and yells, "Hey! Don't do that!" She does not hit, but the woman flinches. She jerks her arm up to protect her face.

Startled, I say, "Don't yell at her! She is already frightened enough."

Pooja responds as though talking to a child. "She is not the one speaking. It is the ghost inside her."

After a few days, seeing no effect from the pills, her family takes her home. The staff says that they will probably hire an exorcist when what the woman needs is to stay in the clinic. A week later I stop into the kitchen to ask her mother-in-law how the young woman is doing. Her daughter-in-law is much better now. The ghost has left her body; she is calm.

For people not caught up in wild movement, lines of footstep cross-hatch time and space. Sanjana walks back and forth, crossing the width of the ward with body and language. Beads in hand, she prays under her breath, her callings to God circling the room as they cycle through her breath. I ask which prayers she repeats. She tells me the phrases. She is not sure what all of the prayers mean, she says, "but they are in the Koran."

Amina also spends longer stretches of daylight in prayer, though hers is less kinetic. On her bed, combed and cleaned, she reads from the Koran. She boasts, "These days I am spending more time praying. Yesterday it was four hours. Two in the morning, two in the evening."

This kind of prayer requires other attentions and preparations, it leaks into other parts of the day. In the mornings, Amina irons the starched scarf with which she covers her head when she reads.

Prayer is an activity of conflicting meanings—it is pathology, and pacifying, or something one might feel driven to when there is little else to fill canyons of time. I ask Sanjana if she prays more since coming here. She used to pray, she says, but never so much. There had not been time for it at home.

"Does it bring you peace, relief?" I ask.

"It does." (I later write reproachfully in my notes, "What kind of question is this? What else would she have said?")

Prayers reach beyond the ward. They can do what their speakers cannot—escape cinder block and fly to the places where gods and saints live.

Sanjana's religiosity, the nature of her renewed observance—pacing, praying, and requesting prayers at shrines—is innervated by desire. Her slow footfalls and the pull of her thumb along the beads strike me as turns of activated longing that string together losses. At times I feel strongly that these repetitions are part of her descent, but then I think perhaps this idea comes from a bias toward seeing desires as entrapping. Were my tendency more Freudian (and less Buddhist), to see desire as needing room to move and its containment as restrictive and festering (rather than as part of life and its sufferings), what might I find worrisome—or liberating—in what she does?

As Sanjana's drugs change and her release is deferred, her religious activity becomes more intense and she is in worse shape by the day. She feels this way too. I write in my notes that pacing and prayer seem not only to rehearse desire but to mark slow time, to reiterate futility. On some days I write strongly of this. "If she had something else to do with her time, her space, her thoughts, her legs and hands, she might be distracted from this active desire and its double bind—the fact that relief came from an activity that enhanced the very emotions, the velocity of desires under daily review." Or do I channel Mrs. M. and others who say the key to avoiding depression is "keeping busy"? Or are they right? What is gained or lost in reading Sanjana's movements this way, in looking in them for meaning and effect?

One afternoon, while I am discussing local shrines with Pooja, Sanjana comes over. I ask what she thinks about dargahs (Sufi shrines), whether she puts faith in them. "Yes," she says, and asks Pooja if she will offer a prayer for her at the shrine near the railway station. Pooja looks away, unresponsive, then turns back angrily. "I work very hard here," she says to me. "I do twelve-hour shifts and then go home to take care of my children, because I don't have anyone, a husband, a mother-in-law, no one. How can I go make duas [prayers] for patients?"

I say I will be going to the shrine that week and will offer the prayer. From then on, Sanjana inquires about the shrines I visit and asks that I make a dua for her, as though by proxy I might deliver pieces of her longing as my forehead touches the cool floor of the saint's tomb, or bring back solace in my spoken words and token objects.

Sometimes it is the first thing she asks when I come in.

She tells me she had visited a nearby shrine, an especially beautiful one whose *pir* (saint) had been alive in living memory. She did not know why, but she could not help but cry when she entered its space. The feeling overwhelmed her. This was before her divorce, before her troubles.

I ask if that often happens at *dargahs* and she says yes.

"What do people cry about? Is it the saint, is it the world, is it one's own life?"

"People cry about their own lives. I cried about my own sorrows."

On a slow, still day when most of the women are asleep, Sanjana sits on her bed shelling peanuts. She asks me to make a prayer at the shrine for her husband to take her back. She says all she thinks about is her husband, about how she wants him to let her come home to her child. She says she prays all day that he will take her back. I write in my notes that this is a change from her earlier attitude, from a feeling of having been wronged. It seems like a bad development.

Some days are pleasant, some are excruciating. One afternoon I write, "One can almost feel the frantic bump of Sanjana's thoughts winging around the room—as though the intensity of her suffering and desire has filled the room like bats. The expanse of the rest of the day, the way the meal marks time, divides up an otherwise undifferentiated span, makes this space feel suspended somehow."

It is as Deleuze writes, we are "given over to something intolerable which is simply [our] everydayness itself" (1989: 39).

"This place is hell, Sarah," Sanjana says.

This is a day that, it turns out, will not be far from her release from Moksha. It is chaotic this morning, but also boring, a void of time, space, and language that can suddenly erupt into excess and just as quickly subside into nothing, into stillness.

Amina comes over and tells Sardar jokes, jokes at the expense of Sikhs. It is her new genre, her new habit, and seems to come from nowhere. Isma sits at the table reading from magazines I had brought, her eyes and nose running with a cold. Riti tells me her father came to see her yesterday. He stayed for a half hour and didn't bring much news from home, but it had been nice to see him. Sanjana and Riti say their families must have been phoned by Moksha last Tuesday, as is the weekly routine, and we discuss whether Kajol had said she did or did not speak to Sanjana's mother. Riti and Sanjana talk to each other about when they will be discharged. Sanjana says she will probably be discharged next week, or that at least the decision will be made this week, relaying what Kajol had told her earlier.

There is a new patient whose hands are bound with a chain and padlocked to the bars on a window. I have not seen this kind of restraint here before. I comment to Sanjana, who nods but says nothing. Pooja is yelling through a bathroom door at another new patient, named Rekha, who came in angry, accusatory, soaring above sleeplessness, yelling accusations. She calmed during the night, but remained in bad shape. That morning we sit across the table from each other. The shoulder-length hair of this middle-class housewife who "ran away" from home is matted into felt. From it lice are jumping. When they fall to the table, she desultorily squashes them with the back of her thumb. On the rides home these days I pluck fattened lice from my sleeves, my bag, my shoulders.

Sanjana and I move to the window by the entrance; while we talk and not talk, Rekha, who has taken the soap of another patient, Giti, comes out of the bathroom and stands at the sink scrubbing her head, though she doesn't seem to have wet it. The stench of her rotting scalp reaches us fifteen feet away. Women occasionally look as though they might vomit. These are not performative retches. People are, in fact, trying to hide their reaction to the smell.

After Rekha leaves the sink, Giti goes over to inspect it, leaning in from a distance. "Oh my god! Look at all the lice in here."

The doctors come in briefly, talking to Pooja about the new patient. They say they will send over lice shampoo. Pooja tells them angrily that shampoo is useless, they need to send a barber to shave her head. "The patient is in an awful state; the entire ward will become infested; the smell is unbearable."

The doctor turns to Sanjana and says he won't bring medications for stomach acidity until she changes her eating habits. She shouldn't eat so much. He reminds her that she had a paratha and omelet for breakfast.

"They never listen," she says when he leaves.

Pooja is again yelling at the new patient, who has now locked herself inside the bath stall where she is washing her hair. Holding an open bottle of shampoo (regular shampoo—the doctor has promised to send medicinal shampoo), Pooja bangs on the metal door and screams at her to open it. Eventually she does, but just a few inches. She is fully dressed but drenched.

When she refuses the shampoo, Pooja thrusts her arm through the door and pours the bottle on top of her, yelling about the smell and pushing the back of her head.

We are all vaguely watching and not watching.

Riti says, "What must her *ghar-walle log* [the people in her household] be like to keep her in such dirtiness, to let her get like this."

Sanjana says, looking down at her hands, that this place is awful, and looks again like she might cry.

For some reason, I choose this moment to ask if Pooja hits the patients like this a lot and she says yes, all the ward attendants do.

Drying off, Pooja leaves to get the lunch. Amina comes over to the table and tells more jokes. When Pooja returns, I say goodbye to everyone and leave. Outside the ward, I look down the hallway on the opposite side of the building to see if any of the doctors are around. All the doors are closed, the padlocks locked. Kajol must be in the men's wards, and I think that the other social workers must not be here today. It is dark and empty.

I write in my notes, "It was only two and a half hours in the female ward—seems like nothing, but lasted forever."

This shred, too, appears in my notes, uncapitalized, disconnected from sentences or paragraphs, between scattered descriptions of Moksha and fragments of observation about Eve's adjustment to life and her play habits in our temporary city:

"How people can make a home anywhere . . ."

The windows of the ward are painted over in blue, offering shadow and underwater glow in place of oppressive sunshine for most of the year, a sense of shade and respite and a feeling of being somewhere deep below.

In winter this effect amplifies a feeling of removal from things that give warmth.

In the summer there is a constant flapping of small things—paper, edges of fabric—in the current of the fans. Air is motion, hair tickles a cheek, pages rattle. At the same time, the thickness of the atmosphere makes it difficult to move once one has decided to sit.

Winter may still bodies, but outside in the sun it also means the frenetic motion of flies, the need to wave them off skin, or resigned willingness to let them stay.

When it is colder inside than out, Pooja takes everyone outside to "eat the sunshine," all but Ammi, the old woman who stays in her corner bed, too old to venture far. We bring empty rice bags to sit on. The cement is warm, though the sun is wan and reticent. We form a misshapen oval, a natural configuration for playing cards. As I deal, Sanjana reminds me that Giti and Poonam will not be able to play properly. I say it doesn't matter, they can play how they like. We deal and pick up our hands. The wind is blowing hard so I put a rock on the deck. We play three rounds. Sanjana wins the first. I win the second, and Isma the third. Sanjana is right. She, Isma, and I play around Giti and Poonam's methods and moves. Poonam holds tight to her cards until someone tells her to go, at which point she puts them on the ground in rows, face down. We say OK, collect them, and move on. Giti puts one card down, picks one up, over and over, without looking at what's on the cards. She comes and goes, bored and antsy perhaps, but not frustrated.

I see Sanjana's mouth bend into the smallest shadow of a smile when I say I am used to playing with seven cards and find it hard to keep track of thirteen. She asks me to give the cards to her to look after when we finish playing. She doesn't say why, but I know it is because she thinks Pooja is likely to pocket them. I think she is probably right. Even though Pooja says she doesn't know the game and doesn't seem interested in joining us, she eyes the cards. She takes them out of my hands after several play attempts and holds them proprietarily. "These must be very expensive."

"No, not really," I say. She asks if they are from "there"—America. They are. My husband brought them. They are new.

Sanjana has already commented that the cards are nice, which I agree they are. Nothing special, but solid and secure seeming, thickly coated with plastic. In comparison to Indian playing cards, they look as though they have more of a purchase on time. I ask for the cards and give them to Sanjana and Isma. They play, turning their faces and loosened strands of hair away from the wind.

Pooja is sitting close to Riti. They are play-slapping each other. When they finish that game, Pooja sits easily with her hand on Riti's lap, and they seem to be lazily chatting, though I can't pick up the thread of the conversation. Giti starts to sing. I ask Riti to sing when Giti's song is over but she says she is not in the mood. Riti and Pooja try to play a children's hand game; Riti gets it wrong at first but eventually learns.

Giti stops, her mouth open in a screamless rigor. She pushes her jaw, saying, "My mouth won't shut."

Pooja yells "Shut it!"

Giti says, "It won't shut. I can't!"

"Shut it, shut it!" Pooja yells. Giti shuts it a bit, but not all the way. Pooja says, suddenly calming and gentle, "*Itna, bas.*" Just that much, enough.

We walk inside. Pooja and Rekha, whose head has finally been shaved, argue over who will walk last. Rekha wants to, but Pooja has to be the last to enter the building to make sure no one runs away. On the slow shuffle, we slide into our bodies, slouch into the scenery, slink into the ward, where we have left Amina asleep in bed.

Another day, we play cards inside. Sanjana gets up and sits back down repeatedly. She seems distracted. I assume it is because she is supposed to be giving up tobacco, which is difficult for her. It is as though she rises to get something, then comes back empty-handed. This happens several times. I ask if she is OK. Yes, she says, but after a few more rounds of rummy she doesn't want to play anymore. She leaves me with Giti, Poonam, Rekha, and a deeply surreal game. We all play different games, by different rules, with our thirteen cards. Rekha wins, but only to the extent that others do not. Her sudden pronouncement of "Rummy!" comes in an aggressive exhale. When we fold our hands after congratulating her win, she says she won't play anymore. "Playing cards is wrong. It is immoral work."

When Sanjana returns to the table she says her throat has been burning all morning. Her acidity is acting up. I realize that this is what has been bothering her. She argues with Pooja about getting medicine. The problem is her eating, Pooja yells. She has to stop asking for so many things.

From the other side, it feels like this: You walk through a white hallway to the back of the building, through a corridor with windows on one side and, on the other, framed phrases extolling happiness and serenity. At the end is a large metal door with "female ward" written in English in something like marker. You knock on the door. If you are a doctor you say you have come for rounds. You listen for the rattle of keys, the timpani of the bolt. You are let inside. You hear someone singing, dropping in and out of verse over the thrum of an electric fan. You see, as you come in, that the song is that of the girl who mops the floor, spreading hard-scented antiseptic circles under your feet.

You go to the far side of the room first. Five women lie in their beds on lightly stained sheets. Two people in white are attending to one of them. She is skinny and drugged, or maybe catatonic, wearing a sleep-rumpled yellow sari and staring beyond the reach of the nurses who hold up her wrist as it falls limp in their hands. They palpate her arm, looking for a vein. The woman to her right is plump. She lies next to the part of the wall where a high-powered fan (the kind attached to forced-water coolers) is at her knees. Its protective screen is missing. The roar of the massive, unshielded blades floods the channel of beds with air. She is attached to an IV.

You look down on her, you ask if she has eaten today. The ward attendant stands behind you, ready to offer details. She tells you this patient would not eat today, but she had tea last night. The patient does not answer. The woman in the bed next to her preempts your question. She tells you she, too, is not eating. She has pain in her teeth. You nod, and move a few steps further, to the third bed. You ask if this patient is eating. "A bit," she says. "I don't really feel like eating."

You move to the back of the room where two women occupy beds. The older woman, who, from her dress and the sound of her speech, you recognize as a villager, not a city dweller, responds to your questions. Her daughter, the patient, lies silently in bed. She slowly sits up as you ask about her eating and sleeping, about whether she is taking her medications, as though in response, as though, in spite of the effort, politeness is demanded. You ask if her period has come. The mother tells you it came the night before.

You go back to the other side of the ward, walking carefully over the spots where the concrete floor is still wet. Another immense metal box of an air cooler sits in the middle of the room. This one is dead. Women sit on their beds. One is at a table. Another squats on the floor at the far end, bent over an iron she moves across fabric spread on a stack of folded towels.

You ask the woman at the table how she is feeling. She is wearing a pink maxi—a long housecoat—and slumps in her chair, saliva hanging from her lip, looking at no one in particular. She has been here for years. You would be surprised to see any change. "*Thik*," she says, without looking up. Good. You ask if she has eaten. She says yes.

You go to the last bed, where a young woman with glasses and a *selwar kameez* much nicer than the others' is sitting up. You know from her attire and speech that she is more educated than the rest, that she lives in a city, in a middle-class household. You interact with her in slightly more familiar terms. She seems more like you.

She is drawing a picture in a notepad with a ballpoint pen, a pretty scene of the sort common in children's sketches, but with more shading and depth. Palm trees, a beach, mountains. You ask her, too, if she has eaten. The woman at the table calls over to tell you this woman has taken her pen. You should give her a pen too, she says, so she doesn't always need to take hers. "This is not true," the woman with the notepad says. "But she keeps saying that." You tell both that you will have pens sent over for them. The woman on the bed says, "There is no need. See, I have two here. But she keeps saying that."

You ask the woman on the floor, whose back is to you, what she is doing. "Ironing," she says. You ask if the iron is hot. The woman turns it upright and taps its surface quickly. Yes, she nods. You tell her to be careful.

As you leave, the woman making the picture calls out to you, "Hey, look! Don't you like my picture?" You return to her bed and tell her with the sweetness you'd use with a child that it is a pretty picture. Next she will make a picture of a wedding. A very good picture, she promises. She is four months pregnant and has been diagnosed with mania. You made the diagnosis yourself, observing her condition when she came into the ward, brought by her father, sleepless for weeks, and unable to stop speaking, wandering in the streets at night. Treating her is not easy because of the pregnancy, so you are happy to see changes, happy to see her looking calmer. Her name is Bulbul, and this is her second stay in Moksha. She left her young daughter in the care of her husband and in-laws. She will not have told you many details, except perhaps in a flood of symptomatic speech. You will not know or remember that she is sent by her husband to live with her parents for the duration of her illnesses. In fact, you will assume this to be the case. You may not know or remember that she lives there nearly all the time now, or that she has taken a job, or that she has become used to long stretches without visits from her daughter, or that she feels this situation is for the best.

If you are not a doctor, but a visitor from another country, the woman in the glasses asks you where you are from and compliments your Hindi. You laugh and say your Hindi is not that good, but that you try. She smiles and says, "That's all we can do is try. Nothing is difficult in life." You are not sure you understand what she means by this. You say, "Yes, as long as we try and work hard nothing is difficult."

"No," she corrects you, "You don't even have to work hard, you try and you move forward. Nothing is difficult."

On most days you come in before the doctor. You stop at the entrance booth just inside the main gates and might be offered chai by the man, a former patient, who signs guests in and out and who insists on speaking

English to you with practiced severity. He has taken a sip already from the flimsy, disposable plastic cup, but he offers the cup anyway, and you don't care. The tea is warm and sweet and you are happy to walk inside with it. In the entryway, the attendant from the female ward is having her tea and joking with the young woman at the front desk, whose name you cannot remember. She engages in a play tussle with the cleaning woman, who walks through pulling a bucket of gray water. They slap each other on the head and dodge each other's hands. You finish your tea with them, and though the ward attendant is obviously in no mood to return to the ward, you say you are going back. "No, not yet," she whines with a mock frown. "Do I have to?" The young woman at the desk says, "Take her back," pointing to you and laughing. "She needs to do her work." You go down the long hall and notice that the ward is locked from the outside. The padlock hangs open, looped casually through the closed bolt.

January, very cold, and the outpatient department is empty and dark. The weather keeps people home, Kajol jokes with another social worker Jaya. There is some confusion about whether Dr. K. is actually in. No one seems to know.

We talk about this and that. Jaya tells me about the way they use pento-thal—"To put the patients into a hypnotic state in which they tell every-thing." It is a form of therapy that frees them to talk all about what has happened in their lives, to share the things they are not yet telling. I ask if the patients can remember afterward what they have said. "No," she says, not unless she tells them. "It is very interesting and very useful."

They joke that the patients think that Dr. M. is "like a don," a mafioso. "They are all scared of him."

They discuss the coming week's schedule, and Kajol jokes about the senior physicians. "They take advantage of the patients, they take advantage of us."

I ask what she means by this. She smiles. "They take advantage of the patients because they take their money and keep them here."

In the ward, bodies are burrowed under thick white quilts, stilled into sleep by cold, retreating into darkness under the weight of cotton batting. Riti tells me later that at night even these quilts, though they press heavily on the chest, are not enough. She has a thin *dupatta* (scarf worn with *selwar kameez*) tied around her ears like a woolen scarf.

Isma asks Pooja for hot water. "I shouldn't drink cold water with this illness," she says.

"You have to go to the kitchen for that, and no one there will be able to heat it up for you right now. Who has the time?" Pooja says, not unkindly.

I offer to take Isma to the kitchen.

"No," Pooja says. "You have not understood. She can go by herself, but the gas is being used right now to make rotis."

I have brought a pile of magazines. Some days I stop at a newsstand on my way. Before I wave down a shared vehicle going to the intersection near the hospital (from there it is either a harrowing rickshaw ride on a road thick with trucks, or an even more nerve-jangling walk), I pull as many magazines as I can carry out of the piles arranged on a threadbare sheet. I buy the newest editions, though months' worth of cheaper older ones lie overripe beneath them. I don't know why this matters, though it is what I always do. In the ward, the effect of newness is shimmer and slipperiness. Riti and I leaf through. We point to pictures; we comment on clothes. Riti sees a cartoon depicting her "father" and comments about the cruelty of journalists. The magazines slide across the table. Often when I arrive, the previous bounty is gone, except for one or two that have slipped under a mattress or into a suitcase beneath a bed. Sanjana says Pooja takes them home. The social workers say this is probably true. Even if she doesn't, every time I come in with these blueprints of desire I feel more and more unsure about the meanings hiding in their weight in my arms. They offer activity but also evidence of its futility, of futility in general. At worst, they bear unintentional cruelty. This is especially true of the homemaking magazines. Glamour magazines present lifestyles out of reach. But publications for housewives portray practical, reachable goals, pleasures in small accomplishments, or joy in fulfilling the modest desires of others. This stuff of domesticity is what we lack here.

But there are attempts. A basket of green beans is brought in, along with two knives. The idea of threat, adjudications of risk and harm are absent. Knives are an everyday presence on wards where fruits and vegetables need to be cut. The beans are long and rough, end-of-season holdouts. But they are crisp and green, and Riti and Pooja get down to chopping. We discuss recipes, all the different ways of cooking beans, okra, potatoes, carrots.

I say that if there were another knife I could cut and trim some as well. "*Arey*, no," they say, as though I am a guest in their house. Riti tells Pooja that she wishes the kitchen could make rotis from gram flour. Pooja says, "When they are making food for at least fifty people how can they stop to make something different to suit one person's desires?"

On the "nonacute" side of the ward, I notice that Sanjana has made a tidy, even homey area for herself, stacking her belongings on a metal side table. When I approach, I ask if she is sleeping.

"No, this is what I do all day—lie here in bed." She sits up and offers dried chickpeas her mother brought on her last visit.

I ask what her hobbies are when she is at home. Reading, she says. What kind of books? I asks. "Self-help. Like Dale Carnegie's *How to Win Friends and Influence People.*" Another is interior design. I ask if this means she sews, and she says, no, she likes to look for things for the house, to buy things and shop. "Every single piece in the house is carefully chosen."

When the beans are finished, Pooja says the day is too cold to stay inside. Outside, we sit, as always, under the half-discarded old sign for the hospital. Dr. S. comes over to say hello. He asks Sanjana what she is chewing. She says it is a peanut shell and refuses to spit it out. He insists, and she spits into his hand a few small things that look like wet matchsticks. He says, to no one in particular, "These are pieces of a broom, pulled from the inside."

Then to me, "She likes to chew on them because of the way they feel, they feel like something in her mouth, and she is so addicted."

Though addiction was not among the things Sanjana was admitted for, it is now accepted as fact that she will not be released until she gives up paan. He tells me I should give her a lecture about how bad it is to chew paan because I can speak Hindi (he does not mention—he probably does not know—that Sanjana speaks English). After he goes inside, Sanjana comes back from the tap where she cleaned her mouth. I don't bring up the incident and neither does she.

Later, inside, I sit at the table trying to start some singing, but nothing takes. Giti comes over and sits down, gets up, sits down, gets up. We manage to have a bit of conversation, which is unusual. Her medications make her sleepy and she struggles to keep her eyelids up and her mouth from falling open.

Riti says she doesn't like being dependent on people, that she wants to get a job when she leaves Moksha so she is not dependent on her family. I ask what kind of work, and she says, "Something like sitting at the front office and letting people in and out, or maybe filing papers, something that is worthy of me, something good, that I can do."

Pooja says she wants a different job. "I don't like this one." She asks if I will look around for her. Giti says she wants to do a painting course. Riti says she would like a job that involves "caretaking [*dekh-bal*], not cleaning [*jaru-ponchne ka kam*, the work of broom and mop], but something *dekh-bal*." She says she put in a form at the railways but never heard from them. Sanjana talks about how much she enjoys interior decorating, shopping for things like pillows, curtains, bedcovers, plants.

The conversation comes around to the possibility of Giti marrying. Riti says that Giti could never work because she is *mandbuddhi*, of weak mind, but that she could marry.

Giti asks, "Do you think I could marry? Can I get married, what do you think? My family says I can't get married because I am mandbuddhi. But I think I can." I ask if she wants to, and she says yes. There is a pause. "I can cook vegetables. Ask me how I make *bhindi*," she says, smiling. I ask, and she describes her recipe.

She asks Riti if she thinks she can get married, and Riti says, "Yes, of course you can, ask your mummy."

Lunch comes in on a big tray, brought by Pooja. Women slowly arrive at the table. Some sit on the bed behind it, most sit at chairs. Pooja dishes out the food—*biryani* and *dahi* for some, *sabzi-roti* for others. Some receive spoons, others eat with their hands. A few complain there is not enough food. Aggravated and tired, Pooja argues but gives them more. She has been on duty for nearly twelve hours. She won't eat now, she says, though she is hungry. She will wait until she goes home in an hour. "A mother usually prefers to eat with her children."

I would find this noteworthy if it weren't the same thing I am thinking—I should head home too. The journey is long and thirsty, and I would like to save my hunger for my home space. My little girl will have eaten, she may be off playing, but I would rather eat in the space she occupies. An older patient says the rice is undercooked. She asks if I want to eat, and I say no. "Come, have some. You are too thin." I laugh and say that I too will go home and eat with my daughter. She nods in understanding. We desire less the arrival of what is new than holding on to what is already ours. We prefer recipes to fancy clothes.

We are sitting outside, closing our eyes into the dim sunlight. Pooja asks Riti to sing something. Riti says that since she has been here she hasn't felt like singing. She used to know so many songs and poems, but now "it's like they just left my head." Isma begins reciting *ghazals*—couplets about sadness, grief, and love. It is difficult to make them out. Her voice is soft and the traffic is loud. But phrases are clear: moths drawn to flames, burnt in the fire of love; worshipful longing.

Pooja, responding to a particularly vivid one, says, "That's *galaat kam* [wrong work]." I ask what is wrong about it, and she says "that kind of *shadi* [marriage], *shadi* from love [as opposed to love emerging from marriage]." I ask, "What is *shadi* then?" She says it should be two people who share a life together and have a family and are responsible for each other.

Riti says, "Sometimes there just is love, and then what do you do?"

Giti keeps trying to get up and go back inside, and some of the women say they want to go inside too, and Pooja says no they should stay outside until the food comes, until it is lunchtime, for another half hour or so, in order to get some sunshine. Giti yells, tired, feeling sick, and very frustrated, "I'm going!"

Pooja calls back, "The door is locked." They argue. Pooja tells her to come sit in the middle of the circle. Giti's eyelids are heavy. She lies with her head in Pooja's lap. Pooja picks through her hair, pulling out lice while Giti falls asleep.

One afternoon, before I have stopped trying to meet with Dr. M., I am told to sit in the waiting room until he is free. The lights are off, and I settle into one of the space-age chairs, feeling drowsy and expecting a long wait. The television is showing an old gangster film with the sound low. A few men with the distinctive look and attire of drug company reps sit on the other side of the room staring into space. A young woman with the distinctive look and attire of a new wife sits not far from me. A few seats to her left is an older man I take to be her father-in-law. After a few minutes he gets up and walks out of the room. She gives a slight smile and nod, which I return. We sit in the hum of the fans and the faint pop of gunfire, screaming, and punches from the TV, looking at nothing in particular.

Bulbul comes out from the ward. She is often given dispensations like this. This is her second stay in Moksha. Her diagnosis is bipolar disorder, and her manic episodes have meant that she now lives with her parents, while her school-age daughter stays with her husband and his family in another city. She is not well enough to take care of her daughter, she says, and is better off with her own family.

She sits between me and the young woman and turns to her.

"Have you been here before?"

"Yes," the woman replies.

"Did you stay here then?"

"No, I only came in a month or so ago, to see the doctor."

"Oh, so you are here to meet someone."

"Yes, Dr. K."

"Are you having some problem? What is your problem?"

The woman does not seem at all bothered by the questions. In fact, it almost seems she is relieved to have someone to talk to.

"I have so much tension, here." She touches her forehead. "And no desire to do anything—nothing at all. No desire to eat, to work, to do anything, I have been feeling very bad these days."

Bulbul nods. "You should try to do something to keep busy. You need to keep your mind active. Read magazines, watch TV, cook food, go to the bazaar, read books, chat with friends. It is very important to keep yourself busy."

"Yes, but how can I do that? I try, but what can I do? I don't even want to cross the door into the kitchen."

"Get out of the house. Take walks. How is your husband's family?"

"They are fine. But," she looks out into the hallway, "they don't like me to go out by myself."

"These things are hard, but still, you have to keep the mind active, you have to make sure you are always doing something, your desire to do things will come back, you will see." The woman nods, and the two continue talking, now about the attachments and labors of everyday life—children, their ages, where they go to school, what a day is like. Bulbul tells her that it is good she has come in. "The doctors are very good." I have heard many variations on this way of managing sadness, but am struck by the way Bulbul adopts the role of an advice giver, an authority by virtue of—rather than compromised by—time spent in the ward. It is hard to interpret such confidence, but her advice is well received, though it is, ironically, advice it would be hard to follow in the female ward. I am once again struck by the contrast between empty time and the mandate to "stay active."

There is an old black phone in the middle of the ward, aloft on the ledge dividing the room. Inside call, one ring; outside, two. We seldom hear a double ring. When I first begin visiting, patients ask me to make phone calls for them from my cell phone. Some plead. Some quietly hand me a slip of paper with a number written on it. Doctors have warned me against this. I feel terribly torn. Phones are markers of presence and absence, of the distance between here and there, the structure—and suffering—of desire. They emphasize separateness while promising connection. This one seems to pulse with potentiality, with unrealized contact, with the uncertainty of existing or severed bonds. Many patients ask the doctors if they can make calls, sometimes with a story or an explanation: "My mother said she would be coming in this weekend," "I need to ask if everything is OK at home." The answer is always no. This phone can receive calls. It cannot call out.

During her daughters' visit, Amina asks them repeatedly if she can use their cell phones to call her brother. Khadija gives in during their first, brief visit. The next day, worried she will be caught by the ward attendant and thrown out, she refuses her mother's requests to use the phone. Other patients are also asking if they can use her phone. Khadija and Ruksar have to say no.

Before their visit, Amina writes her daughters a postcard and gives it to the social workers to send. As her daughters cannot read Urdu, she shapes the letters in careful Devanagari. Months later, glancing through patient records, I come across the postcard stapled to a piece of paper, its unsent effort grafted to Amina's file.

After another week, Rekha's hair is grown in to a close crop and signs of lice are gone. In air stinging of fresh Dettol, we sit at the table and page through magazines. Riti reads recipes under her breath, and Pooja looks at *Saheli*, a women's magazine.

Rekha pushes the magazines around on the table. "These are all useless."

She goes on, "You look messy today. Your jewelry is cheap." I pull at my bangles, skinny green metal ones with gold ridges. "Where is your husband? "

"In the U.S."

"What, are you divorced?" Her tone is not kind. She snorts and rolls her eyes. I don't know what to say.

"He is working."

"You should be home taking care of your husband. Look what you have done to your daughter. You are ruining her life, wasting her time, taking her out of school there, putting her in school here, taking her out again after six months." I fear this too. My usual defenses—"But she is learning a new language; but she is experiencing a rich life in a new place; but she is seeing the world"—seem flimsy.

She asks about my research and I explain.

"This is not research. This is not quality research." I suspect she is right. I try to say nothing, knowing this is not a time for defenses. It is not easy.

Riti asks what Bihar is like. I must have mentioned once that I had been there. I tell her how much I liked it and explain about my earlier work.

Rekha gives small, knowing grunts. This is illness, I tell myself. Don't take it to heart.

"You shouldn't have studied that," she says. "*Dais* [midwives] and birth. That was worthless research." She explains something nonlinear and difficult to recall about the way the *shastras* (holy texts) say birth will unfold depending upon a specific capacity of the mother's body, like whether she needs vitamin A or vitamin C. "It's all in God's hands anyway," she says, which makes me laugh. I spent so much time thinking about just those words, but never in quite this way. "It is useless to do a second project now."

I say, lightheartedly, "Well, it's too late now—that book is about to be published."

"No, it's useless to do this research. You should stick to one topic." She may be right about this, too. "I know these things." She says this often, an exclamation mark at the end of harsh words. "You think I know nothing but I know these things." I wonder who she is "on the outside"—a professor? A writer? A poet? An activist?

My recorder, which these days is mostly off, is lying on the table.

"What's the point of this useless thing? To take what we say and take it away and use it for your own purposes." Yes, perhaps. "The people here are all stupid and will put up with it, but not me." I tell her I will keep it turned off, and she looks at me knowingly.

"And I am not mental, I am not mad, I was put here by force. I was put here because of my hair. I am not at all mental, and they fill me up with medicines but I am not sick." She gets agitated and angry and yells and I think something violent might be about to happen, and somehow it is connected to my research and to my presence here, this moral question about her, about her madness, about who she is and who is sick. She says, "Anyway, *mansik*, that is not what I am, that is like having your m.c. [period], that is something different, and not connected to me." She has confused *mansik*, "mental," with *masik*, "menstruation."

Isma and Poonam are called to the kitchen to cut vegetables. Another woman comes over, but when Rekha starts in on me, she gets up, quietly walking away from madness in the same way older generations in my family whisper the word "cancer." It is hard to read these exits. They are resigned, maybe? Maybe they have heard all of this before and are tired of it. Or they are embarrassed and don't want to witness any more. I begin to taunt myself with guilt and bitterness: Why don't I get up and leave too? Why am I still talking to her? I am not recording, I am not "getting anything." I probably shouldn't "use" these interactions anyway. Isn't that what this is for? "Use"?

Isma comes and sits with us for a bit. She says her cold is still bad, but that otherwise things are OK. Rekha continues her rant. Isma leaves the table. I get the sense that she has had enough of the secondhand embarrassment. I don't feel embarrassed by the abuse (though I can't help feeling beaten down by it, sad and defensive) so much as by the sense of a sympathetic audience, the idea that I might, or should, or must be embarrassed. Perhaps I really am humiliated.

Rekha keeps asking if I will play cards. I defer, remembering how hard it was the last time but thinking how silly it is that I should feel frustrated because she always "wins." Why does it matter if the game is futile, it's not like it has any meaning, and what difference does it make if it exceeds the rules, why would it feel frustrating when it is pointless anyway? What is the point of a game?

It is decided that we will go outside for whatever sun there is. Riti looks over pityingly as I sit in the wash of Rekha's words. We all try playing rummy. It is frustrating, but for everyone in a different way. Riti is having trouble understanding; Sanjana and I are the only ones playing correctly; Giti can't understand at all, far more so than Riti, whose problem is only that I don't explain properly. And Rekha is playing smugly and will win. She jumps her turn but one can't say anything. She bugs me to go if I don't play fast enough. And she wins, and her hand is almost right—three sets, and one "almost" set. I wonder if she normally plays by different rules in which one needs three sets instead of four, or if she just couldn't wait.

She asks why I am wearing glasses this time and wore lenses last time. I feel it as accusatory but can't figure out why. She says I must be lying when I say I didn't put in lenses because my eyes are so blue; the last time I must have worn colored lenses. She asks what my nose ring is made of, or someone asks—maybe it is Giti, when we are looking in the magazine at suits we like (Riti says she likes the one in the middle, but only if it could be made with longer sleeves because her father won't let her wear short sleeves). I say my nose ring is a diamond, but then I feel like I shouldn't say it is a diamond, so I say it is probably not really a diamond, but glass, and Rekha says, assuredly, "No, it's not a diamond. It is definitely glass or something fake." I have heard similar observations from women in the "real world," but with less direct and more passive aggression. One of the little psychoses of domesticity?

Riti asks if we can play a different game. Though I have a hard time understanding, eventually I get it, and it is actually fun. When we finish, Rekha pronounces the game stupid and says, "Let's play rummy." Neither Riti nor Sanjana want to play, so I play with her alone. When we finish (she wins, quickly) I say I will play with Riti now, thinking I should alternate between the two people who actually want to play. Rekha explodes, "What is this? I am just playing for time-pass, not *dil phailana*," not to spread one's heart. "I don't do this *dil phailana* thing, you two play. I am done with cards."

The abuse goes on. I lose track of topics. The other women look away, close their eyes. I am trying to be friendly, to let it wash off, to laugh a bit, to ignore it, but she comments on my efforts to endure or ignore as well. Finally someone asks what time it is. Though it is early for lunch, there is a wordless collective decision to go inside. When I go home later, I will nap for hours, sleeping off the abuse.

As we get up, Rekha tells me, "What are you doing here anyway? Don't you have a husband? Don't you have a child? You are ruining their lives with this useless research. You should take care of your home, take care of your husband and child. Leave this stupid research."

Much of my time is spent waiting. Embarrassingly long hours pass in states of deferral. For one excruciating month, before I find Moksha where I had left it, I wait every morning, forsaking all travel, for the man paid to install my Internet cable. I call daily and am promised his arrival in a few hours. Daily he does not show. I sit on the bed that serves as my sofa, with the doors to the balcony open and the small surrounding panes of amber-painted glass filling with light as the morning rises. I drink tea, read and write, clip newspaper articles; I watch through trees below my balcony the gradual rise and fade of political rallies, the drift of banners to the ground and strings of flags flapping like loose teeth; I respond to small emergencies, like the family of monkeys that takes a bath in the rooftop water tank. Until the last morning minute when it becomes late night in Boston, I punish myself by waiting for phone calls from the person I had thought was a new and redeeming love. The calls don't arrive, or, when they do, they come with cruel descriptions of outings with pretty, young students. I wait for the ten o'clock hour, when I can phone Moksha, trying to locate it, or reach other doctors in other hospitals. At night, I wait for the bulldozers to finish their midnight excavations, for the new buildings to crystallize out of brick and sweat. For a few weeks Eve and I wait for our eyes, benighted with pinkeye, to open, to lose their grit. I wait for the next day.

Waiting replaces order with sensation, lines with dots. I feel I am swallowed by time rather than the one who consumes the hours. In Moksha, before I make the female ward my first and eventually my only destination, I wait for hours for appointments with doctors and for someone to call me to observe in the outpatient clinic. It is confusing, and I make long, elaborate notes on the shape, feel, smell, and sound of the waiting hall. It is very easy to feel, in the dim light and quiet hum, that the waiting room is time itself, that "it is we who are internal to time, not the other way round" (Deleuze 1989: 82).

The same is true of the ward where we are compressed and extended in body, thought, and spirit. This is a place where stillness is both enforced and criticized, and where people move in and sometimes out of choreographies they both do and do not choose. Elusive arrangements direct bodies into meaningful action—picking stones from rice, pacing while praying—as well as into acts of indeterminate meaning—sitting against a wall in the winter sun, lying still under a quilt, pedaling a stationary bike that has no tension. Such movements are not limited to their ability to be meaningful; their primary importance is not what we make of them, or what it falls on us to interpret. Power arrangements are uncertain, ways of being are confusing and erratic, forms of scrutiny fall short of being systematic, and human expressions are changeable. Such fleeting durability offers to notions of agency a powerful conundrum—poor treatment and enforced confinement happened as much in micromoments of accident as in organization, in atrophy as much as systematic scrutiny. In all of this there is movement, a kind of presence visible always and only in its moment of burn.

This is connected to the kind of harbor Moksha is, as well as to the kind of containment it enforces. There are few places in the city for women starting their lives anew or needing momentary refuge between catastrophe and settling, flight and groundedness. Moksha is a halfway house with the halves in the wrong places. It is half a setting for acute care, where women in need of constraint, care, and control might be attended to in medical terms that could reasonably include some degree of restriction; at the same time it is a living space for people who need no restriction but who benefit from a bit of care. The temporalities of each, as well as their spatial configurations, collapse and are often confused.

Kajol tells me about a government institution for "destitute women," those who "can't be with their families" or who are in "some kind of difficult condition. It is a place for women who," she shifts to English, "have had a lot of mishappenings." I think about this ontology of a happening gone wrong, and wonder if Moksha is also a space of mishappenings, those of kinship, those of life, those of medical practice, those of bodies in motion among other bodies in motion.

There may be mishappenings in ethics too, the framing of which— medical or research ethics, or ethics in general—shapes choreographies of confinement in Moksha. It incorporates the idea of research, who people become when we look at them a certain way, and where and how we may look when people become a certain way. It involves the presence and mispresence of language as well as the happenings and mishappenings of bodies, the passage and mispassage of time. And it relates to the ways movements in and out of Moksha are regulated, to the way consent works here, and to women's place in relation to research, to medicine, to Moksha, to me, and to each other, crossing from the literal to the conceptual. In other words, if the language of consent, as the marker of the private, rights-bearing citizen, "bears the signature" of globalization and of a distinction between public good and private rights (Das 1997: 101), a different ethical orientation exists in Moksha, where the public good is not at issue at all, and neither is personal suffering; where admission is not mediated in terms of harm but is always "voluntary". This is a setting of full consent; it is also a setting of utter restriction. And it is a collection of spaces filled in by movements, efforts, resignation, desires, and futility between those poles. Such movements might be haphazard, accidental, disorganized, and non-narrative, even as they are also deeply impactful and undeniably systematic. Indeed, for all the clinical scrutiny of women's paranoia about husbands, it is not this clinical practice that bears the most impact on women's lives. Rather, the habitation of time and space on the ward, the shifting and irregular (or numbingly regular) mesh of movements, interactions, and sensations establish the terms and stakes for dissolutions. These elements are difficult to locate as part of global systems of regulation, surveillance, economy, and knowledge production, though they do, of course, participate in them. At the same time, certain aspects of long-term involuntary confinement are all too easy to understand as the corrupt and illegal practices of a rogue institution operating at the edges of legitimacy. Neither approach is entirely sufficient in grasping the kinds of presence and crisis taking place in Moksha.

Moksha, like other choreas, might be at once spasm and dance, perhaps a dance of missteps, if we think of dance in Paul Valéry's terms, as "a body which suddenly as though by the effect of an internal shock, enters into a kind of life that is at once strangely unstable and strangely regulated, strangely spontaneous, but at the same time strangely contrived and, assuredly, planned" (1988: 56). For Valéry, the dancer's singularity is flooded by her dance (though this is an idea dance theorists have long contested, it has compelling resonance for the inpatient ward); for the dancer "there is no outside"; action itself is a system of containment. Women in the locked ward occupy a similar conceptual landscape, locked into space and choreographies that indicate a world of estrangement and a world estranged, at the same time that they engage in accidental and purposeful patterns of movement that make habit, familiarity, and presence out of estrangement. They do so amid—and because of—the constant press of an outside that they imagine, suggest, dream about, discuss, and mourn.

Just as speech is less important here in what it signifies than for how it comes to signify, movement is important less for what it means than for how it both invites and defies interpretation. Shifting our sense of recognition from knowledge production to movements that punctuate time in never entirely scrutable ways, we glean something more than interpretation from sensations and movements in and against Moksha's walls. We gain a sense that important work takes place at the edge of legibility, and that "the body's unanticipated gestures" (Foster 1995: 4) tell us that confinement is more than restriction on movement, and movement more than performance. Bodies and persons appear beyond their creation as certain kinds of subjects, beyond their "genre" (mad, female, Indian, abandoned, disciplined, resistant, etc.) (Foster 1995). In this dance, bodies are disciplined, but only partially; legible, but never fully; "still capable of generating ideas . . . of writing as well as being written upon" (Foster 1995: 15).

This is also a space of catastrophe, of the mishappenings of Moksha and the anxieties and suffering they produce. And there is intimacy and aggression in it, in ways that cross boundaries between mad and sane, pathological and normal. These are choreographies in which spaces are inhabited as unlivable, while referencing the spaces they are not—the horizons beyond the locked ward that may themselves be livable or unlivable. There are temporary intimacies and bonds here, connections that may extend beyond the clinic but in all likelihood do not. Subjecthood is undone here. To say as much is not to undermine women's desperate states of existence or the injustice of their confinement. Indeed, it may offer access to aspects of those injustices that are more difficult to locate in critiques emphasizing subject-making. In the locked ward, movements, like language, continually speak to the possibility that presence—of loved ones, of love, of oneself—is, like "happening," a matter of degree. Here, in the intensity of sensation, including the sensation of time, one encounters the possibility of one's own disappearance, the fact of dissolution.

Often, on my journeys home from Moksha, I worry my own wounds. I repeat to myself my life's echoes of Sanjana's life. I tell myself I know about exile, and that my exile is as breath is to gale in comparison with what she has endured. Nonetheless, I think about what it feels like to pack a suitcase and a child into a car, to run from home into darkness uncertain of the possibility of return. I think about making temporary homes—in an ice-laden New England February, in a steamy north Indian September. I think about the subtle hallucinations—wobbling walls, undulating floors, birds in the edges of rooms—that come with sleep deprivation, how the breakdown of love is a kind of end of days, an insanity that empties truth from language. I think about the sheer and bodily *force* of love coming undone, the way the emotions it involves can erupt into violent expressions, can take over a body, occupy its arms and hands, ventriloquize a voice, make quiet souls roil and slender arms flail.

I think about the slow kill of lying, the negotiated nature of reality, and the way speech grapples for purchase on truth through obsessive repetition, by telling a story, by giving an explanation over and over in order to make it true, or by pleading in a voice that ascends to shrill hysteria. I think about the way it is difficult not to perform madness in moments of desperation and loss. I remember what it feels like to not be believed, to be called crazy and accused of making bad choices, to long for a home and fear it at the same time.

I also think that I do not know what it would be like for these things to also mean my child will be taken from me, or what it would be like for this to unfold in a world in which I could not live on my own or support myself, in a setting in which there are many obstacles to doing so. I think that there is some solace in the heroic status attributed to single motherhood in the United States. It is my shiny medal, my little reward and I-told-you-so. There is no such mythology in India. And I think that I do not know what it would be like for all of this to be followed, even pursued, by clinical judgment, by doctors who either watch too closely or not enough. Or what it would be like for the basic suffering of the end of marriage to come with the burden of having to disavow the stories that enable me to survive love's breakdown.

After my husband's departure, the elderly *dhobi*, the washerwoman who lives behind us, the tiny, palm-wine-drunk woman we call Mata-ji, burns herself on a fire while warming her legs. The synthetic fabric of her petticoat melts to her skin. I visit her one afternoon. In the shadowy light she shows me the burn stretching the upper half her leg. It is black and bubbled like the skin of a burnt pepper. She stays inside for weeks, eventually emerging, carefully and infrequently, to sit in the sun in the driveway. Her hands shake from pain and lack of alcohol. When she returns from her trip, Mrs. M. buys a small bottle of brandy for her, something to soothe the detox.

The children spend the winter playing with rounds of puppies. Each litter comes and goes. The children understand that puppies are not creatures of this world. Few of them make it through the coldest nights, fewer to a hardy and viable size. Most are too scared to venture out of the bushes where their mother lies tired and milk-full. Boys tie rotis to the ends of strings and drag them along the ground. Some of the children hang back, having seen the long needles with which siblings were punished after dog bites. Eve runs away quaking when a puppy gets close to her, taking very seriously my strong warnings. I worry that I have put her off puppies— which once seemed a natural childhood thing—for good. Others are bolder. One girl Eve's age pets one of the tiniest dogs and then, copying her older brother, starts tormenting it. She pushes down hard on its back and pulls its tail until I tell her to stop. Her little brother, barely two, wants so badly to pull the puppy's tail, but stops when he sees me coming. Two of the older boys alert me when puppies die—from cold, from "fever," hiding inside the perimeter wall or in the junglelike area bordering it. The older boy points to a puppy that is sleeping in the sun and tells me this one is sick too. It won't last long, he says.

Eve's Hindi begins to astound me; her voice is indistinguishable from those of the other children, and she unwittingly corrects my grammar when she responds, correctly, to my poorly phrased questions. She has become skilled at making sari pleats with my *dupattas*, and I notice that while she once dressed up with one *dupatta*, wrapping it around her waist and over her shoulder, she now ties play saris with two, folding perfect pleats into one, tucking them into her waist band, then tossing a second one over her shoulder. I buy her a pile of cheap and colorful scarves from the bazaar. Her new abilities and this bounty of fabric allow her freedom of movement. She can run in her "saris."

She spends more time with children than with me, and has adopted from them and from her schoolteachers the habit of hitting, both in jest and with real force. When I scold her for one infraction or another, she enfolds herself in Prem's arms and says, "Hit Mummy!" Prem says, "I'll hit Mummy. It's OK, I'll hit Mummy," and swats at me. I take the gentle blow. I am allowed my anger. The message gets through. Eve is comforted and allowed her injustice. It's a passable division of labor.

In the winter, dust coats everything in our open household. It leaves an oily film, weighty with the sweat of exhaust and the steam of tar and whatever goes into the buildings rising around us. It coats the plants like cheap makeup and is impervious to water and difficult to wash out of clothes. Our hair is dry, heavy, and tangled. Our clothes are dirty even when clean.

Just before ending my time at Moksha and returning, for a brief hiatus, to Boston, I begin to visit the lawyers and activists at a local women's legal organization. I talk to them about Moksha and what is happening there, I listen to their accounts of working with women without mental illnesses trying to leave marriages; to cope when they have been left; to deal with the return to natal family; to fight for custody, for maintenance, for an inheritance; to protect themselves from angry husbands, fathers, brothers, brothers-in-law. I follow cases involving families' persecution of couples in love marriages, reading files on young men and women pursued and abused by kin.

And then I get sick. My breath gives out. My time with the lawyers is cut short. I sleep through a fever for a week, maybe more, I don't remember. People around me take care of Eve, they feed her and keep an eye on her. She has become amazingly competent and independent in our time here, well beyond what would be expected for her age at home, but perfectly attuned to the lifeways of the children who make up the little band she spends her days with. At times, in my fevered wakefulness between long sleeps, I do not know where she is, but in my wheeze and fog I trust she is safe with Prem or Mrs. M., or with other mothers and older children. There is no other option. For a month I do not leave the house except to go to doctors and labs. For a month Eve's father calls daily to see how I am. He sends an enormous burst of roses—three dozen. Like most Indian flowers, they smell more pungent, sweeter, than American roses. These acts empty my heart.

Two years later I find the following thoughts, a heap of metaphors, buried in the last notes I wrote before I got sick:

> Desire and madness, home and confinement/security/abandonment indeed. It's a jumble of these things—abandonment, confinement, security, independence, and yet those things are at once structured and live too close to each other, slip too dangerously into one another to ever be completely defined, structured, situated. I suppose most of us, in most of our lives slide along with things in some kind of arrangement where these categories are in place, we don't think about them, they live on top of each other, but they don't chew each other's heels. But it doesn't take much to set them snarling, to make it collapse into a heap, and when that process is set in motion, the things and people and processes and institutions and structures that are supposed to put those categories back in order (in whatever form they live and work and don't work in different settings, which would be the role of culture, to establish that situation and the rules that hold the categories in place) seem to scramble and scramble and only barely succeed at putting it back into place. But yet it is so hard to see the fragility of those things until they fall apart. With madness, with divorce, with violence, with fear, with paranoia, with shame, with too much or too little force or strength or authority . . .
>
> And then what are we left with? The *dargah*, the field, sex, adultery, the ward, praying, madness and lice and pleading with doctors and social workers who tell lies in the two minutes a day or a week that they might give you. Places and actions into which desires are poured and sadness comes rushing out. . . . Longing that comes in repeating the names of the dead, in pacing, in weeping at one's own sadness when one enters the place of calm and healing.

I manage to pack Eve's and my things in an enormous aluminum crate, install it in the storage room in Mrs. M.'s house, and coordinate our return to Delhi and then to Boston. I am helped by friends, residents of this city and others like me passing through for work, who hoist me into rickshaws, phone doctors, mail boxes of books, and pack our belongings. Meanwhile, the woman I had intended to stay with during the short stay in Delhi before our flight to the United States—a wealthy American public health specialist who lives just a few blocks from me in Cambridge—tells me Eve and I are no longer welcome in her home given my illness. I tell her tuberculosis is unlikely and that I desperately need a place to stay in Delhi. No, she says, it would be too risky. She promises to help me find somewhere else but never phones back. I scramble to find a place for the few days on our way home, somewhere I can sleep through the afternoons and Eve can play safely. The friends who had welcomed me in my disheveled sadness in September tell me they have experienced, in one way or another, nearly every kind of sickness, and let us sleep in their own bedroom.

Before I got sick I did not know where Eve and I will live on our return to Boston: in the home I took us from a year, nearly to the day, earlier or in a new place I have yet to locate. It is a terrifying, adrift feeling. Being unwell, I decide that for the time being we will go "home." I feel immediate relief, and also fear. This is no heroic or triumphant return. I walk through the arrival hall doors into the winter coat my husband has brought, bearing no big, India-effected life decisions on the mess I left behind—the divorce I can't bring myself to follow through on, the house I may or may not lose, the angry emails and long silences that are the disintegrating hulk of my affair. All these waterlogged ruins, and my rooftop in the city so far away.

I end this phase of my work exhausted—by the uncertainties of my own dissolving family, by the weight of my mistakes, by the elusiveness of home, by the ungraspable state of language and meaning in Moksha, by the deeply unsettling feeling of passing in and out of the locked ward, and by what increasingly feels like the counterhuman constraints of "research." But more than any of these feelings, I end convinced I have not done nearly enough for Sanjana, Amina, and Isma.

In a month's time I will be back, having settled Eve into a new school and life with her father, who repaints her bedroom the turquoise blue of a warm ocean—a paler version of the color of the window glass in Moksha. On my return to India my body will be flush with antibiotics, my lungs working again, and I will plunge into work in a place an experiential universe away from Moksha, one with strict time frames, open spaces, and different circuits of language. One with different mishappenings. I will race so manically through the days that I will be all but unaware of the oppressive heat. It will feel more like "research." I will go back to Moksha, but only sporadically. I will spend less time in shrines.

I will not know yet that time will bring, at first, less articulation and more dissolution, and then, not until years later, a new love who will offer kindness and sanity, overturning—easily, gracefully—everything that I have come to fear is true about love and home, and much of what I write here.

But before all this, when I return to India, without Eve I lack many things. One of them is the following: on most days I come home from Moksha exhausted, thirsty, hungry, and wrung out. I bring a late lunch onto my roof balcony, listening for the shouts of children below to tell me where, in this large compound, this small, small universe, Eve is. I yell over the back wall and listen as the call moves down the row of doorways, resonating in one voice, and then another, and then another until it reaches its destination: "Evie, your mummy is calling." "Evie, your mummy is calling." "Evie, your mummy is calling."

Chapter 4

On Dissociation

> A fissure opens in a once silent body and from it flows an
> unstoppable, uncontainable speaking as we cast our bodies without
> thinking into space.
>
> —Elizabeth Dempster, "Women Writing the Body:
> Let's Watch a Little How She Dances" (1995)

The psychiatry unit of Nehru Government Hospital was at the edge of a large campus, just beyond the traffic of a busy thoroughfare. Not far from the old city, Nehru gave a sense of being in the dense middle of things, of having arrived at a center. Through grand gates, its main buildings were reached via a driveway lined with lawns on which families set up temporary shelters—tents, beds, and makeshift kitchens. Here were Nehru's oldest buildings, their cupolas and domes recognizable as signs of the city's fading stature. Across the road pulsing with food vendors, barbers, dogs, and rickshaws, the psychiatry unit was behind a brick wall, through an inconspicuous vine-covered gate.

The unit was a gathering of buildings of varying ages embodying eras of psychiatric care. The newest building, just inside the gate, contained the emergency ward, administrative offices, doctors' offices, classrooms, and a library. The outpatient clinic, a short walk away, was a humble single-story structure with an ample courtyard, reached by a path lined by wild growth—flowers, bushes, trees, and towering marijuana plants (which a resident said must have grown from a laborer's unfinished joint). Between the outpatient unit and the road, the neurology building occupied a crisply new structure, its metal and concrete entrance a shiny announcement of modern science. Farther back was a decrepit building that had once housed Nehru's original psychiatry unit. A building of several levels with a colonial feel, its shuttered windows and doorways led off verandas into dark rooms and hallways piled with broken plaster, brick, and trash. Though it felt uninhabited and many of its rooms were empty and locked, it contained social workers' and occupational therapists' offices.

Nehru, one of the city's three large institutions for psychiatric care, was also the city's oldest and most prestigious medical college. Though I began pursuing research there around the time I started working in Moksha, accomplishing clearance was slow bureaucratic work. This was in stark contrast with the absence of procedures that—disturbingly—made entry into Moksha easy and instant. Whereas Moksha was often empty, and doctors could either welcome you into their offices or make you wait for hours, the doctors at Nehru had packed days, busy hours filled to the minute with a routine of activity. Finding a time to see them was difficult, but a few moments spent in the crowded hallways made this understandable. Once an appointment was earned (and once I learned how to bypass the aggressive gatekeepers who manned doctors' doorways) I became part of their schedule and never waited for long.

I met with senior physicians and passed through Nehru's human subjects review process, instructed that on every page of my application I should write "Through Proper Channels." After months of waiting, news that I had received clearance came, but only after my return to India from the United States. Though approval had been granted a month earlier, there was confusion about who was to inform me. After a month in Boston trying not to put down exhausted roots, I settled Eve into American life and returned to India, hoping to begin work in Nehru, but uncertain when and if this would happen.

Winter was over. Holi had passed, the spring festival of raucous color marking the approach of summer giving way to increasingly parched anticipations of monsoon. On my return, I passed through Delhi in a matter of hours and spent a jet-lagged week tying up loose ends, figuring out who was still around, who had left town, who was sick and could not meet, who had returned or was now ready to work with me. My nights were soaked with whiskey in attempts to find sleep. The roughest hours were the warming dark of early morning. During the day, I raced around making appointments and locating contacts, but as the day dimmed, I began a descent into the raggedness of failed sleep.

I had only been away for a month, but much seemed changed. People I had been working with were gone. Efforts to make appointments failed. I was told by the receptionist at Moksha that Dr. K. had left and now "sat" at Nehru (though I never saw her there and doctors did not recognize her name). The receptionist said the only staff psychiatrist was Dr. M., and though she could not give me an appointment, I was welcome to visit the female ward. My heart sank when I found Sanjana and Amina still there. Riti had gone home but was returning for "day-care."

It was difficult to be in the city without Eve. I was no longer staying in our apartment—there was no reason to take up so much space—and rented a room in the lower part of Mrs. M.'s home, sharing common spaces with other visitors. My room was cavernous. It had once been one of the house's two drawing rooms. It had no exterior windows but high louvered glass vents to the outside and a glazed window onto the enclosed veranda where we took meals. Deep in the house, there were no flash floods of children; the calls of trains and summons to prayer were not audible; I no longer needed my cook and companion Prem. I missed the open doors; I missed Prem; I missed naps with Eve, shouting children, and the lively wake of our life.

But I had more freedom of movement. I could come and go without plotting around school schedules or meals for a picky six-year-old. I could stay out later. I didn't feel like a mother; this left me feeling relieved in some ways, amputated in others. People did not seem to make much of this, or to grasp the emptiness I felt. Being separated from children was a fact of life. I recalled Bulbul's apparent ease with the fact that her daughter lived with her husband while she stayed with her parents for the foreseeable future. I thought of Indian parents I knew who sent their children for months-long stays with grandparents so they could work or travel. Being with and apart from children was a matter of pulsation. It still felt strange.

At the same time, something had shifted. Unlike when Eve and I first arrived, seven months of a slower pace and modest tasks had calmed me, and, though missing our shared life, I could now feel its effects. I could lie alone with my racing mind without feeling the earth dropping away. There were a thousand small worries, but no looming fear, less sense of loss.

But work was elusive, and I felt aged and jarred by what a childless life threatened to mean. In my first days back, I spent an evening with one of the foreign students I had made an acquaintance with, listening to stories about the excesses of the city's rich sons. "It's all the same party," she said, "only different DJs."

I decided to leave the city for a while.

Tulsi was in the country, so I planned a trip to visit her and Ammi. I passed a pleasant week in their company, spent a day at a large shrine, and took a trip into the mountains to pay respects at a favorite goddess temple. In temple and shrine, I watched women untwine their hair and go into trance—for release from spirits at the shrine, and for their entry (so the goddess could "play") at the temple. Phoning Nehru, I learned that my approval had been granted and a senior psychiatrist, Dr. C., was ready to work with me. I bought a train ticket and said a reluctant goodbye, heading back into the plains, anxious for busy days and predictable work.

So regular was my schedule that after a few days of making the same journey—by cycle-rickshaw to the auto-rickshaw stop, then onward in a packed auto to the hospital—a rickshaw-wallah began to meet me at the gate. Small and old, he had difficulty getting passengers so tried to reach them before others could. His pace was slow but I contracted with him for daily trips. Apace with our wheels, a pack of dogs raced us from Mrs. M.'s house to the auto stop, a twenty-minute journey that included skirting trucks and buses at a complicated crossing. It made my heart race even without animals weaving through the traffic.

I assumed the dogs were following me, that someone like me had fed them once. No, the driver said sheepishly. He gave one food. It started following him, and others joined, to the loud amusement of other rickshaw pullers, who cheered at us as we rattled by with our team of barking strays. The auto drivers began referring to me as "the tall lady with the old rickshaw-wallah and the dogs." Determined not to be embarrassed, I imagined us background characters in a Fellini film.

Meanwhile, the heat grew intense, the rain still months away. I wrote in my notes that the atmosphere felt like "a leather blanket of heat, a slick, sticky humidity, like cane syrup, like soup, weather to steal your soul." Like many before me, I found much to make of the weather, too many associations to describe it. At Nehru, though, I hardly noticed it. There was little time to feel the air. In Moksha, the atmosphere had been overwhelming, cold or hot, raucous or still, sensation was oppressive. But Nehru was worlds away from Moksha. No one was locked interminably; some patients asked to stay longer. Doctors were busy, attentive, and present. The doors to the wards were open; in fact, I wasn't sure for some time if the men's ward even had doors (it did). Where the ground floor was damp with the smell of earth and cleaning fluid, the women's ward on the third floor had a breezy sense of elevation, a door that closed (but seldom was), and a wall of screened windows letting in a mottled green. The vendors' calls and bus horns that punctured the men's ward were, at the altitude of the women's ward, just a distant wash of sound. Calls to prayer rose in regular intervals. Time came with sound; both were predictable and paced.

Time was also steadied by regular visits from practitioners. Students came in and out in groups—nursing students in starched uniforms, white-coated medical students on rotation, social workers who chatted with patients and ward attendants and offered curt advice. Residents, new psychiatrists, mostly men and a few women in their mid-twenties, trained in medical schools all over India, came through several times a day. Though they did not wear white jackets, they were no less recognizable in their pressed gray trousers and button-down shirts or tasteful *selwar kameez*, and especially their black, rectangular-framed glasses. I began to feel I could recognize psychiatrists in the city by glasses shape alone.

Accustomed as I was to Moksha's empty sense of exile, it was comforting to find Nehru full of families. On a given morning, a father might be changing the bag on his daughter's IV, a man might be asking the mother of the patient in the next bed to look after his wife while he went out to buy medication. Sisters, brothers, aunts, and uncles might speak in low voices around a teenage girl while her mother brushed her hair. Another mother might be refolding *dupattas* she had ironed for her daughter, who lay on the bed.

Given shortages of nursing and other support staff, patient care was dependent on kin. It was extremely rare for patients to come in without family. At least one family member—the "attendant"—was required to stay with each patient to manage their medication, interact with doctors, bring food and snacks, and look after hygiene. At night, only one additional person was permitted to stay on the ward. Others went to a *dharamsala*, a lodging house, where they stayed for around five rupees a night, a meager sum. Patients without family or legal guardians—often brought in by the police—were categorized in official terms as destitute and required court order for hospitalization. Some were referred to the psychiatry unit from other departments, a process that was slow, confusing, and rife with paperwork. Some waited for days to be transferred to trauma or neurology units; others moved quickly. One patient, a "destitute" with a gruesome head wound, was moved back and forth between the trauma and psychiatry wards several times during the course of a few weeks.

The feel and rhythm and sheer comprehensibility of the place could not have been further from Moksha.

Early in my visits, a female patient and her husband sat together in the sixth bed from the door. The woman, introduced as Kavita, had come into the ward days before I began working there, having traveled a day's journey from the village where she and her husband's family farmed and ran a shop. At night, Kavita's husband slept on a mat on the floor, though ward rules said he was supposed to sleep downstairs. During the day he read the newspaper and brought fruit, biscuits, and meals from vendors outside. At times he cooked for Kavita on a small stove in one of the open areas behind the building. They ate together and attended to labors of daily life, napped in the afternoons, and in the evenings took walks around the grounds.

Kavita complained of pain, especially in her arms, and "heaviness" (*vajan*) in her head. At times she grew wild and unrecognizable, panting, and staring intently through half-lowered lids, yelling at her doctors and her husband. At times she spoke as though she was someone else, referring to herself in the third person, asking why Kavita was being "kept" in the hospital. Later, she began to speak to herself and, as residents put it, "mimic" other patients, a sign, they said, that she was smart and observant but manipulative. The residents diagnosed her with dissociative disorder, what one referred to as "in common language, hysteria," and admitted her for observation to rule out schizophrenia. Most were confident of their diagnosis—there were no positive symptoms, and Kavita's possession episodes were distinct from the aural and visual hallucinations of psychosis; they saw this arrangement of symptoms all the time.

Much in this case had to do with control. Unlike the intrusions of psychosis, Kavita's afflictions were "under her control," residents said. Indeed, they were an effort to gain control of others. Dr. C., Kavita's consulting psychiatrist, said, "With schizophrenia the symptoms are beyond the patient's control; with dissociative disorder, it all depends on how much control the patient has over other people. If a person begins to slip out of that control, the symptoms will increase."

Kavita was treated with an escalating barrage of medication, but also through her husband's monitoring. He was not to "give in" to her desires, not to offer her "secondary gains." Achieving insight and understanding her agency were essential to Kavita's improvement. I couldn't decide whether I felt this process to be punitive or confessional, or neither, or both.

Several things struck me about Nehru. The first was the constant presence of kin on the ward. Where women in Moksha lived separated from families, in this setting the messiness of kin life, intimacy's borrowings from affliction and vice versa, was no less present than in homes. As in Moksha, doctors made particular use of relationships, especially marriages, questioning relationships and feelings about relationships to gauge illness and the effects of drugs. But unlike in Moksha, this happened in the constant presence of kin. It was complicated, interactive work.

Rare in Moksha but common in Nehru were ailments classed as dissociative disorders but referred to by doctors as "hysteria," or "like hysteria," or "also known as hysteria." This was a distress understood and treated as agency gone awry, often amid (or causing) fragile relationships. The word "hysteria" seldom made it to case files, where diagnoses were recorded in ICD-10 code (the International Statistical Classification of Diseases, the diagnostic manual used in Nehru) or as "dissociative," or, less commonly, "conversion" disorders, but the term was very much present in along-the-way conversations and explanations.

Signs of dissociative disorder included unconsciousness, unexplained pains, headaches, anger, clenched teeth, and visitations from spirits or deities. In unmarried women and girls, affect read as aggressively sexual might be a sign—lipstick too bold, a top too tight, a *dupatta* draped across the neck instead of modestly covering the torso, dress beyond one's station in life. Bangles, with their colorful ability to be piled on and their jangling insistence on being noticed, were often made note of. I was never convinced that these were things families cared or even thought about. But for doctors, these were signs of disorder. They could indicate other things, too—mania, in particular. But together with other signs, and without positive symptoms of mania or psychosis, they suggested dissociative disorder.

In the United States, when I shared this observation, the usual response was a mixture of surprise—that hysteria was still diagnosed—and lack of surprise that this happened in India, hysteria diagnosis being taken as a sign of India's backwardness or, as one person put it, "the last gasp of the nineteenth century in India." As every anthropologist should know, even those unfamiliar with South Asia, this is an insufficient understanding of the non-West and its histories of medicine. But as might not be as obvious, this is also an impoverished understanding of hysteria.

In contrast, Indian psychiatrists, especially those familiar with diasporic patients, were neither surprised nor particularly intrigued. Dissociative symptoms were not unheard of with South Asian patients outside of India, and dissociation, as one colleague put it, tongue firmly in cheek, could be considered "the psychiatric diagnosis of the Third World." Medical anthropologists are well acquainted with the idea that beyond Europe, disorders such as neurasthenia have remained viable ways for social crises to be "somatized" as bodily experience (Kleinman 1986). We are accustomed to thinking about dissociation, conversion, and similar diagnoses as continuous with possession, trance, and mediumship, means of access to power and expressions of distress, like hysteria in Euro-America, the bodily voicing of unspeakable critique.

How, then, to understand this difference between Moksha and Nehru? Was Moksha, with its old problem of dumped women and its asylum feel, a more modern space of diagnosing? Or was it simply that its clientele were of higher social classes? Was Nehru, with its internationally known psychiatry professors and bustling distance from anything asylumlike, "backward," or were its poorer and less educated clientele more likely to still have this old disorder? Not only are the answers equally no—Nehru saw plenty of middle-class and even elite patients, a great many with hysteria presentations, and Moksha received many from the lower ends of the middle-class spectrum—the questions are wrong. This is not to say that hysteria has nothing to do with modernity or that modernity is pure imaginary where hysteria is concerned. But questions like this miss the complexity of hysteria's ontological status, the peculiar *thing* it is; they assume that hysteria, if it has not disappeared, is on its way to obsolescence, first in the Western world, then in the rest of the world as other places "catch up."

Instead, hysteria is a shape-shifter, calling into question the nature of its own existence, and destabilizing formulas for truth, especially as they materialize on the ground of women's lives and afflictions.

The common wisdom that sees hysteria as a fading (or obsolete) diagnosis requires thinking of psychiatry as on an ever-forward march away from minds and stories and toward brains and chemicals, and an ever-backward retreat from morally loaded diagnosing. But sciences (and anthropologies) of trauma and social stress leave room for the possibility that, however we might feel about the term "hysteria," the distresses it captures may reveal something about power, about people's relationships with others in given times and places. Similarly, anthropology's attention to the symbolic aspects of even the coldest-seeming biological explanations do not oppose moral orders to modern medicine. They share with feminist arguments the idea that hysteria may be a kind of expression (of acquiescence or resistance) amid symbolic orders. They leave room for the possibility that wide-reaching gender conditions may be as potent in shaping distress as things deemed biologically universal.

Importantly, hysteria is not only a disorder but a clinical operation. That is, it is something doctors and clinics do, not something they find or invent. It is a disorder of performance par excellence. In naming and treating it, medicine has long generated—at times to the point of minstrelsy—its ways of making knowledge and the inequalities and disavowals that involves. Hysteria makes these things obvious. According to some, it also *makes* them, being not only exemplary but inaugural of medicine's power plays.

In Nehru, as in other places and times, these clinical operations were vividly gendered. The treatment of a disorder understood as female (even in men) by doctors who were in most cases male, or the scrutiny of a woman in deep distress by a room full of men, or the kinds of questions asked and behaviors made note of made Nehru a stark tableau of Indian psychiatry's gender arrangements, and allowed dissociative disorder to expose the heavy gendering of Indian medicine's performativity. That hysteria was also an epistemological crisis—a crisis of truth telling—steeped in female desire gave these gender plays even wider implications.

Where was Nehru Hospital in this slippage in what hysteria is, or whether it exists? If Moksha's gendered crisis was involuntary commitment and the enclosures and estrangements it involved, Nehru's was something different, but to say it was a crisis of "hysteria diagnosing" or to call hysteria diagnosing a crisis is to mistake the revelatory potential of hysteria presentation for a medical lie or cultural figment. At the same time, taking hysteria out of its historical and context, separating it from a century of global conversations, and rendering it simply a culturally shaped somatic response to social stresses denudes whatever was happening in Nehru of its epistemological complexity and, thus, of much of what it might expose about gender in the global clinic. Truth itself seemed to be constructed in ways of bearing, knowing, and treating hysteria, a gendered truth that was also a medical one. In this, too, the dissolutions and vulnerabilities of lives with others—and ways of telling about them—seemed to be at stake.

Just as Moksha represents one aspect of the history of the asylum and its ends, Nehru's psychiatry unit embodied other aspects. In India, amid the flux of restructuring and deinstitutionalization, government hospital psychiatry units were pillars of constancy. Even before large asylums changed around them, altering structure, name, and ethos, by the 1970s government hospitals were taking on more patients as philosophies began shifting away from institutionalization and drugs became more available. Government hospitals bore the paradox of simultaneous growth of primary-care infrastructure and efforts to move psychiatry out of large institutions (Jain and Jadhav 2008). Over time, hospitals saw fewer patients in inpatient wards and more thronging outpatient clinics.

The pressure on doctors in government hospitals can be shocking to outsiders. At Nehru, the head of psychiatry, Dr. A., estimated that the outpatient department saw 200–250 patients per day, including approximately 125–150 patients for follow-ups and 45–100 new patients. Ninety percent of patients were treated on an outpatient basis, he estimated, and out of the approximately 250 patients who passed through the department in a day, either in the outpatient clinic or emergency room, only two or three were admitted.

Dr. A., an internationally known specialist in child psychiatry and highly regarded practitioner, witnessed the decades of change in Nehru's psychiatry unit, the rise of new buildings, transitions in patient demographics, and cultural changes inside and outside clinical practice. The biggest cultural change involved perceptions of the role of the family in care for patients with serious mental illnesses. Consistent with current thinking, his view was that caregiving should be the family's responsibility. Families should not be dependent on institutions and, likewise, the institution "can't completely take over." Medical residents described differences between Nehru and private institutions (including Moksha, which no one at Nehru thought highly of) as the difference between modern institutions and asylums. As one explained, "This hospital is not like an asylum. It is a teaching institution. But other hospitals, like Moksha, are more like asylums. There the staff takes over the responsibility for the patient."

In the past, Dr. A. said, doctors were more inclined to hospitalize patients, and families more likely to hospitalize kin for longer periods of time. A popular ethos associated mental illness with long-term institutionalization, and this was also common medical practice. In the 1970s and 1980s, he said, the inpatient ward at Nehru was overflowing. But at present, hospitalization happened only when absolutely necessary, wards were seldom full, and stays significantly shorter. Though attitudes about mental illness had shifted, he said, changes in family life were the real source of change. The family stayed in the ward in "those days" too, and there had always been staff shortages. But "family structure was different." Patients came from larger households and family members were more easily sacrificed from domestic labors. Now, networks of social support were shrinking, the joint family was less common, and more people worked outside the house. Bringing a family member to the hospital meant losing someone whose labors were essential to household survival. "People have to work," he said, "It's not a matter of choice."

For patients coming great distances, the burden was increased—kin could not rotate shifts, nor could they go home for an hour or two. Families' willingness to seek care had little to do with stigma, he said, and more to do with demands of time, money, and labor. (A doctor in Delhi once observed to me, "You Americans always come in asking about stigma.")

Dr. C., with whom I spent the start of most of my days in Nehru, was more cynical. He noted with amusement the irrelevance of the old stereotype in which patients were held for long periods. Here, patients often asked to stay longer. "The ward may not look like much to you," he said, "but many of our patients come from poor environments, villages and slums. The conditions here are good for them. There are fans, lights, running water."

Unlike situations in which longer institutionalization involved loss of contact with family and signified abandonment, here, institutionalization required extensive family involvement and signified care. Patients who stayed for short periods did so because there was no family to care for them in the hospital. The results were two-sided—on the one hand, patients were surrounded by kin and cared for by loved ones; on the other, whatever conflicts and stresses were present came into the hospital. Interpenetrations of love and affliction might retain their timbre, be intensified, or be transformed as people found new ways of being together in the busy community of beds. Sometimes new freedoms and intimacies became possible away from household pressures, while at other times the embrace of family life meant persistence of whatever had contributed to illness in the first place. Control and care were jumbled together.

I got to know Kavita in an episodic way, during rounds mediated by the third-year resident Akhil, to whom I had been assigned by Dr. C. Most mornings I went on rounds with a trio of residents (senior psychiatrists seldom entered the wards) and shadowed Akhil in one way or another. Akhil was an earnest and cheerful young man from a small city some distance from Nehru. He often spoke in aphorisms and found in his work material for optimistic philosophizing. As we walked from ward to ward, he asked me questions of personal and soteriological nature. Was I interested in spirituality? What is a person's goal in life? What is the purpose of being alive? One morning, he sang me a song whose message was, "You win some, you lose some."

Rounds involved "phenomenology," taking stock of patients' states of being through questions about eating and sleeping, changes, improvements, and new difficulties. Residents asked which drugs patients were taking, when, and how much, making certain they understood correct amounts and timings.

Often, as in Moksha, questions involved how patients felt about their loved ones—were they suspicious of spouses, did they feel their families were "against them"? Establishing how people should relate to each other was integral to clinical practice. Social orders offered models of behavior, and living up to them was both diagnostic and therapeutic, tools for assessing a person's sense of themselves in the world. Was their behavior appropriate to their station in life? Was it overreaching? Did it show disregard for rules? When a male patient offered his hand, Akhil said, as I reached out, "Never shake hands. In this country, culturally, they do not shake hands, especially not with a woman. But this patient has tried to shake hands with you because of his grandiose mood, because he has this feeling of superiority." With another patient, he asked how he was behaving toward his uncle and grandfather, with whom conflict preceded admission to Nehru. "They are senior [lit. bigger] to you. You should show them respect. Do you touch their feet?" He turned to me, "He has grandiosity now, but when he is better he will understand that it is important to know his position."

Kavita and her husband encountered similar questions. They had come into the ward via the outpatient department, traveling by bus from their village where they left their four daughters in the care of Kavita's in-laws. I was told that Kavita was in a "dissociative stupor" when she arrived, unable to speak and "unresponsive to all stimuli." Her husband reported that she had taken to extreme behavior, shouting and crying. She was angry and demanding. "She demands people do what she says immediately, she feels she is always right, she can be abusive even to her own father," according to Akhil. From time to time she fell unconscious. She had tried to run away but was brought home by neighbors. The resident asked Kavita if she heard voices or saw people who were not there. Her husband had said no. But when asked if a god or spirit had been coming to her, the answer was yes. A goddess had been "grabbing" Kavita and demanding food, especially meat. He showed residents prescription sheets from a bout of illness after the birth of their second child, when Kavita was put on antipsychotic medication.

The residents gave her antianxiety and antidepressant medications, typical treatments for dissociative disorders, as well as the vitamin supplements with which they often padded prescriptions. The additional pills gave patients a sense of being treated well, they said, and most patients ("especially women") could use the supplements anyway.

Often we found Kavita sitting calmly on her bed, peeling bananas and offering pieces (something Akhil also saw as grandiose). At other times she was angry and accusatory. A few days after her admission, she was sitting up with her husband and looking, I wrote in my notes, "quite floridly psychotic." She looked up with a hint of a smile, lowered lids, and what I described as "an accusatory look." Her husband told residents she had been yelling all night. She said she had pain in her arm. The first-year resident, Azim, said perhaps this was because she had recently had blood drawn.

"No, she says it is in her whole arm." She pulled away from Akhil's examination.

Complimenting her on "doing her duties," he observed, "You have done your work very well today." She did not respond. Akhil explained that Kavita had washed her clothes by herself.

Though Kavita was diagnosed with dissociative disorder, he said they were having a hard time "assessing her problems."

"It is likely that she has multiple problems, including a personality problem, like narcissism. She has very narcissistic behavior. But we have been unable to do an objective personality assessment because she is not cooperative."

In a teacherly voice, he told Kavita the story of the villager who raised false alarms about lions, a "crying wolf" tale, then explained to me that that Kavita's pain had to do with her "hysteria."

"This kind of patient often complains of pains that aren't there. It is important to tell them that if they keep complaining then when they have a real problem no one will believe them."

He reminded Kavita to eat.

"You eat!" she said.

On another day, she asked, "Why have you brought me here by force?," the refrain so familiar from Moksha. She looked up accusingly. The ward attendant sitting by her side explained that Kavita's four daughters were not with her because of "this problem."

"Perhaps she is upset about that," she said softly, her hand on Kavita's upper arm.

I said, "Oh, I have a daughter, too."

Kavita's voice ascended, "They are not your daughters, they are my daughters. Why do you want to take my daughters away?" I tried to reassure her that nothing could be farther from the case, but I left feeling intrusive and ashamed of my naive assumption of shared maternal identity.

Later, hearing about this encounter, Akhil said, "It's fine; she should talk to you. It will make her feel better."

"Perhaps another day. I don't want to force her."

"Sometimes even we have to force them to talk. When we are trying to take a history and they are not cooperative, we have to make them talk."

I asked what they did. "We talk about neutral topics, like family life, their hobbies. We try to explore the problem in a different way rather than asking in a direct way 'What is the problem?'"

Though that seemed reasonable enough, his next comment was troubling. "Or we can threaten them with ECT," he said. Shock therapy. "Everyone knows about *bijli ki sikai* [electrical warming] and they are terrified of it. There is also a big stigma with ECT, so we use it as a threat to get people to talk and give the history. It is a strong aversion therapy, especially for dissociative patients. We also use it for these kinds of patients to get them to let go of their symptoms. You can threaten them with ECT if the symptoms don't get better and then they often improve. We also have the patients assist in the ECT of other patients, or watch. That can be enough for the dissociative patients to give up their symptoms. Rural people are very frightened of ECT, they know about *bijli* [electricity] and they are extremely frightened about it."

I asked if patients always comply.

"There are definitely times when families and patients refuse ECT, and they have to get the consent from the attendants [family members caring for the patient], but usually families comply."

In the quick shift from "patients" to "families," I recalled Dr. A.'s comments about consent: "Consent is not just between the doctor and the patient, and medication can be given more easily against a patient's will. This may look from one side, from the international human rights side, like it is illegal, and it is illegal, or it may look like it is against the patient's rights, but at the same time, it is what is better for the patient, it works out better for the patient. So even if they resist initially, when they are very sick, they get those medications and then maybe a month later when they are a bit better they are happy that they have taken the medications."

One morning, the second-year resident, Virinder, said Kavita had had an episode the previous night. "She pushed her husband and attacked him." He fell to the ground and required stitches. A decision was made to put Kavita on "typicals," older and stronger medications that were often first-line antipsychotics.

The next day, Kavita was subdued. She did not respond to Akhil's questions. Turning to her husband, he said, "You should give her a slap if she does that again." He flashed me a look that suggested he regretted his words. He softened his tone. "Or you can tell her we will tie her to the bed."

On rounds the next week, Kavita looked much improved. She was sitting up, and, I wrote, appearing "not nearly so accusatory or suspicious." I realized later how evaluative my notes were, how much they depended on my interpretation of her emotions and how little on the gestures, moves, and enunciations in which I read them.

Akhil told her she looked better. "This is a very good thing, because there is going to be a wedding in your family soon and you people will be going." He reminded her to keep taking her medicine and explained to me that as well as being on antipsychotics, Kavita was "on behavior treatment," which meant doctors encouraged her to perform her own "self-care," to wash her clothes and prepare her food. "The problem is because of her own behavior and her own personality."

I was confused about Kavita's diagnosis, writing in my notes, "Kavita is dissociative disorder according to Akhil, and Dr. C.'s approach to her delusions is to try to keep her close, verbally, to reality, without directly challenging them, but to encourage her to at least be consistent and 'not keep springing out with new stories.' But she is also on antipsychotics and Virinder tells me her diagnosis is paranoid schizophrenia." At this point, Kavita was on an arsenal of medications: trifluoperazine, a typical antipsychotic; trazodone for sleep; lorazepam for anxiety; the antispasmodic trihexyphen; and several vitamin supplements.

One afternoon, as I walked through the ward, I saw Kavita and her husband on the bed. She was drinking tea and leaning back in his arms, a casual, public embrace all but impossible in the household.

The outpatient clinic is flooded with people. When I arrive in the morning, the waiting area is full. Residents are certain it gets busier as the temperature rises. Patients and their families sit on hard-slatted benches or on the floor, or they lean against the wall when there is nowhere to sit. People press to the edge of shadows as sunlight empties the courtyard. This is a dry space; there is no running water in the outpatient department. Dr. A. has been arguing with the hospital administration for months to get it repaired.

Patients are triaged by a senior resident, who directs them to a hive of residents in cells along the edge of the veranda. The furniture in residents' offices is often broken—chairs are missing slats, wood hangs from windows. Each room has a sink, but they are impotent, and many are broken and filled with used plastic cups, paper, and syringes.

At first, I alternate days with Akhil and Virinder. Later I sit with a second-year resident, Kareem, in part because he seems to especially understand what I am up to. He explains his questioning and occasionally asks, curious to see if I am learning, what my diagnosis would be. A day is a nine-hour stretch, a hungry span peppered with shots of chai delivered by a former patient who has a business selling snacks to doctors. Though the feel is factorylike, and also exhilarating, there is evident, even remarkable, patience and care in residents' voices. They listen with intensity and focus, and seldom seem distracted. I begin to sense that Akhil's recommended slaps and paternal tone are unusual. Mostly I listen and write absurdly fast.

One day with Akhil brings the following patients:

The first is a young girl, fourteen, here with her father. Her eyelids droop, she looks drugged, or tired. She answers for herself, telling Akhil her "chief complaint" is pain in her chest, but there is also "heaviness." Her father has taken her to one of the new hospitals outside the city, which may explain the look of antipsychotics in her gaze. Akhil explains to me that many women with depression complain of somatic symptoms like pain and heaviness first, depression only secondarily. "We also see a lot of somatoform and dissociative disorders, things like hysteria," which can have similar presentations.

Later, after several other patients, a woman comes in with her husband. A "negative *bhasa ati hai*," a negative language, comes to her. Her family will not "let her go out." "In eight years," she says, "I have not gone out," which Akhil understands to mean she has not been permitted to go to her *maike* (natal home). Akhil asks, "*Kuch apke upar ate hai?*" Does something (a spirit, perhaps) come to her (literally, from above)?

"My family comes to me. They don't speak to me, but they inhabit me."

Her husband says she has "had problems" for some time. Recently, when she returned from a family picnic at her *maike*, the "negative language" started. She began saying that her family had "come to her."

"But they don't bother me with things, they tell me about their own work but they don't give me trouble."

She gets angry at times, her husband says, and tells people abusive things, like to "drink phenyle" (a cleaning solution), but only since returning from her *maike*. Akhil writes, "trance disorder?" in her file.

Another woman, also middle-aged and with her husband, has been referred here. For fifteen years she has had pain in her chest, but doctor visits have proven inconclusive. She feels a lot of *gabrahat* (anxiety) and "gets dizzy and falls unconscious."

"Has anyone ever told you with confidence that this is a problem?"

No, they say. No one can "give an answer."

Akhil says to me that this is clearly somatoform disorder. "When a patient goes to another doctor all the time, with lots of problems that have no real reason, and wastes that doctor's time, often the doctor will refer them to psychiatry."

He says to the patient, "There is no definite cause for me to explain."

"But what about the anxiety?" she asks. "And the pain in my hands and feet?"

From now on, Akhil says, he does not want her to go to a doctor with complaints, to seek any more checkups (*janch*). "You have to stop this." He says to me that she will be put on antidepressants for somatoform disorder.

Two young women come in succession complaining of headaches. The first has had pain for two years, "water falls from her" (probably leukorrhea), she is weak (*sust*) and has no appetite. Akhil asks if she feels depressed. She nods. The next patient has had headaches for four months. She also has no appetite (*bukh*, literally hunger) and, after some questioning says she experiences depression. She is often sick, very weak, and cries, and she is terrified of going out and hates being with people. A man I take to be her brother says she often cries out, "I will die, I cannot be saved." I note that she "looks like she is on antipsychotics." Akhil tells me this is likely a phobia, and possibly depression with somatic complaints.

"We have to see if the pain is real or if it is depression."

A young woman comes in with her father. She reports her own symptoms—pain, unconsciousness. Sometimes, after taking medication, she cannot see. Her prescription sheets show that she has seen Dr. C. in private practice and that she is on diazepam, or Valium. "The medicine is for depression," she tells us.

"Her unconsciousness is a dissociative fit," Akhil tells me, "And so is the way she talks a lot about her symptoms, including pain, but does not seem concerned about them."

"With hysteria patients you often see that they seem happy and not concerned about their symptoms, even as they are reporting them. It is clear from how she looks, and especially from her dress that she is hysterical. The difference may be too subtle for you to pick up on." He compares Indian hysteria cases to those in the United States, where, he says, disorder is more evident in the ways patients "dress provocatively." Here it is more difficult to discern, but one can still see it, he says. "You look for bright colors, nicer dress, dress that is different from the family's economic status." This patient's outfit does not match the appearance of her father, who looks as though he is "poor and plain." "But she is dressed very nicely, in bold colors, and provocatively." (I write that it is hard for me to see what is provocative about this, to me, normal looking *selwar kameez*, though she is indeed wearing eye makeup and her suit and jewelry look nice.)

Akhil takes the group to Dr. C. Though new patients get at least twenty minutes of residents' time, with Dr. C., who sees all the patients triaged among residents, sessions are minutes long and conducted with with assembly-line efficiency. Residents sit at his side as patients and attendants are brought in. While one group interacts with Dr. C. the next is placed in the back. When the first have finished, they are rotated to the front and the next in line are brought in.

Dr. C., "the lion" according to residents, is charismatic and commanding. A tall, handsome man in his late fifties, he speaks with a booming voice and is known among residents for his firm tone, for the way he yells at patients to sit properly and not speak out of turn, and for the rhetorical questions he asks with a disciplinarian's edge. In his presence, residents are nervous and reticent. After exercising confidence with patients, with Dr. C. they are cut down to size, chastised for being unobservant or for incorrect diagnoses.

We take our place along the wall. Akhil presents the first patient and reports his diagnosis—somatoform disorder. Dr. C. turns to the patient. He tells the woman she should continue with her medication for high blood pressure but that she is too preoccupied with the pain in her body, saying to the husband, "There is basically no sickness inside her" (*Uski andar* basic *koi bimari nahin*). He tells her that her lorazepam is "not a good drug."

"If you had a real illness, it would have come out in the tests and checkups, and second, if you had a real illness, would you be seeing me today? Would I be treating you? But don't think you don't have an illness. Someone has a headache and it is from a tumor, another person has a headache and it is from tension. You have an illness, but it is not a physical illness. It is from mental tension, but it doesn't mean there is no illness. But don't give her pain medication," he says to her husband. To Akhil, "We need to treat the cause, so we will treat the cause."

He writes a prescription for a different antianxiety medication and sends them out.

A young woman comes in. After explaining her pains and fear of social interactions, Akhil says he has diagnosed her with a phobia. Dr. C. asks about her fear. She says she doesn't fear going out in general, especially if with friends, but she doesn't like crowds. When she feels pain, she says, her father gives her an injection.

Dr. C. gives Akhil a look of cutting disdain. "Why do you say phobia? There is no phobia. No one likes to go in a crowd. Didn't you explore dissociative disorder? If there is no increase in pulse or BP [blood pressure] with paining, it could be dissociative, because with real pain you will usually see an increase in pulse or BP. Your phobia diagnosis came from asking leading questions. If you ask leading questions from a hysterical patient they will all pick up those symptoms. She says that the pain lasts for four, five minutes, why are you saying an hour? No one could endure panic or pain like that for an entire hour."

Akhil turns to her. "Didn't you tell me before that you had pain for one hour?"

Dr. C. erupts. "You don't ask the patient, 'Did you tell me this before?' You ask what is happening with them now. This is a leading question. It puts the patient in a jacket and makes them answer in a certain way. So, why does the father give an injection?" He looks at the girl for a moment. "You should have control, madam." He writes a prescription.

The next patient is brought in. Akhil reports that she has had headaches for two months and experiences mild depression. The patient says quietly, "There is dizziness in my mind."

"Do you feel *udas* [depression]?"

"As long as I feel pain, I feel *udas*."

"Is the problem headache or *udas*?"

"The problem is entirely headache."

Dr. C. asks about the timing of the headaches and if she sleeps at night. He asks if there are problems at home. She answers that everything is fine.

"Do you feel like doing housework?"

"I work very hard," she says.

He asks what work her family does, whether they live in a joint family or "alone."

"We are farmers and we live separately."

"Does your husband take alcohol?"

"No."

He tells Akhil the diagnosis is depression and writes a prescription.

Another woman is brought forward, accompanied by her husband and father-in-law. Akhil explains that she falls unconscious "because of tension," and that there have been tests for pain but "nothing has come out of them."

Dr. C. yells at the older man for sitting with his feet on the chair. The man adjusts. He says they had taken his daughter-in-law to a doctor in another city. The doctor prescribed medicine and said she should have an operation on her throat.

"Are you a doctor?" The man looks blank. "Should the hospital admit her?" Dr. C. goes on, sarcastically. "Look at how you treat her. You should send her to her *maike* to get better, for a year, a year and a half." The woman's husband starts to argue, but Dr. C. cuts him off, "Should we admit her?" He shakes his head, writes a prescription, and waves them out of the room. After they leave, he turns to me and says that this is "a case of dissociative disorder, hysteria, and the father-in-law is supporting her in these symptoms. Some doctor in [their city] wants her to have an operation, and he wants her to do it!"

We are nearing the hour when Dr. C. leaves his post. Things speed up and Dr. C. reminds us we are nearly out of time. "We have to work fast." He tells residents to be shorter in their reporting. There is no time for extensive questioning.

Another woman comes in. Akhil reports that she falls unconscious. Dr. C. asks if she has pain. Yes, she has headaches. He tells Akhil she is "dissociative, hysteria," writes a prescription and sends her off.

Another day in the outpatient clinic, this time with Kareem. A girl, about eighteen, comes in with her father. I write that she is "obviously already very agitated and intense looking." Kareem asks what the problem is.

"Fear," she says, "A lot of fear."

Her father says she sometimes cries, and that she has anxiety and unease (*becheni* and *gabrahat*). She cuts in, "I always feel frightened."

"She doesn't eat. Before she used to be very good in her studies, but for eight years she has had this problem."

"Have you taken her to another doctor?" Kareem asks.

"No."

"[School] exams can cause a lot of tension, and there is a lot of this kind of illness these days." Kareem says to me under his breath that he thinks the father suspects she is faking her illness to get attention.

"Is there any unconsciousness?"

"No."

Kareem is called out of the room. The girl turns to me and says in a mix of English and Hindi what sounds like, "This death is eating me. It is eating me from inside." I ask her to tell this to Kareem, and when he returns, I say she said something I could not understand. He asks what she said and then repeats it back to her, also uncertain of what she is saying. "Some deficiency?"

"This 'def' is eating me." She goes on, now in English, "Anyone doesn't believe me, doesn't believe whatever I say."

Kareem says quietly to me that this is probably a case of dissociative disorder. "It looks like she is trying to manipulate her father."

She hears this. "No one believes me."

"Does her voice ever become like a child?" Kareem asks her father.

"Sometimes."

Kareem turns to her. "You have to fix this problem, this illness. Because if you don't, you will have so many problems in life. You will have problems with marriage [with finding a marriage partner], not just with exams."

He says to her father, "If you don't listen to what she says does she get angry?"

"Yes, she is always angry. When she doesn't get what she wants she yells, she cries."

"You are going to get an insanity certificate [*pagal ka certificate*]. Is that what you want? Then you will have problems your entire life."

Through all of this, the young woman has been leaning on the table with her head on her hands. Hearing this, she slouches into her chair. Kareem says, "Sit properly, sit up straight." (I write, "But not in a mean voice or as sternly as Dr. C. would.")

"Sorry, sorry." She sits up.

"Don't you want to get better?"

"Yes."

"How do you get better? You sit properly, you eat properly, you respect your elders, you work hard."

"Yes, I want to get better."

Kareem turns to me and says quietly, "She is overexpressive."

When I write this down, she gets angry. "You two, sitting there, I know you are saying this is not real, but no one is believing me."

Kareem asks what she wants to be in life.

"I want to be a DM." A district magistrate.

"If you get a *pagal* certificate how will you be DM?"

"Bhagwan," she says. God.

"Yes, but God helps those who . . ."

"Help themselves, yes, yes, I know, I know, God helps those who help themselves." She goes on, "There is a person in my neighborhood coming after me. It is a eunuch."

"Has anyone else in your family had an illness like this?"

"No," her father says.

"In your neighborhood?"

"Yes, there is someone in the neighborhood. An older girl."

Kareem turns to me and says firmly, "This is all manipulative behavior. There is someone in her locality with a mental illness and she must have picked up the symptoms from that person, she has learned how to have the symptoms. It is dissociative disorder, not schizophrenia, because it is all conscious [*jan-bujhkar*]."

"I know what you people are saying," she interrupts. "This eunuch is real. This means I won't get a mad certificate."

"Yes," Kareem says, "this is the thing."

She starts to laugh.

"Then maybe you will get ECT, an electric shock."

"This is because I know everything."

"She is doing all of this knowingly," Kareem tells me, "all of this to manipulate people. Because her family is all following after her then." He turns to the father. "There is no illness. You have some woman in your locality who has this illness and your daughter has learned from her. She has learned all the symptoms to manipulate. There is no cure [*ilaz*], *this* is the cure." The cure happens in telling her that her illness is not real. "You need to stop this behavior. There is no illness, and you just need to stop behaving in this way."

Kareem finishes her case sheet and closes it, nodding toward the waiting area. As they leave, she repeats, "Sorry, sorry, sorry."

Hysteria is outmoded. Hysteria is an invention. Hysteria is a tool of patriarchal oppression, a means of moral discipline. Hysteria is a form of resistance, a voice for the oppressed. Hysteria is a trauma response, a bodily expression of the unspeakable. These are common understandings of the thing we call hysteria.

Also common, as I have mentioned, is the idea that hysteria has disappeared. Accounts of hysteria's obsolescence vary, though most settle on the idea that medical modernity has made hysteria irrelevant. In one story, as psychiatry's mid-twentieth-century shift to neurochemical explanations and pharmaceutical cures fissured understandings of distress between "brains" and "minds" (Luhrmann 2000), hysteria disappeared from diagnostic manuals. In another, hysteria disappeared once it was disarticulated from wombs and masculinized as shell shock, transforming into posttraumatic stress disorder (PTSD) (Fassin and Rechtman 2009, Young 1995) and dissociative identity disorder (Hacking 1995). Another history sees hysteria as transforming, in diagnostic currency, into conversion disorders and trauma or stress responses, becoming, like PTSD, increasingly provable in biological terms, something found in neurons related to fear and empathy. Another scientific story traces hysteria through conversion disorder and out of existence, by way of its transformation into histrionic personality disorder, recently removed from the Diagnostic and Statistical Manual of Mental Disorders, the gold standard source for psychiatric diagnosing.

Historians have also contributed to the disappearance of hysteria. That is, they have effected that disappearance themselves, but in epistemological terms, by reducing it from a universal category of knowledge to a historical and cultural construction (Mitchell 2000), a thing of times and places, context bound. In this domain, hysteria becomes an idea, a historical construction and tool of critical thought, something to think with in finding critical undertows in master narratives. But seen amid wide-reaching cultural memes and social structures (like marriage, or patriarchy), hysteria can also be seen as an effect of what Gayle Rubin described as a sex/gender system (1975), an all but universal symptom of a broad system of power (returning us to biological notions of trauma response).

The more I accompanied residents on rounds and in the outpatient department, the less sense hysteria's obsolescence made. I came to see hysteria as they did—a universal but distinctly Indian diagnosis, one that called into question differences between the universal and particular basic to scientific knowledge. In a clinic that saw hundreds of patients a day, residents joked that conditions of scarcity made their training the best in the world. Indian psychiatrists were good at diagnosing, they said, because of the sheer numbers of patients they saw. They were especially adept at diagnosing dissociative disorders, common in India but not in the West, and one resident told of a friend working in the United States who described the way American doctors could not recognize dissociative cases that he could diagnose immediately. Hysteria was neither a Western category imposed on Indian phenomena nor a historically specific diagnosis, an anachronism hanging around the postcolonial world, but a configuration of global and local processes involving common human biology and culturally specific social orders.

There is a danger, of course, in conflating hysteria with dissociative, somatoform, and conversion disorders. They are not the same "thing," to the extent that any diagnostic category is a thing and not an idea. While doctors' use of the term "hysteria" may not justify linking what happens in

Nehru to the history of tangled ideas about hysteria, its categorical slipperiness overlaps with the medical idea that, in hysterical or dissociative states, patients' experiences and expressions are mutable, their expressions of fact shifty. Whether or not dissociative disorder (or conversion disorder, or somatoform disorder, or PTSD, or histrionic personality disorder) is or is not hysteria misses the point that specters of hysteria, in a flock of historical formations, abide in contemporary psychiatry in ways that are social, performative, cultural, and epistemological. My sense is that these contemporary appearances of this old category matter very much.

Hysteria's signs over time have been multiple: fatigue, pain, paralysis, muteness, contortions, unconsciousness, fits, and emotional afflictions from melancholy to agitation. Its origins are typically located in Hippocratic theories of the uterine source of female fragility and emotional excess (though there is also evidence of hysteria-like afflictions described in Ayurvedic texts). In nineteenth-century European medicine, though no longer attributed to wandering wombs, hysteria remained associated with female biology. New ideas about neurology and trauma grew from the study of female patients in Charcot's Parisian Salpêtrière; a short time later, women treated by Freud (a student of Charcot), made hysteria formative for psychoanalysis. Without hysteria there would be no "talking cure" and, arguably, no unconscious.

Hysteria has long been a matter of fungible reality, a disease that calls into question the nature of truth telling. It is of great importance that this happened on the ground of female biology at least until the early twentieth century. In hysteria, the body may speak truths that voices cannot; or it bears a particular kind of truth, one that is experiential and at the same time fabricated and hollow. Hysteria's relationship to trauma, on the one hand, and kinship and desire, on the other, have long called into question the nature of truth, particular as voiced by women, as in, famously, Freud's switch from a trauma etiology (the seduction theory) to the Oedipus complex to account for his female patients' symptoms and stories of sexual abuse. As post-Freudian psychiatry pursued trauma neuroses in "male hysterics," neurological models separated the facts of trauma from the brain's reaction to it, extending into biology (and away from women) the instabilities of truth telling created in Freudian models of hysteria, and beginning a process both political and medical that would continue throughout the twentieth century to revise the relationship of memory to trauma (Leys 2000; Hacking 1995).

The idea that hysteria is distinctly Indian is nothing new, and neither is hysteria's appearance in India. Since psychiatry's nineteenth-century arrival in India, many doctors, Indian and non-Indian, described hysteria as particularly Indian or as having distinctly Indian forms. Distresses akin to hysteria in what would come to be called indigenous medicine (including *ikhtinaw ar-rahm*, or "suffocation of the womb," in Islamic medicine; Attewell 2007) encountered British colonial efforts to institute "scientific medicine" as a moral mandate (Ernst 1991). Indian physicians (*daktars*), practicing in spite of policies asserting the superiority of British medicine, treated Indian cases of hysteria, portraying it in advertisements alongside semen loss (*dhat*) as a threat to family well-being (Mukharji 2009: 240); European patients showing similar afflictions were sent home (Ernst 2001).

In the nineteenth century, hysteria in India, and states of being associated with it, was both a testing ground for the scientific status of new practices and a means of moral referenda on Indian society. References to India appeared in European and North American medical journals; the development of hypnosis, key in hysteria's European history, was informed by missionary reports of Indian religious adepts; and mesmerist journals cited Indian examples of treatments for hysteria and the induction of hysterical states as a form of cure (Winter 1998). In an early version of clinical experimentation, an East India Company surgeon tested hypnosis—"induced hysteria"—as pain treatment and anesthetic (including on surgery patients) in his Bengal hospital, touting his successes to British audiences (Esdaile 1846: 1). Decades later, European and North American practitioners of mediumship found soteriological potential in dissociated states "discovered" in India, while religious movements in India, including Pentecostalism, theosophy, and spiritualism, used hysteria and trance as well as more overtly religious practices to debate theology, divinity, and suffering (Blavatsky 1888; Monroe 2008; Curtis 2007, 2011). Scenes at Pandita Ramabai's mission of young women in hysteria-like dissociative states inspired American missionary Minnie Abrams to develop the practice of glossolalia (speaking in tongues), a divine communion that came to characterize Pentecostalism (Abrams 1906). Meanwhile, Abrams's defenders used psychological models to distinguish medical disorder (hysteria) from religious experience and demonic influence, invoking Indian examples in cautioning practitioners to guard against unconscious influence (Curtis 2011).

As Christians used hysteria in India to evaluate doctrine, Indian religious leaders took up hysteria less as a site of analysis than as a distinctly modern health problem, one whose treatment lent legitimacy to newly institutionalized indigenous medical systems. In the early twentieth century, a period of both invigorated nationalism and religious reform, distinguishing hysteria from spirit possession while asserting the rationality of Indian practices was just as important to these efforts as it was for Christian missionaries. For reformers of Unani medicine, hysteria was a problem of modernity, one to which urban, literate women were especially vulnerable given their "uncontrollable carnal desires" (Attewell 2007: 46). With national and religious identity at stake in concepts of modern womanhood, these reformers made moral hygiene integral to medical attention to women, combining visions of religious and scientific modernity (Attewell 2007: 46).

Indian psychoanalysis found other ways to make of hysteria a contest of legitimacy. In the early twentieth century, for British psychiatrists—even those working to establish the profession in India—psychoanalysis offered a language for finding in Indians attributes "notorious . . . of all Oriental character": weakness, tyranny, and "quarrelsome" behavior (Berkeley-Hill 1921: 336, in Akhtar and Tummala-Nara 2008: 12). British theories about hysteria, menstruation, hypochondria, and mother-child dynamics suggested the vulnerability of Hindu psyches, using psychoanalytic models to assert British superiority (Dangar-Daly 1930; Berkeley-Hill 1921). Meanwhile, Indian psychiatrists were busy altering those tools to probe both Indian cultural realities and the "secret selves" of the colonized (Nandy 1995), recuperating, though not explicitly, a selfhood compromised by colonial rule. Psychoanalyst Girindrasekhar Bose, finding in his male patients less evidence of castration anxiety than gender-switching fantasies, revised Freud's Oedipus complex, drawing on Hindu mythology and religious texts to develop an Indian model of the ego (Hartnack 1999; Nandy 1995).

After Independence, hysteria in India became a matter of ethnological interest, a way of negotiating difference in medical, psychological, and cultural terms. Midcentury discussions of trauma compared reactions of British and Indian soldiers, observing hysteria's predominance in the subcontinent (Abse 1950). Anthropologists and psychologists charted the cultural parameters of selfhood in analyses of hysterical experiences (Freed and Freed 1964, 1985; Carstairs and Kapur 1976; Obeyesekere 1981; Kakar 1981), while scholars asked what it was about the Indian family that engendered hysterical neuroses (Kakar 1981). Together, medicine and anthropology came to view hysteria as prominent in India with specific manifestations embedded in the cultures of family life, especially mother-child relations, even as elsewhere explanations were shifting away from families and toward traumatic neurosis. Rather than connecting hysteria to historically specific trauma responses, psychologically informed ethnographic literature (and ethnographically informed psychology) was more interested in relatively ahistorical vision of Indian cultural formations, including the way they shaped historical events (and acts of violence) (cf. Kakar 1996). While anthropologists began tracking relationships between spirit affliction and patriarchal kinship (Freed and Freed 1964), for the most part, hysteria (invoked as a global category) remained associated with kinship (as cause) and religious practice (as expression). Artists and writers reflecting on Indian gender norms found female resistance at the intersection of hysteria and religious life (cf. Clément and Kristeva 2003). It was not until the writings of psychoanalytically informed postcolonial theorists brought these elements together in a web of mutual influence that the "gentle violences" of political systems; the outright violence of acts like rape, mutilation, and pogrom; and the social insecurity they all generated might be considered part of a science of Indian psyches that addressed cultural means of grappling with trauma (Nandy 1983; Das 2006).

Thus, while notions of hysteria in the West were moving simultaneously toward trauma and historical configurations of power, in India (and in relation to it), hysteria remained a universal ailment that, at the same time, was inseparable from the idea of Indian culture, translatable into Indian forms of life, and involved either subordination or resistance. Hysteria's relationship to religion and kinship in anthropological, psychological, and feminist literature on India muted somewhat its potential to reference either trauma or political conditions—gendered, colonial, postcolonial, or otherwise—even as clinically hysteria remained, indeed flourished as, a crisis in female truth telling. Hysteria came to relate to cultural conditions and, in medical terms, gave increasing attention to constraint (as in the way doctors noted that "life in India is very difficult for women, which is why we see so much of this"). Yet, it did so at the same time that etiologies of dissociative disorder retained hysteria's sense of the female body's undisciplined desire and inability to tell the truth. Rather than separating the social from the biological, Indian psychiatry's attention to hysteria rendered the two inseparable. It did so in ways that had clear consequences for the figuring of truth, desire, and control in its care of women. In other words, bringing patients to an understanding of the falseness of their pains by

recalibrated control, or bringing families to an awareness of the manipulative nature of their patient, or bringing desires under the control of the
family—amid doctors' awareness of the struggles, violence, and inequalities
women face—may have represented less an overt aim to reassert gender
norms as morally right than an effect of a long history of medical and
scholarly understanding. In that history, culture, trauma, truth, and illness
were organized in specific and self-consciously "Indian" terms.

Thus, while an obvious approach to Kavita's symptoms might ask how
they are culturally appropriate expressions of social distress and crises in
agency (this is a reasonable thing to suggest), another might ask how clinical conditions, and their long history, configure women as agents, bodies,
and figures of culture, and as sites for vagaries of agency, through their
management of such symptoms, how, that is, they participate in the cultural construction of the thing that is dissociative disorder in India, neither
creating it ex nihilo nor managing something entirely given. In this is room
for the reordering of desires and relations gone awry (in some cases in ways
that encourage women to take more control in their relationships, in others
to exert less control) and genuine concern for women's mistreatment in
families. Discipline is not separate from doctors' understanding of the ways
women respond to constraints in their lives. That understanding is bound
to the idea that through mimesis and deception women experiencing those
constraints, consciously or not, complicate trajectories of truth.

Divisions between minds and brains or social and biological explanations are often seen as defining Western psychiatry. These divisions are
reordered in Indian psychiatry. So are divisions between the universal (biological or psychoanalytic) and particular (social or cultural). Kavita and her
sisters in diagnosis enacted this reconfiguring and shouldered its consequences. They did so in ways that show medical attention to hysteria to
articulate a clinical destabilizing of truth with "cultural facts" about wom-
en's lives. Hysteria remains like the patient herself—shifty, mimetic, performative, susceptible, spongelike, and instrumental.

Yet, as residents knew, one can learn to see it as something objectively
real. To the question of whether dissociative disorder is (or is like, or is
enough like) hysteria, we can summon Freud, who, in his account of Dora,
wrote, "J'appelle un chat un chat" (ironically, to describe his conviction
that female sex organs should be called by their proper names) (1997: 41).
In other words, like Freud's pussycat, we know something when we see it.

Around the same time that I was working in Moksha, a film called *Bhool Bhulaiyaa* (The Labyrinth) came out. It was advertised as a light comedy with some scary moments, and so Mrs. M., her daughter, a friend in town conducting research, Eve, and I went to see it in a new shopping mall cineplex. The film was scarier than I expected, but also beautifully shot, full of singing and dancing, and a pleasure to look at. Eve took it all in, including the raucous whoops of young men in the audience during the modest love song, and sang along with the songs, which she already knew by heart. As the tone of the film darkened, I watched closely as her eyes widened, asking repeatedly if she wanted to leave. She said no (she was not the youngest child in the audience) until the climactic sequence, a melodramatic exorcism, when she looked up at me in confusion, hid her head in my shoulder, then resurfaced to say, "What was that about?" Agog with the rampaging spectacle of so many themes close to my interests, and equally wide-eyed, I said I wasn't sure myself.

A Hindi remake of a Malayalam film (see Halliburton 2005), *Bhool Bhulaiyaa* involves a palace haunted by the ghost of a dancing girl who killed herself after the king, besotted with her, murdered her lover. Into the palace come newlyweds Siddharth, the palace's heir, and Avni, fresh from America and flush with the stuff of progress—video cameras, a dam-building project, a love marriage, and declarations of rationality. Though discouraged by the caretaker (Siddharth's uncle), Siddharth and Avni move in, skeptical of things like curses and ghosts.

Curious about the house's past, Avni enters the courtesan's forbidden quarters. Soon, creepy things happen—mirrors shatter, footsteps sound, the shadow of a woman with disheveled hair is seen. A trio of bumbling priests is brought in to seal the cursed rooms, but the ghost disturbs them. They run away terrified.

Siddharth suspects these are the actions of his uncle's daughter, whom he suspects has gone mad. He calls in his friend Aditya, a psychiatrist from the United States. Initially, Aditya is as inept as the exorcists—he is poorly suited to Indian life and stumbles into one minor catastrophe after another. But as events escalate, he proves his abilities. Even ritual practitioners, initially mocked, appear rational: we meet an exorcist just returned from having delivered a lecture in England ("Exorcism the Indian Way").

After investigations, Aditya tells Siddharth, "The ghost is none other than your Avni," whom he has diagnosed with "dissociative identity disorder." Every night, he says (but not to Avni, from whom they conceal knowledge of her illness), she takes the identity of the dancer Manjulika. This is a response to childhood trauma—separation from her beloved grandmother (and India) when her parents took her to live in the United States. Without immediate action, Manjulika's personality will consume Avni, he says, but Western medicine can't cure her. Only an exorcism will convince the dancing girl (or Avni's delusion) to leave Avni's body. Western biomedicine may have the capacity for explanation, for knowledge of "what is wrong," but only Indian practices—exorcism—can be effective. This pragmatic portrayal of Indian medicine resolves the postcolonial dilemma of global medicine—how can one be modern and Indian when modern is defined as what India is not?

It does so, however, by reasserting a profoundly conservative structure of gender, one in which female sexuality bears, painfully, the capacity for disordered kinship.

A final dance sequence precedes Avni's exorcism. It is a dazzling display of male discovery of female disorder. Following the sound of ankle bells, Siddharth, Aditya, and Sharad (the poet that Avni/Manjulika believes to be her lover) find Avni's clothes strewn on the threshold of Manjulika's chamber. From its inner room, they gaze into what was once the king's reception hall, where Avni is dancing wildly. Shots of her dance alternate with those of the three men watching—through windows, from behind screens, and over banisters—gloriously portraying thresholds between viewer and viewed, subject and object, knower and known, male and female, rationality and madness.

Siddharth sends Sharad to Avni. As the two transform for the film's viewers into Manjulika and her lover, the hall illuminates and fills with men in old-fashioned finery. Images alternate between Avni in disheveled clothes and smeared eye make-up, dancing in shadows in awkward moves, and her counterpart in delusion, the beautifully attired Manjulika, dancing perfected moves with her lover for a brightly lit audience.

The king (embodied by Siddharth) enters and marches toward the throne. When Sharad spins toward him, the king takes out his sword and beheads him. The scene abruptly reverts to the empty hall and to Avni, face smeared with vermilion, the red sign of Hindu wifehood streaking her face like blood.

Sharad beckons Avni outside, where she is grabbed by four men in clinical (or priestly—it is not clear) white, who drag her to the exorcist.

"Who are you?" he asks, throwing explosive powder into the fire. He commands her to sit, hitting her with a stick. He will help her kill the king, he says, but only if "you, Manjulika, leave Avni's body." Avni violently beheads the king (a dummy that looks like Siddharth), then falls unconscious as his family looks on (this is her *sasural*, affinal home, after all).

In the next scene, Aditya wakes Avni from her trance. He holds his hand above her face as she reclines and reminds her who she is, merging her name with that of her husband: "You are Avni Siddharth Chaturvedi." The dancing girl is purged from the family scene; the wife is healed.

To understand Avni's past, Aditya takes a trip to Avni's hometown. But why not ask her? This hysteric, like all hysterics, "ushers the articulation of knowledge" (Wajeman 1988, 3). At every turn, she is under consideration of male characters, performing with opulent clarity Laura Mulvey's (1975) dictum that the framing of the cinematic gaze is inherently objectifying in starkly gendered terms. As in Charcot's nineteenth-century medical theater, knowledge of a woman's madness offers spectacle as scientific knowing. At the same time, that disorder is the product of a kinship arrangement, a crisis of relatedness with a familiar narrative. Of course it is the new bride who is mad. Of course the good wife is inhabited by a courtesan (and the heroine by the "item number," the dancing girl of Bollywood film who, disarticulated from plot, offers the audience sexual spectacle while allowing the heroine to retain her moral virtue; Kasbekar 2001). As Avni's disorder becomes objectively valid through spectacle, multiple viewers (Siddharth, Aditya, Siddharth's family, and the audience) consolidate patrilineal, medical, and voyeuristic gazes. Science, kinship, and the pleasure of seeing converge in a single look.

Though not lacking in female characters to share the sleuthing, *Bhool Bhulaiyaa*'s male characters solve its riddles while women are objects of gazes, capable of disorder but not objective understanding. Suspect (not detective), patient (not doctor), the female character who tries to know is driven mad. Just as the film echoes the gendering practices of the nineteenth-century sciences of hysteria, in which scientific knowing depended on the (often dancelike) spectacle of female disorder, so it is enchained to expressions across genres that reference the outsider status of the daughter-in-law and the disruptive nature of women's presence in kinship. When Avni becomes Manjulika, a moral order is exposed, one evoked every time ankle bells are heard, when *payal* (a married woman's anklets) are indistinguishable from *ghunghroo* (the courtesan's dancing bells). Manjulika's appearance exposes multiple family secrets: not only the way women disrupt the family scene in their status as outsiders, but the way kinship depends on control of female sexuality, the exchange of women, and double standards of desire.

In *Bhool Bhulaiyaa*, crises of modernity do not come overtly gendered: little is made of Avni and Siddharth's love marriage; Avni does not choose a job over childbearing or do anything suggesting a conflict of modern womanhood with traditional values. The conflict of a woman's madness embodies overlapping formulas for knowing, treating, and desiring.

But the audience is not always complicit. At times it shares Avni's view. Early on, Avni holds a video camera, allowing the audience to witness scenes through its (and her) lens. Her camera is destroyed the first time the ghost appears, smashed by Avni herself, who nullifies her own gaze when she becomes disordered. Likewise, in the dance sequence the audience participates in Avni's fantasy, a reality not accessible to either husband or doctor.

In the same way that Indian histories of hysteria reorder the relationship of universal to particular at the heart of science, *Bhool Bhulaiyaa* reconciles postcolonial paradoxes at the heart of Indian medicine. It does so with a psychiatrist who calls on an exorcist (who is an international lecturer), and a pragmatic vision of healing that trumps the universality of medical knowledge. But it does this on the ground of a vision of gender that reiterates splits in female subjectivity created by structures of kinship and reasserts both the movability of women and their potential to disrupt those structures. It summons global grammars of disorder to produce a vision of Indianness and to resolve concerns about the limits of knowledge of and in female madness.

A young woman came alone to the outpatient clinic (an exceedingly rare occurrence). She had not slept for three days and had begun hearing voices. Having failed ninth grade once and tenth twice, she had come from her hometown some distance away to finish her education in the city. Lacking the fees to reserve a place at college and the money for a place to stay, she was staying at a *gurudwara*, a Sikh temple.

Virinder described her as *tez*, a term that means sharp, but can imply intelligent or manic. I understood him to mean the latter. She frequently heard the voice of a girl who wanted to "see the world," and felt that everyone was laughing at her. Though these positive symptoms suggested mania, Virinder suspected dissociative disorder. "She is very intelligent," he said to me, "And it is easy to answer these [diagnostic] questions yes or no, and she may have figured out which way to answer them." They would give her antianxiety drugs, "but that's it."

Later, Dr. C. asked, "What do you want to do in life?"

"Actually, I hear voices," she responded. "They say 'Come, come, help me.'" She told him she came here for medical training.

"Your problem is with your future plans." Dr. C. turned to Virinder and me. "She wants to pursue studies but has financial difficulties." He recommended a fifteen-day course of a benzodiazepine.

"Your problems are imaginary," he said to her. "These things are part and parcel of life." He told her that the hospital would help her find a place to stay, and mentioned the Lions Club. "They train ladies and may be able to get her some skills training," he explained to Virinder, "so we will give a social intervention."

After my first, ill-fated effort to talk to Kavita, I had pleasant interactions with her when I began going into the ward and sitting quietly among the women. In long periods between residents' visits, she was calm and lucid. There were no outbursts, no arguing, and little discussion of her pain.

She told me her symptoms came after her first *vidai*, her move from *maike* (natal home) to *sasural* (affinal home). Kavita's move was less gradual than many. Her husband had been married before. His first wife died of an illness before she could bear children. As Kavita adjusted to life in her new household, she began receiving visitations from the ghost of the first wife, a woman who had also experienced pain, unconsciousness, and visits from ghosts and goddesses, disturbances she shared with Kavita. When these afflictions flowered after the birth of Kavita's second daughter, Kavita's husband took her to shrines, brought in exorcists, and took her to a general practitioner, who put Kavita on antipsychotics.

Kavita's in-laws blamed her family for concealing her illness during marriage negotiations. Her natal family insisted she had never been sick before. During her first illness, Kavita returned to them, leaving her two daughters in her *sasural* with her in-laws. But her natal family "would not keep her." No one had any interest in taking care of her, she said. Her parents sent her back to her *sasural*, where her symptoms abated. Kavita had two more children—both daughters—and did not "get sick" again until this latest bout. Her parents did not want her to return this time.

Kavita's narrative was familiar, even predictable. In South Asia, just as psychologists have probed "the Indian family" looking for clues to personality, ethnographers have long observed the emotional effects on women of patriliny, virilocality, and village exogamy. This is well-mapped territory: in-marrying women—daughters-in-law—threaten the coherence of the patrilineage in their desires and claims on their husband's affections and time, while their sexuality is threatening to the patrilineage and its moral coherence (Mandelbaum 1988; Raheja and Gold 1994). The lower social standing of wives in the north Indian Hindu context (bride-givers are ranked lower than bride-takers) exacerbates their otherness. These threats are somewhat mitigated by the birth of a child, more so if the child is a son. In this is a strong sense that "madness," meant both medically and morally, comes especially to young brides. The undoings of daughters-in-law may be indicative of their vulnerability as well as of the new forms of love and responsibility they encounter as wives. Even more than in the natal home, in the affinal household, expressions of anger and desire both embody distress and destabilize family harmony.

Less discussed in these accounts are motions between households, and the ways they involve constantly unmade and remade bonds and feelings that can include a sense of being unwanted as well as familiarity and care. Such passages are a repetitive choreography of north Indian kinship, taking on different tones in times of illness and uncertainty or happiness and celebration. In them, women's separation from children is a practical matter—a child who may travel with his or her mother to her natal village for a wedding is likely to stay in the paternal household if she is sick. This is practical, and may be welcome, but it may also involve a sense of loss or be posed as a threat. Such flows are common. Children move in and out of households as they climb on and off laps. But these movements can lend precariousness to relationships with children, echoing the fact that in patrilineal systems women reproduce for kin who are never fully their own. In spite of celebrations of motherhood and the fulfillment of wifely roles, and in contrast with psychologically oriented understandings that note the binary of nurturing and devouring mother or the permanence of the mother-child bond (Kakar 1981), the precariousness of parental bonds in times of illness indicates that motherhood is far from durable. Such vulnerability may erupt through the veneer of roles and ideals, showing the limits of maternal ideology, the extent to which motherhood hinges on things like "control" (over anger and desire), or the way mother-child bonds may be under threat by the very kin structure that holds them together.

In a dissertation on "clenched teeth illness" in Varanasi, Jocelyn Marrow makes the trenchant observation that doctors and patients' families differentiate afflictions (clenched teeth illness, dissociative disorder, and spirit affliction) in spite of overlapping phenomenology and resonance within diagnostic categories that might not otherwise distinguish these bodily signs (2008). Different diagnoses map onto different kinds of social crises, that is, the different ways crisis is felt to impinge on female selves, within the kin unit or involving threats from beyond it. Different afflictions embody different locations for female agency, as women's bodies and psyches bear different interpersonal conflicts, and tensions with different stakes for the coherence of kinship. In "clenched teeth illness" among young, unmarried women, Marrow notes that families attribute afflictions to crises of agency (2013). Obstacles to young women's aspirations, especially as they relate to labor in the public sphere, represent the challenges of new social conditions, manifesting as too much or too little "power" (Marrow 2013). This was also the case in Nehru, where young women's studies and career goals often entered clinical conversations about their dissociative symptoms, and problems tended to involve too much or too little agency (typically in the idiom of "control"). To these observations, I add that clinical scrutinies of unmarried women, especially of their appearance, involved gender imaginaries linking aspiration to female sexuality, even where doctors were sympathetic to obstacles young women faced in their efforts to pursue work, studies, and careers.

Where Elaine Showalter refers to (European) hysteria as "the daughter's disease" (1985), in India it is also very much "the wife's disease." In each, terms and causes are different. For married women in Nehru, though agency was at issue, crises involved relationships and agency within them. For them, hysteria-like afflictions had less to do with aspirations in public and more with the stakes of relationships and the structure of family life. Married women were less scrutinized for their appearance (unless the marriage was in question, as in the case I discuss in the next chapter) and seldom expressed complaints in relation to work, studies, or life goals. Their ailments expressed the conditions of marriage and motherhood. (It is noteworthy, here, that the heroine's emotional turmoil in *Bhool Bhulaiyaa* involved kinship, separation, and the disruptive capacity of female desire and anger.) As Marrow suggests, these different formulations offer the possibility that in India, in spite of common etiologies and symptoms, there may be many hysterias; the dissociations, pains, unconsciousness, and visitations of young women assessed for excessive behavior or understood in terms of life goals may be clinically grouped with, but different from, those of women embedded in affinal kin life.

In her ethnography of a south Indian household, Margaret Trawick (1992) observes that marriage prescriptions may not necessarily decide actual unions, though they give shape to possibilities for emotion, as kinship ideals provide a sense of what is desirable. At the same time, they shape vulnerability, both as part of their patterns and in the way those patterns threaten to dissolve, even where they seem stable. Many wives in north India may feel vulnerable in the ways their placement is contingent or their location one of movement, even if they remain in one place for decades. And movement can involve rich passages as well as things less solid. Strife and illness enhance these uncertainties and are, at the same time, expressions of multiplying vulnerabilities. When a woman becomes ill, or divorces, or is "sent home," her children may not move with her, or her welcome may be mixed, at best. In Nehru, married women's afflictions at once materialized, exacerbated, and invoked kinship's inherent precariousness, embodied in lives of movement between households, as well as its vulnerability to outside pressures (which include the afflicted woman herself). Not unlike the double-bind experienced by Sanjana, expressions of distress that may be brought on by married women's persistent dislocation (in a social status supposed to be eminently locating) may be the behaviors that activate that movement, separation, and instability. Through a life structured by movement, real or actualized, a woman made mad by the precariousness of her relationships may, in her madness, jeopardize those relationships.

One morning I sat with Kavita on her bed. Her husband had returned from a trip to the village, bringing back their four-year-old daughter. The girl leaned against her mother, resting in her lap while Kavita oiled her hair into tight braids. Finishing, Kavita patted her on the back and commanded, "Go play." She picked up a large knife from the shelf and began to peel a pomegranate. The ruby seeds fell loudly into the metal bowl. We ate them together, offering the little gems to her daughter.

I asked if Kavita had any brothers or sisters. Two brothers, she said.

"There was another brother, but he died. It was my fault. I played with him a lot, and one day I think I played with him too much, too hard; maybe I lifted him up too much, or shook him too hard. He got sick that evening and a few days later he died. Was it my fault?" I could not tell if it was a genuine question and said I doubted it was her fault.

"What happened to him before he died?"

"Fever, diarrhea, vomiting."

I said that I doubted that her playing with him had anything to do with it. It sounded like a sickness that came from drinking unclean water, or from another child.

"Really? No, I think it was my fault. All my life I have known this is my fault."

Through my newly practiced diagnostic screen, I felt this to be the thing that held diagnosis together, the "originary trauma" residents looked for in diagnosing dissociative disorder, though they lacked time to look into patients' pasts (which may have had to do with why cultural explanations replaced specificities of patients' lives). Kavita's sense of culpability for the death of a brother, in the kind of rural setting in which I had heard many times that "babies just die like this," connected one loss to another, forming a web of broken effort and vulnerability, containing all it might mean to be a woman or girl in a family, to be connected to others. In previous fieldwork, I witnessed women's exchange of stories of infant death. Some elaborate, some just breaths long, these stories forged bonds across hierarchies even as they established new ways of othering. They fell into two categories—accounts of intense effort and institutional failure, or those in which "nothing happened, sometimes it is just like this." Both described crises in agency; in both sustained grief was social commentary; both brought to light flaws in government promises that good outcomes come with proper action (Pinto 2008). Kavita's sense of blame suggested something other than the common statement that closed so many of those stories: "Everything is in the hands of God." The blame I heard dissipated into critique in the use of this phrase was, for Kavita, turned inward. There was no "sharing the grief" here. Instead, grief may have connected to other kinds of losses.

In all of this work, I did not anticipate that loss of children would be integral to women's afflictions, especially not as the chords of anxiety that resonated in so many cases. I did not expect to see grief and parentage entangled with hysteria or psychosis—depression, perhaps, but not these ailments, with their instabilities of truth and reality. But this should not have surprised me. Where loss of children represents a crisis in agency, too much (in cases of infanticide or withheld medical care) or too little (in accounts of death in spite of effortful action or due to inaction), and destabilizes fetishizations of human will, hysteria does something similar, especially when it appears as a disorder of control, control over the self, control over others, control over one's own symptoms, mind, and body. As a crisis of female desire (especially as it relates to kinship), hysteria also involves the ways women bear the vulnerability of relations in the specter of lost children. The presence of Kavita's daughter in the clinic, jarring to a Western sense of psychiatry wards as inappropriate places for children but utterly normal in India, may have suggested intimacy sustained in this structured anxiety, connection fostered where it was also most at risk.

Oddly, I was reminded, in the way Kavita pared fruit, in the child dancing nearby, of Lucas Cranach's sixteenth-century images of melancholia. Representing the moral disorder of acedia, the wasting of the will, a woman sits at the edge of the frame, whittling with a knife and surrounded by babies—dancing, playing instruments, sleeping. Behind her, nude riders on horseback form a devilish horde of witches performing a reversal on the masculine, productive hunt (Zika 2003: 341). In Nehru, too, in a distant context, a woman sat at work with a knife, shadowed by spectral forces, surrounded by children, living and remembered, communicating crises of will while disrupting the order of things.

Every other day, Kavita and her husband were brought to meet with Dr. C. The doctor's office was a place of contained chaos, a mess of papers, books, people, and voices. His desk was covered with doodads from drug companies, stacks of paper, coasters for coffee, and piles of books, and more piles of books and papers surrounded it. The office was often filled with people—three or four members of his drug research team, residents three at a time, one or two assistants, a secretary, and a "peon" to regulate the entryway and make tea. Calendars, posters advertising drugs, and various inspirational placards hung on the wall, as did plaques announcing honors and awards, photographs of Dr. C. inaugurating events, and pictures of imaginary landscapes.

(Dr. A.'s office could not have been more different. Open and uncluttered, its pale blue walls were bare and the desk was clear of baubles. Dr. A.'s and Dr. C.'s personalities were as different as their work spaces. Where Dr. C. was charismatic and loudly intimidating, Dr. A. was serene and reserved. Where Dr. C. announced the end of meetings and sessions with a loud, "Go!," Dr. A. signaled with a barely perceptible nod of the head.)

Residents sat against the wall to the side of Dr. C.'s desk while I sat on the other side, sidelong to the patients, who sat against the wall opposite the desk.

The residents reported changes in Kavita's symptoms. While earlier she showed signs of pain and "stupor," she now appeared to be in a state of "trance and possession."

"You can tell this is the case because she speaks about herself in the third person," Virinder said: "'Why did you admit Kavita?' 'Why did you put Kavita in the hospital?' We have begun to cut out her secondary gains. We have told the husband not to talk to her when she is in a trance state."

Dr. C. asked Akhil to interview her. Akhil seemed nervous. He asked Kavita to tell Dr. C. what she had reported to him the day before, and observed, "But this does not match what you are saying today."

Frustrated, Dr. C. cut him off. "It is important for the doctor to talk to the patient in terms of today, not in terms of what they said yesterday or the day before, but for what is happening to them right now. If the patient is unwilling, then you have to say 'We need to understand what is happening with you so that we can help you get better, and you need to talk to us. We need to talk about your problems in a mature manner. And we need to talk about your problems today.' The patient should know that you mean business. The words you use to ask the questions should not be directional." I often felt that Dr. C. enacted with residents the tone he wanted them to use with patients.

Dr. C. nodded for Kavita to continue.

"I don't feel like eating," she said.

"It's OK if you don't eat. Some people fast for thirty days. Muslims, at Ramadan, they fast for thirty days and only eat after the sun goes down. But if you stay in this state you are in now, there is big danger." He asked what the people in her *maike* were like.

"The people in my *maike* will not keep me [care for me]. I won't go to my *maike*."

Kavita began to breathe heavily, a half-smile visiting her face. "Why do you keep asking me questions? You have all the knowledge." She waved her hand, implicating the scenery.

Dr. C. called her name as though summoning her from a distance.

"Kavita is not here," she said.

"Who are you?" (the same entreaty used by exorcists).

"Kavita is not here. Why have you brought Kavita to this place? Today Kavita is gone. Today Kavita will die."

She stood abruptly, throwing herself against the desk and knocking a pile of papers on the floor. Her small frame was grabbed quickly by one of the research assistants. She shook him off. Dr. C. lurched back, but waved off the assistant, who let her go.

"If you are a goddess, go sit up on the top of that wall up there, by the ceiling. Tell us what the room looks like from there."

"You are the god," she said, leaning again over the desk, breaking the invisible wall it demarcated around Dr. C.'s island of authority. "You know everything. You are god. You have everything. I have nothing. You are God. I am neither man nor woman. You know everything, you can do everything. Look, you have so many things. I have nothing."

She sat. Dr. C. turned to her husband. "Does she become like this often?"

"Sometimes. When she does, she asks for a lot of things."

The doctor reminded the residents that patients like this are in control of their symptoms but that families must be encouraged not to give in to their demands. "We must confront her, to ask, 'Who will take you seriously if you behave this way?'"

In the emergency clinic one afternoon, I took notice of a poster on the wall. Advertising a drug company, in the center was a familiar image of Freud, cigar in hand, and beneath it the caption, "Only he could put the 'ego' in its place."

The irony of the poster was that through the dominance of pharmaceuticals, Indian psychiatry had written off psychoanalysis as an explanatory or therapeutic framework. But it retained a scrutiny of women's distresses that bore elements of Freud's attentions to his own hysterical patients, a sense of their disruptive passions, crises involving control in and of the family, the idea that fantasy and mimesis might outpace reality. Its performative elements also resembled those that flourished before Freud, in which physical rigors were evidence of an untruthful mind. However, dissociative disorders-cum-hysterias in Nehru, while steeped in somatic effects, resembled less Freud's Dora, or even Charcot's Augustine, than Robert Carter's hysteric, described in 1853. For Carter, hysteria related to escalating crises of emotion. First, women denied erotic discharge could experience an acute reaction—the "dam could burst" (Porter 1993: 262). This hysteria, Carter said, played itself out without the aid of medicine. A second kind of hysteria was provoked by memory, producing "compensatory pleasures" in memories of suffering. In the third and most extreme form, the hysterical woman represented "the appalling depths of moral depravity, contriving to manipulate all around her, so as to gratify her whims and domineering spirit, and enable her to bask in the 'fuss and parade' of illness" (Porter 1993: 263). This hysteria was a matter of will dispersed into soma, and cure was a matter of self-discipline (Showalter 1993: 300).

In Nehru, while physicians reminded residents that the hysterical patient must not be coddled, and her desires must be disciplined, this did not mean they failed to recognize insecurities and demands specific to women's social conditions. Indeed, "culture" was everywhere they looked, and I found myself, like residents, invoking and discounting it as part of what dissociative disorder was all about. For the residents, reordering power relations encouraged patients to persist in unyielding worlds, suggesting that self-control was a sort of acceptance, even if it came with unforgiving outcomes. Doctors sought to remind patients of what was real and what was not, and to reiterate to families that symptoms were "in patients' control." In some cases this had to do with thwarted aspirations, in others it involved the effects of potentially disintegrating bonds.

In Nehru, hysteria was a caustic agent dissolving relations, upending what was functional and effective. In other words, it was not that women's dissociative symptoms were a threat to normal life, or to morally legible relations, but rather that they threatened the social in general. The reinforcing of moral norms may have been an effect of this, but it was not an aim. To reiterate, in this there was a doubling. While caustic to the social, women also bore the brunt of its fungibility. Thus, for married women, vulnerabilities (remembered, actualized, and threatened) inherent to kinship included those within normative marriage, junctures between one home and another, between rootedness and dislocation; for unmarried women and girls they involved life in natal homes (including possibilities for abuse in them, which I have not yet touched on) and efforts in public, junctures between home and world.

Where Western histories of hysteria emphasize the extent to which it might involve responses to trauma or enforce moral norms, hysteria's appearances in Nehru emphasized dissolution within the social, the responsibility for and effects of which fell on women. Medicine participated in this process. Just as Moksha may have caused some to feel more acutely the distresses it was intended to cure, systems that addressed dissociative disorder shared an uncanny ability to produce the thing they sought, to generate what they claimed to discover.

Hysteria is a knowledge structure, a power structure, a medical structure, a gender structure, and a kinship structure. It is "asking a question," the name given to the "object which cannot be mastered by knowledge, and therefore remains outside of history, even its own" (Wajeman 1988: 3). For Kavita and others, these overlapping orders and evasions involved a particular kinetics, borrowing from vocabularies of spirit visitation, the history of psychiatry (as captured in paint, ink, and film), and even dance, that may be similarly interrogative, less a mode of resistance or its opposite than habitation, tentative or bold, through voice, body, and sensation, of memories, constraints, and possibilities. It is a way of being amid difficulty that is at once knowledge's creation and that which defies knowing.

Many of hysteria's paradoxes lie at the crux of symptom and artifice, and, by extension, at the blurry boundaries of agency. In restaging iconic photographs of Charcot's star hysterics, artist Tejal Shah explores the relationship of pathology to artful movement. With herself and a ballet dancer as subjects, Shah's reenactments blur distinctions between intentional and unintentional movement, original and cultivated expression. Her work suggests moments of conjuncture, when what Jessica Benjamin calls the "unconscious communication" of hysteria is transformed not into the "active subjectivity" of language but that of movement, of bodily habitation (2001: 41).

Such movements are symptom and artifact of clinical knowing as well. In well-known images from the Salpêtrière, historians have found evidence of science's dependence on performance. In André Brouillet's painting of Charcot's theater (which hung on the wall of Freud's office), a gathering of male doctors and students watches as Charcot displays a patient, whose eyes are closed and bodice opened as she swoons into the arms of a nurse. The scene is jarringly reminiscent of moments in women's care in Nehru. In the troubling photographs Shah reproduces, what is captured is not just a contorted body, but a contorted gaze, and not just the "twisted" gaze of the hysteric, but the gaze of medical science (Didi-Huberman 2003). These moments of encounter make hysteria a "face-off" with science, both recreating and undoing its penetrating gaze (Didi-Huberman 2003: 129). Together with Brouillet's paintings, the photographic images from the Salpêtrière can be read many ways—as the capture of real suffering, as performances of patriarchy, as a kind of pornography, as scientific performance, as a contract between patient and doctor that affirms the latter's status, as the violent eroticization of medical knowing (Didi-Huberman 2003). As "representations of anguish," they suggest that, in such "visual-ized silencing," the body may enact something language would "efface," "traces of a traumatic knowledge" that are "never only a representational game" (Bronfen 1998: 199). This is a tensile position, and for Kavita and other women whose pains, rigors, paralyses, visitations, and fluxes of con-sciousness emerge from worlds dense with vulnerability, the body enacts something more than a clinical performance that affirms the superiority of the doctor. There is in this both proof and the undoing of its terms (Bron-fen 1998: 184).

In Kavita's rages and her doctors' scoldings were a paradoxical moment (one characteristic of hysteria) in which cause clashed with effect and action met passivity as "the patient's autonomy emerges out of the identification with the analyst's authority, which she accepts" (Benjamin 2001: 46). At the same time, such acceptance was rejected all the time, in theatrically bold ventriloquy and quieter utterances. It was almost as though Kavita knew her feminist psychoanalytic theory: "And for the patient, certainly, [the doctor] may appear to be the god who denies only this particular sinner the redemption she seeks" (Benjamin 2001: 52).

Possession, in anthropological terms, shares with hysteria this contour between action and inaction, constraint and resistance, outrage and accep-tance. This is true in its bodily grammars and verbal discourses, and in the kinetic nature of its exorcisms. Some describe it as a way lives are ordered to specific demands (Nabokov 1997), and others regard it as a means of pushing back against those demands. Yet others read possession beyond this structure, or rather, don't read it at all, refusing to textualize the body (Stoller 1995) or translate it into "resistance," "power," or anything else. In other words, possession, like hysteria, may demonstrate through ventril-oquized desires the boundaries of a constrained will. But it also kicks at walls. It lunges at observers. It breaks the proscenium.

It is no accident of Bollywood convention that hysterical psychosis is represented as a dance. This theme extends transnationally; think of Darren Aronofsky's *Black Swan* or the plot of many nineteenth-century ballets (or see McCarren 1998). In Shah's image, the hysterical arch becomes legible as ballet's back *cambre*, part of an aesthetic vocabulary rather than grotesque contortion. Shah brings to pathology the possibility of not only the aes-thetic but the pleasure of the body, or at least an element that is neither pleasure nor suffering, but intense habitation. It is not unlike the way anthropologist Julie Taylor describes the Argentine tango, as an art at once combative and demanding submission, one that incorporates a history "of human ties destroyed" without remaking them into something liberatory or retrenching their violences (1998: 61). Such ways of moving are, for Taylor, means of habitation—of histories of violence and its unspeakable memories; of what it is to be a body from which one may be alienated, a self who can be alienated from others; they allow the intensified possibility of being alive in spaces of destruction and self-negation.

This might be too much to read into Kavita's situation or in those where clinical management overwhelmingly focused on reinstating control. But recall that in *Bhool Bhulaiyaa*, Avni's madness flourished as a beautiful dance, one that gave a glimpse into her own reality, or that before that mad dance she carried around a video camera, the manifestation of her gaze already present in a film that would, scene after scene, deny her perspective. That the Indian cultural landscape, including its popular entertainments, has room for *this* configuration, *this* habitation of agency, desire, inscription, and reinscription, illuminates the way sciences of the mind and the rituals of medicine, like care in the household, participate in dramas of control—control of women, to be sure, but also control as a feature of relationships, and intersubjectivity more generally, in which women bear specific eventualities. Here, medicine intervenes not where control must be established against freedom, but where control is a feature of care and relationship making, and both its lack and enactment are not discontinuous with neglect and loss. This is a painful space eloquently revealed by the body in a way that blurs distinctions between pathology and expression.

Hysteria is notoriously slippery. Distant from the stuff of homemaking and the comforts and demands of life with a child, living out both aspiration and separation, I grappled, in Nehru's dissociations, with the way it blurred boundaries between critique and sympathy. Challenged in my thinking by the dramatic differences from Moksha, I was relieved by Nehru's order and attentiveness. Yet, in this order were efforts, though often partial and unfinished, to repair social lives in the very terms that may have wrought damage. Here I came closest to finding shades of the asylum in the clinical disciplining of women, though I suspected that something else was also at work, something intrinsic to relationships and intimacy more generally, though always in what doctors felt were "Indian" terms. That was the nature of hysteria, to be a thing of times and places.

But hysteria also seemed to be everywhere I looked for it, in myself as well as others, in transnational connections and hyperlocal distinctions. It felt, indeed, that "there doesn't seem to be anything medicine has not said about hysteria: it is multiple, it is one, it is nothing; it is an entity, a malfunction, an illusion; it is true and deceptive; organic or perhaps mental; it exists, it does not exist" (Wajeman 1988: 1). The latter binary—around the uncertainty of existence—made the most sense, in the way women's afflictions marked interstitial spaces where existence (of a disease, a pain, a spirit, a self) was, like presence, a matter of degree, and undeniably real as an expression of the stakes of social and medical arrangements for women.

Following hysteria's ever-expanding chains of mimesis, I was and continue to be sucked into a wash of self-referential effort—grasping something using the thing itself, critiquing it using its methods for undoing. Feminists have long used hysteria to unpack hysteria, remaking the master's tools before using them to dismantle his house. This illness, representing crises in truth telling, agency, and interdependence, all embodied in the female patient, offers a rich blueprint for self-referentiality. It becomes possible to recognize in hysteria the kinds of syntax, the symbolic arrangements, the contracts of truth and relatedness that bring a woman to her feet to call her doctor a god in an office that looks disarmingly like Charcot's theater, instead of being pushed to her knees to touch his feet, as patients not in the throes of dissociation do on a daily basis.

Chapter 5

Making a Case

> The dream acquitted me of responsibility for Irma's condition by
> showing that it was due to other factors—it produced a whole series
> of reasons.
>
> —Sigmund Freud, *The Interpretation of Dreams* (2010 [1901])

Among the many scenarios Eve and her friends enacted in their play, the
most popular was *shadi*—wedding. Transforming my *dupattas* into saris,
turbans, and dhotis, expertly folding, pleating, tucking, and wrapping, they
played bride, groom, and priest, hosted ceremonies, songs, and the sobbing
departures of new brides on my balcony, painted magic marker patterns on
each other's arms, offered leaf garlands, and took turns at walking around
a "fire" of unlit sticks. The brides took turns touching a lucky groom's feet.
In a *shadi*-mad world, for Eve, becoming a north Indian kid meant learning
to play wedding; learning the complex actions and obligations of a wedding
was part of the work of childhood.

In the final month of my work, long after Eve, back in the United States,
had forgotten the rules of *shadi*, I spent days dense with busy interaction in
the hallways, wards, and offices of Nehru. It was hot, and my memories of
that time have a background of sound—the roar of helicopter-like ceiling
fans. Those days were bookended by sweaty rushes to make the quickest
transition from one shared auto to the next along a series of linked routes
home.

Whereas earlier months felt given over to forces beyond my reach,
memories of this last month are now laced with the pounding regret that
comes with bad decisions, though at the time I felt exhilaration. I had gone

home again for several weeks and then returned, again without Eve. But the peace of mind I felt on returning to India in the previous trip had given way to frightening groundlessness. This time, the man I had become involved the year before was also in the city. Eight months of purposeful forgetting was undone, and my fall back into a relationship with a person I knew I disliked—a relationship that I allowed myself to think would bring security and release from the difficulties of a dissolving marriage—proved instead to be a source of ever-expanding insecurity, of anxiety and odd jealousies that felt cultivated through little acts. Other women might have withstood it all with fortitude, even humor, or walked away. I did neither. Though it seems crazy now, there was hope in this recklessness.

My work proceeded at a breakneck pace. Notebooks filled with reams of observations. But evenings were consumed by sickening waves of panic, a sink of deception and self-deception, lies so consuming I could feel them like sharp stones in my chest. I began to experience vertigo. A memory of Eve or reminder of the fresh wounds of my still undoing marriage—mention of a book or song or place—set off rushes of dizziness. Unlike when I was working in Moksha and mixed personal reflections with the things I was seeing there, now thoughts about my circumstances did not easily meld with field notes. I needed to separate them out, to hold one thing apart from the other lest competing truths about who I was and who I wanted to be collide. I kept different files for each. Where notes from Nehru are overabundant with energy, frantic with people and details, my personal notes from that month are sparse and evidently unhappy. I was at once aware of the darkness of all this and strangely accepting. I wrote with resignation, as though I had chosen a path I could not leave. All of that eventually ended—I could and did step away—but not yet, and it now seems fitting that I should have spent those final weeks contemplating love and madness at Nehru while feeling around me growing disorientation, loss of a sense of what was right or true, and unwarranted resignation to what was unbearable.

Things seemed to be changing in the city, too. One evening, on our way back from the center of town, as we turned off the main road into our neighborhood—normally a relief of shade and birdsong—a motorcycle pulled alongside our cycle rickshaw. It slowed down just long enough for the driver to reach across, grab, and painfully twist my breast. It took me a moment to realize what had happened, what the stinging was. My first thought was to marvel at the skill of the assault—a deft reach from one moving vehicle to another to a less-than-conspicuous target under layers of clothing. I made jokes and said I was glad he hadn't grabbed my bag. But my companion was vocally outraged, shouldering the victimhood in a way that made me feel oddly betrayed, as though the violation I would—and did—eventually feel was already appropriated.

Earlier in the year, I boarded a shared auto rickshaw for Moksha and, as always, was pressed up against my companions on both sides. Slowly, like a caterpillar inching, the pressure of a hand began to climb up my side. I tried to wiggle away, but by the time I realized what was happening, fingers were on my breast. I yelled for the driver to pull over and got out. My skinny, blank-faced assailant got out as well. The streets were sunny and crowded, but I felt dizzy. I climbed into the first cycle rickshaw I could find and rode to a friend's shop, where my trembling hands were quickly handed a cup of tea. I did not go to Moksha, though I felt guilty for skipping out over so "minor" an incident.

These things were new to me. No one had accosted me in India before, with the exception of one bottom-pincher in a crowded train over a decade earlier, and never, ever in this city. But for the strange attentions that had been occasionally paid to Eve, I had no point of reference. In our first days in the city, as Eve and I walked the short journey to visit a friend in our neighborhood, we were stopped by a man on a bicycle, who smiled avuncularly through red and rotting teeth and commented on Eve's beauty as she leaned against my side. As I made a move to walk on, the man said, "Just one kiss," and lurched forward. Before I could push myself in his way, he kissed her full on the mouth. I ripped her out of his grasp, and yelled. "What are you doing? Get away!"

"It's just a kiss," he protested.

I scooped Eve into my arms. She did not understand this as a violation, which was both a relief and terrifying—what things might a child come to believe is right, if only they are told so? She only said, "His mouth tasted horrible." I shook with adrenaline and felt limp with anger, at him and at myself, as I carried her the rest of the way to our destination. There were other attentions I rebuffed. I held Eve tightly as older female acquaintances insist Eve "kiss Uncle" when she did not want to, rebuking myself for my paranoias but keeping her firmly in my lap. These things could have happened anywhere, of course, and mostly people were surpassingly thoughtful of her needs. More often, people upbraided me for expecting too much of her. "She's just a child. Who can understand what is in a child's heart?"

In that final month, as these brief encounters merged into a wash of experiences, the violences of both intimate and public life were heavy on my mind. While my thoughts away from Nehru were riddled with hollows made by guilt, insecurity, and uncertainties of victimhood (in what ways was I creating my own suffering?), my thoughts at Nehru were absorbed by a woman I call Lata, a nineteen-year-old who came into Nehru under court order, as what residents called an "under-trial." Lata's mother had contested her recent marriage to an older man—a servant in their household—whom she accused of taking advantage of her daughter's mental illness. Lata said she wanted to stay married. The courts required the opinion of psychiatrists to determine Lata's "testamentary capacity"—her ability to testify in the trial and to have entered her marriage willingly. After ten days of observation, a diagnosis would, or would not, be assigned and a letter would be written to the courts. It seemed a straightforward situation; indeed, it seemed easy enough to make of it a "case," to fit it into an available language of critique and reform. It reminded me of cases I had come to know about in my short weeks working at the legal organization, cases in which family intervened in the loves of their children, and biological proof of adulthood and mental fitness were summoned to establish the rationality of will. On paper at least, this seemed to make a clear example for my files.

Lata was born in a rural village. Her parents were Brahmin, and while her father performed some priestly tasks in the village, their main work was raising buffaloes for milk. Lata grew up in a household with three older brothers and a sister, as well as a servant, a man called Amit, also Brahmin, about twenty years Lata's senior, who helped take care of the animals. Lata's father died when she was seven, leaving her mother alone to manage a large household, fields, and livestock.

When Lata was about twelve, her brother began to beat her for one small infraction or another. There was a lot of fighting in the house, yelling between her brother and mother, between Lata and her brother. She preferred to stay in her room but liked the company of friends—"good people" to talk to. Her brother often hosted friends for evenings of drinking. On one such night, one of the older men crept into Lata's room and raped her. According to Lata, the sex was consensual. It was painful, she said, but she "chose it" (by legal definition, of course, sex between an adult and a twelve- or thirteen-year-old is nonconsensual).

Around this time, Lata began a bout of what her mother called "craziness." At first, her mother noticed that she made many demands, especially for new clothes and jewelry. She started wearing tight and revealing clothes, and became angry and uncontrollable if she did not get what she asked for. She soon stopped sleeping for days at a time, and in screaming fits, she yelled abuses at her mother and tried to run away. She cut her arms, slashed off her long hair, shaved her eyebrows, and cut her eyelashes. Her mother brought Lata to the private practice of one of Nehru's psychiatrists who put her on risperidone, an atypical antipsychotic medication, which she took for some time (six months to two years; reports differed). She soon relapsed. She grew argumentative, yelled at and attacked her mother, and tried, again, to run away. She was admitted, briefly, to the large private psychiatric hospital in the city. When she got out, her mother took her a Hanuman temple known for healing the mad. Lata gazed at the deity and received holy offerings, taking *darsan* and receiving *prasad*. Both helped calm her. Her mother then took her to a Sufi shrine, where Lata went into trance, swinging her hair and moaning for release from an afflicting spirit. After this, her condition worsened. She grabbed her mother by the hair and called her names—a bitch, a fucker, a cunt. Her mother took her to a hospital in a different city, a smaller one closer to their village. There, Lata spoke rudely to the doctor. When he felt her pulse she said, "What, do you have a fever?" and when he asked, "Where are you?" she said, "I am in your house." Lata was put back on antipsychotic drugs.

Lata's sister, to whom she was close, got married and moved to her *sasural*. Not long after the wedding, her husband died in a truck accident and Lata's mother was pressed to find her young widowed daughter a husband. The new match was not ideal. The man was much older, and they later learned he had a wife already. Lata's sister continued to live with him and, during this time, began to have sex with other men in exchange for money and gifts. Lata occasionally visited, but she seldom stayed for long.

Lata's older brother married, and after the new bride was brought to the house, he got a job as a laborer and left for a distant city. When Lata was fifteen, Amit, then forty-three, began pursuing her with gifts and physical advances. Soon, a relationship began. Amit gave Lata a cell phone and encouraged her to call his friend, Faisal, who lived in a nearby city. Lata's mother was desperately unhappy about Amit and Lata's relationship and she begged them to stop, threatening to kick them out of the house if they did not. She took the cell phone from Lata, but Amit got her another one.

One night, tired of Lata's mother's objections, Amit suggested they call Faisal and have him take them to his house. Unlike Lata's farming family, Faisal, a government worker, had a motorcycle, and he used it to retrieve Lata from her home in the middle of the night. When Lata's mother awoke, Lata and Amit were gone. Convinced Amit had taken advantage of Lata's mental instability, and concerned about Lata's friendship with a man she referred to as "the Muslim," she went to the police and filed a first incidence report of abduction. There was no sign of Amit and Lata until, a few weeks later, a shopkeeper in their village told her Lata was living in Faisal's house. The three had been into his shop, he said. "They sat right here." Other people were talking as well, saying that Amit and Lata were living with Faisal in a dubious arrangement. There were rumors that Faisal had "bought" Lata for three thousand rupees, that he tended to prey on schoolgirls, and that Amit had procured for him in the past.

When Lata's mother approached the police again, they told her that Lata and Amit had married. They showed her the certificate and said the union was legal and there was nothing she could do. She mustered her resources, selling things from the house, and sought a lawyer. With his help, she filed a case to nullify the marriage, arguing that Amit had taken advantage of Lata's mental illness.

A month after Lata and Amit "absconded" (as the doctors put it—an accurate, if formal-sounding translation of the Hindi *bhagna*, and a legal term that was common in the hospital), a month after Lata began living with Amit and Faisal and having sex with both, Lata's mother located Faisal's home. In spite of having been plied with un-Brahmin things like meat and alcohol, Lata was skinny. Her blouse was torn, and her sari was old and cheap. There was a loud scene—screaming, yelling, threats. But Lata refused to come home. Later, facing a summons to stand trial, Lata was returned to her mother by the police.

While her mother pursued an annulment, Lata insisted she wanted to stay married to Amit. In fact, she wanted to be married to both men. She loved them both, she said, though she held a particular affection for Faisal, who gave her gifts and, in her words, "took good care of her." In preliminary hearings, Amit said he wished to either stay married to Lata or be compensated for the thirty thousand rupees (US$800) he had spent on her for clothes, jewelry, and food. He was sent to prison to await trial.

Lata's mother took the case to the high court, where the judge ordered Lata to be sent to Nehru for evaluation. Results of the ten-day inquiry would either support her mother's contestation of the marriage or support Lata's expressed desire to remain married. Lata's mother claimed that Lata's symptoms persisted: "She doesn't bathe for up to four days; she eats nothing; she drinks nothing; she gets smelly. She abuses me too. She is genuinely insane [*pagal*]." Lata said nothing was wrong with her.

Upon her admission into Nehru, Rorschach and IQ tests showed Lata to have an IQ of 85, what the medical residents described as a "mental age of about thirteen." The senior resident noted that when Lata spoke, she "gave a childish response to questions." But finding a diagnosis was challenging, even with Lata's old prescriptions in hand. They tried out different diagnoses—schizophrenia? bipolar disorder?—but found no clear disorder. Though something was unmistakably "strange" about Lata's behavior, there were no positive symptoms to fill in a diagnosis. Lata did not have hallucinations. She did not have grandiose ideas. Her speech was odd, but not pressured. She did not have fainting spells or unexplained pains. Her mood and affect seemed fine.

But her interactions were "not normal." She said of some recollections, "Yes, I did not tell the truth about that." She changed her mind in the middle of recounting events, laughed at things that were serious, and insulted the residents. Though she frequently changed details about her own life, and though no one was ever certain if Lata was, as her mother said, "telling a lot of lies," days of interviews and questioning seemed to suggest only a personality disorder. The trio of residents evaluating Lata sympathized with her mother, suggesting the best she could do would be to encourage Lata to seek a divorce on her own.

Lata had been assigned to Dr. C., who was often triaged Brahmins, as he was Brahmin and it was felt he might have special insight into their circumstances and better rapport with families. He, too, struggled to settle on a diagnosis. Together with residents, he consulted with Lata's mother about means by which she might dissolve the marriage. Lata's mother told Dr. C. that there was a rumor that Amit might already be married. If that were the case, Dr. C. told her, the marriage could be nullified. Lata's mother sent her son to look into the matter. He returned with the information that Amit was not otherwise married, but that he ran a prostitution ring in Delhi as well as procured girls in their district. Dr. C. explained to Lata's mother that while the marriage could not be nullified, if Amit took money from anyone "for Lata," then "she herself can get a divorce." But she would "still have to admit that she slept with that Muslim man." (No one mentioned that Lata's mother might ask the police to pursue Amit on grounds of trafficking; perhaps they thought it would be useless, or perhaps they didn't think of Lata as a victim.)

After days of interviewing and observation, residents and Dr. C. agreed that Lata did not have the kind of disorder of thought or rationality (an Axis-I illness like schizophrenia) that would cloud her judgment. They did feel she had a histrionic personality disorder (a disorder recently evicted from the DSM). Dr. C. drafted a letter for the courts. It read that Lata had a histrionic personality but no signs of a mental illness that would disrupt her testamentary capacity.

In the early weeks of monsoon, ceiling fans wheezed on the dust of broken concrete and the mayhem of building construction. Throughout the day, laborers broke walls and carried refuse up and down stairs, in and out of wards, hauling concrete in and carrying broken plaster out. These were often women, with bowls heavy on their heads and just-walking infants at their heels. I would occasionally turn a corner to find a toddler sitting alone on the floor or wandering up the stairs.

On the third floor, where female wards straddled a hallway full of rubble, some patients paced, others sat on beds within circles of kin. A young woman cried as her husband loosened the white cloth tying her wrists to the bed frame and put a baby to her breast. A worried-looking father sat next to his daughter's bed while she lay in what a resident told me was a catatonic reaction to the wrong dose of anti-psychotics. In a far corner, one of the "destitutes" reclined in clothes heavy with feces, one arm wrapped around her legs, while the other picked at a head wound. There were complaints about her smell until a nurse cleaned her up.

When the ward had few patients, it was as though sketched in charcoal—dominated by the gray and white hues of fraying supplies and tired sterility. When it was full, its edges were draped with color and cloth—saris, shirts, towels, tunics, and petticoats hanging on bodies or in windows to dry. Beds became roomlike, even homelike, with boundaries between groups marked by bags and shoes. Patients and husbands, mothers, fathers, siblings, sons, and daughters prepared food, combed hair, read newspapers, talked, folded clothing, or lay in stillness, sharing whispers or vacant inactivity. Some cried, some moaned, some sang, some spoke in hushed voices.

The ward was approached one of two ways—via an industrial elevator or up a cavernous winding ramp. The doors were always open and the room was high ceilinged and lined with screened windows. A view onto treetops and the cluttered rooftops of the old city gave a lofty feeling, a softness of green and birdcalls. The room's two doors, one on either end, channeled people in and out: patients and their attendants, laborers, sweepers, nursing students, psychiatric residents in bands of three, ward attendants, social workers, and a range of researchers. Painted on the wall was the admonishment, *"Rishtedar mariz ko janjir-tale se bandh kar na rakhe,"* (Relatives must not restrain patients in chains and locks).

Attendants kept an eye on the female ward through an open window from an adjacent office. When I first met Lata she was climbing through this window. Her hair was wet and her arms held the damp bundle of yesterday's clothes. Chasing her, a ward attendant yelled that Lata had been using the men's bathrooms. *"Badmash!"* she called after her, "Naughty!"

The bathrooms in the female ward had been unusable for a week. As nursing students passed through, they covered their noses and mouths, and patients and caregivers complained about the walk through the courtyard under hot sun to toilets in the building next door. Lata yelled back that the bathrooms were disgusting and she wouldn't walk so far to bathe.

Lata and her mother were accompanied on the ward by two police officers on alternating shifts. In mornings, I often arrived to find the night constable, a fleshy woman who bulged through her uniform, lounging on Lata's bed and chatting, drinking tea and holding out her arm so Lata could draw on it with ink, swirls and flowers like wedding henna. It was unclear whether the constable was bored or enjoying what seemed to be a relaxing duty. She helped Lata organize and fold her clothes or go through the plastic bag hanging from the bedpost in which Lata kept the decorations signifying wifehood—red vermilion for the part in her hair, toe rings, a black-beaded *mangalsutra* necklace. Sometimes Lata wore these auspicious signs, though her mother told her to remove them and the social workers chided her for it.

When the ward was crowded, Lata's mother swept an area clean and unrolled her blanket on the floor. When patients ebbed, she took a cot. Food for Lata came on hospital carts. For herself and the constable, Lata's mother brought meals, tea, and snacks from the vendors outside.

The residents came through in trios of instruction, gray-blue flocks around the beds. A third-year oversaw a second-year; a second-year oversaw the first-year who, after a few weeks of observing, would take on cases of his own. They took rounds in the early morning and again in the late afternoon, when the adrenaline of the outpatient clinic was wearing off and the wards offered relative calm.

On rounds, residents asked Lata and her mother the same things they asked other patients. How was she feeling? Was she eating well? Was she sleeping? They asked other questions, too. Was Lata listening to her mother? Did she know why she was here? Who was she talking to on that cell phone? (Usually Faisal, to whom she spoke most mornings in a cooing whisper laced with laughter.) They reminded her that she was not permitted to make phone calls. And whose phone was it, anyway? (The constable's.)

Lata's words were small and girlish, at times reticent, at times bold. Her sentences crumbled into giggles, and she covered her mouth with her hand, especially when talking to the doctors. Her voice tripped from sweetness to insult, critical observations coming from behind a Mona Lisa smile or the folds of her *dupatta*. She told the first-year resident that he was not hand-some. "Your ears stick out." She told me I had a strange nose. Her affect was difficult to describe—girlish in a heavily performative way, with exag-gerated eye blinking and head tilting reminiscent of Bollywood femininity, but with an edge of aggression and falseness. Often she said nothing and smiled enigmatically. She mimicked questions and the English words resi-dents used, repeating sounds and exaggerating accents in the voice of a child. Her eyelids were often heavy, hanging low in a way that seemed to me to be not unlike other women in the ward, as though psychotropics made it hard to stay alert, though Lata was not on medication. One morn-ing she pulled me aside. "You are from America, right? I saw on TV that in America people eat worms. They open the cans and eat them. This is dis-gusting and makes me want to vomit."

Another morning, her mother preempted residents' questions. "Lata is angry today; she is throwing things and yelling at me."

Lata rebutted, "My mother keeps yelling abuses. Just like at home."

Her mother sighed. "Lata tells a lot of lies."

Lata said it was her mother who was the liar: "Nothing she says is true."

On other mornings, Lata said she was fine and had slept well, but her mother disagreed, "She has been yelling abuses again."

Lata insisted again that it was her mother who was the liar. "It is the opposite of what she says. At home she is always yelling, always complain-ing, there is so much fighting and no escape."

Lata's mother told about a short walk they took to the Durga temple down the road.

On another day, Akhil introduced Lata to me on rounds, "She ran away with a servant at Holi."

The younger resident, Rahul, corrected him. "No, she married him in January."

Akhil continued. "Her mother says she has a history of many relationships with servants and others. She does not have a diagnosis as yet."

Another day, Akhil asked, "Do you think you have a problem?"

Lata said no. She was wearing a long-sleeved, well-tailored polyester *selwar kameez* in a bright flower pattern. It looked new.

"How did you come to be in the hospital?"

There was a long pause, then Lata said quietly, "I don't know. There is no problem."

"How is your mother's behavior?"

"Mummy's behavior is not good. She yells abuses at me; she says that I am crazy."

Her mother, standing behind, gave a pained smile and shook her head.

Akhil turned to me. "She used to demand a lot of things when she first came in. Money, clothes, jewelry." He told the constable that she should be careful that Lata does not run away. He turned to Lata. "If you run away we will put *bijli* [electricity] on your head." He spoke gently and with a smile.

"No," Lata said, "I want to stay here. Here it is very good."

One evening, according to Azim, the first-year resident, Lata demanded "outside food from some restaurant" and got angry when her mother did not fetch it for her. She had been looking at herself in the mirror wearing sunglasses borrowed from a patient. Later, when a downpour coincided with a long electricity outage that darkened the ward, Lata stood in the downstairs entryway looking out into the light evening sky.

Details of Lata's case changed daily for the residents, for whom new information regularly surfaced (and was sometimes forgotten or lost to contradicting information). On one of Lata's first mornings in the ward, Akhil said that hers was a case of abduction and illegal marriage.

"She married outside the community, to a Muslim man who is forty-five years old. There is dispute over her age; mother says seventeen, she says nineteen. Her family says she is of unsound mind and so the marriage is invalid. The mother gave a history of psychotic symptoms, and she was on risperidone for six months, but after this the symptoms are very vague and the history is vague."

Akhil said there were questions about what happened when she disappeared. "But she herself will not talk about it, so we don't know."

Akhil and Virinder told me at different times that Lata was eighteen or nineteen, married a servant and "absconded." "A Muslim man," said Akhil, and then, later, "Hindu, but someone of a lower class."

"Someone much older than her," Virinder said.

Details changed for me as well. The idea that this was a straightforward case of contested cross-community marriage gave way when Lata's mother made it clear that Amit was also a Brahmin. I wrote in my notes, "Main task today was putting together story of Lata M., the young under-trial who is in the ward with both mother and constable for observation because of allegations of abduction and illegal marriage. . . . The story comes together, and also frays apart throughout the day, in different voices, with different practitioners."

Several threads remained consistent: Lata had a low IQ; she had a history of sexual encounters. Indeed, sexual history was important to Lata's diagnosis, and her ways of speaking about it (openly after initial hesitation) were made noteworthy. Akhil and Virinder both observed that Lata "admitted" she had sex with both Amit and another man ("married him," Akhil said; "had relations," said Virinder). He was a Muslim, they both pointed out. Virinder said a few days later that Lata admitted also to a long history of sexual activity. But the slipperiness of the word for "marriage" made it difficult to know what we were talking about. Though *shadi*—which etymologically means "happiness" or "delight"—usually refers to the wedding ceremony and the religious or legal institution of marriage, in some circles it can be a euphemism for sex. "We got married" can mean "we had sex"; "marry me" can mean "make love to me."

Opinions about Lata's diagnosis shifted rapidly and were seldom consistent from one resident to another. On one afternoon, I asked Akhil about a recent diagnostic exam. "It is possible that she has some mania, but the symptoms are very mild and sporadic. It is likely that she has a personality disorder, a histrionic personality. She likes dressing up, showing off her body. Most of the symptoms reflect a personality problem. She wears a lot of bangles. And she is often demanding things—money, jewelry; but there is no diagnosis yet."

Another morning, Virinder introduced Lata as "an under-trial who may have a personality disorder, also with some hypomania and histrionic features." Later, he said Lata had signs of mild psychotic episodes, but that it was hard to make a firm diagnosis of schizophrenia or bipolar disorder. "These could also be signs of personality disorder. Or these things are also signs of dissociative disorder, and a histrionic personality can also dissociate. She wears a lot of bangles." Akhil and Azim also noticed that Lata wore a lot of bangles.

Bangles came up in another way as well. In a personality assessment, residents observed cut marks on Lata's arm. She held out her wrists and said the marks were from bangles broken in a fight with Amit. They pressed her on the details of the fight and argued quietly with each other about whether it was possible for broken bangles to make such marks. Perhaps they were the marks of self-cutting, they said. It was difficult to know.

In reporting to Dr. C., initially there was talk of mania and "hysteria," and Lata's "hyper-sexualized" and "demanding behavior" were mentioned. But other signs were lacking. She did not complain of bodily pain or headaches. She had not experienced a trance episode since her mother took her to a shrine some years earlier.

In these sessions, details of behavior were precipitated into pieces of a diagnostic paradigm—behaviors present or absent, marked or minimal. Interactions that gave everyone a sense of something being "off" were clustered into themes and symptoms—or their lack—in the case sheet and report: "demanding behavior," "occasional inappropriate affect," "no over-talking," "no big talking." For everyone, it was difficult to keep track of the moving pieces, though all agreed that Lata's was "an interesting case," "a difficult one." After a few days, Akhil confessed to Dr. C. that Lata's case sheet had not been written up. (According to hospital rules, it should have been written in the first twenty-four hours after admission. But it was not uncommon for overburdened residents to take days, even weeks to write up cases.)

In all of this, Lata's choices in and feelings about sex remained pivotal. In her personality assessment, Virinder asked, "Lata, what is marriage?" When she didn't answer, he said, "Then tell us, what is a husband?"

She answered with the rising intonation of a question. "A husband is someone who loves his wife, who keeps her inside the house and doesn't show her to others? A husband is someone who has physical relations with his wife?"

Concerned that Lata seemed to confuse marriage with sex, Virinder told her mother she should note that Lata was unable to "properly define marriage," which could call into question her decision-making ability.

With a personality assessment book open on one knee and a well-thumbed ICD-10 on the other, Virinder asked about Lata's life, her feelings, and her experiences with Amit and Faisal, and with other men.

"How many boyfriends do you have?" (A pause, then "Only him," a laugh.) "Do you think it is OK to have sex without being married?" ("Yes? No?") "Do you think you should have a relationship with every man you are friends with?" ("No?") "Would you be satisfied to never have sexual relations?" ("Yes?")

Finally, "This thing you have done, this is wrong," Virinder said.

"Then why hide it?" Lata replied.

It was at this point that Lata said she wished to remain married not only to Amit but to Faisal as well. "When I was a girl I used to dream I would have two husbands—one to give me food and clothes, the other to love me." The residents—and I—had difficult locating this statement on any grid of evaluation, clinical or otherwise.

But while Lata's choices (they were assumed to be her decisions) about sex were deemed important in revealing something about her state of mind, other details slipped off the diagnostic radar. In Lata's personality assessment, she spoke of her first sexual encounter, with the drunk older man when she was twelve. This piece of information did not get recorded in Lata's case sheet, only that Lata had a "history of early sexual encounters." Though Virinder said Lata's responses were useless because she "keeps returning to the core episode" (her marriage to Amit and time with him and Faisal), suggesting an etiology of distress in which trauma might be part, the psychic impact of the earlier episode or of sexual assault in general was never mentioned. Virinder nodded when I asked if Lata may have been raped. "It is possible, but she does not report it." Lata's experience with the houseguest—what I decided to refer to as rape—did not appear in her file, nor was it mentioned to Dr. C.

Two occupational therapists, Dr. P. and Mrs. R., called the women from the ward into their meeting room. Both women were in their late fifties and were warm auntie types, plump and smiling. Their expensive but understated saris and jewelry denoted a privileged social class, and both spoke of foreign travels and family living in the United States.

The meeting room was large and empty except for a large desk, a few plastic chairs, and a metal cabinet in the corner. The patients and, in some cases, their attendants, sat in a circle on a plastic woven mat at the feet of Dr. P. and Mrs. R., who sat in chairs at the desk. From this height, Dr. P. asked in turn how the women were feeling, calling them "*larki*" (girl) and "*bacca*" (baby, or in this case, child). Dr. P. turned to a teenage girl—also named Lata—who had been admitted for *tezi* (mania) and a suicide attempt, and asked her mother, seated behind her, just off the mat, how she was feeling. "Is she still saying she is better than everyone, or ripping her clothes?"

"No," she said.

To this Lata, she said, "Lata, you want to live. Life is so pretty, so beautiful. Look outside. Look at the beautiful birds, look at the beautiful . . ."

The other Lata, our Lata, cut in, as though trying to please a teacher by completing the words to a well-known poem, "A lovely, lovely breeze is blowing."

Dr. P. asked her to be quiet. "I am speaking to this girl now."

In her little girl voice, Lata said, "Sorry."

Then it was her turn.

Dr. P. asked how she was. "Why are you here? How is everything?"

"There is a lot of fighting at home. Between my mother and my older sister."

"What do you fight over?"

"I don't know."

"Why are they fighting? Is it because of you?"

"Yes, because of me."

"Why are they arguing about you?"

"My mother has forbidden me to say."

"What kind of work does your family do?" Dr. P. asked.

"Buffalos. We raise buffalos."

"Who looks after the buffalos?"

"I do, my brother does, my mother does."

"Is there anyone who works in the house?" Dr. P. knew Lata's situation. Her tone communicated this. She was trying to get Lata to tell the story herself.

"No, there is no servant," Lata said.

"No servant?" Dr. P. repeated.

"Well, there is someone who comes to look after the buffalos."

"And did you become friends with him?" The word "friend," *dost*, was loaded. Everyone knew what she meant.

"Yes." Dr. P. asked his name. "And you didn't marry him?" Again, it was unclear whether Dr. P. meant "marry" or "had sex." I took her to mean the latter.

"No. I talk to him. He talks to all the girls."

"That's fine within limits," Dr. P. said, "But your friendship went beyond those limits, didn't it?"

"Yes," Lata said.

"And who objected?" Dr. P. asked rhetorically, pulling the story out of Lata.

"My mother did."

"And Amit has gone?"

"He is in jail."

"Why is he in jail?" Again, a rhetorical question, a call and response kind of storytelling.

"He is accused of abducting me."

Mrs. R. had come in late. She joined the conversation. "It is because of this, because of a reaction to all of this that you are ill." Now I was no longer certain they understood Lata's circumstances. The backstory, perhaps, but not her reason for being in Nehru.

"Let us come to the point, child," Dr. P. said. "What is your trouble? What are your symptoms?"

"Because of all this tension," Lata said, echoing what Dr. R. had said.

"Since you have come here there isn't any new trouble?"

"No."

"Don't you get medicine?" Dr. P. asked. I was now certain they did not understand that Lata was under observation. "What are your symptoms?"

"I see visions. Visions come to me."

Later, I wrote in my notes, "It is hard to know how she understands this question or its stakes—really, she should be saying she has no symptoms but somehow being here it is as though she must, or as though she knows which language to speak, so she speaks it. She is almost like a dissociative patient, maybe manipulative, maybe malleable—here too the two narratives cannot be reconciled—is she manipulative or manipulated?"

Dr. P. brought a *dholak*, a small drum, and finger cymbals out of the cupboard. She handed the drum to the first Lata and asked our Lata to sing a *devi git*, a song to the goddess. As the drum settled into predictable rhythm, women joined with finger cymbals and tried to sing together, losing, for a time, their more obvious symptoms. Shakuntala, a pregnant woman who couldn't stop talking, stopped talking and sang. The first Lata appeared happy to be singing, as did her mother. Our Lata sang loudly.

Between songs, Dr. P. asked Lata what she was chewing on. "Tobacco? Did Amit give you this habit?"

"No, it is just *supari* [betel nut]. My older sister got me started on this."

"Did Amit give you those anklets your mother is wearing?" Lata's mother had strung a pair of anklets around her neck. They argued, and Lata insisted they were a gift from her sister.

"Did he give you the suit you are wearing? Your lovely new blue suit?"

"No, I liked it and got it myself."

It struck me that it was only female patients who were called on to sing, and I recalled the role of singing in many women's lives—the way it brings women together for small and large occasions. The songs women were asked to sing were all religious, and Hindu at that—*devi git*, prayers to Ram—but none from other genres—no *filmi* songs, no *gali* (abuse) songs, no ghazals. In my notebook, I scrawled, "What the drum does . . . rhythm. Order."

But later, I reflected about not only the disciplining order of the drum but the embrace of rhythm, the comfort of shared voices, and the way Dr. P. and Mrs. R. not only encouraged the women to sing and clap in time with the beat but told them to sing out in voices loud enough to be heard. Each action demanded interpretation and suggested easy readings.

I thought too about the presence of mothers in this scene, women whose role can be read in the same double way as the drum—as caring and protective, even, as in Lata's case, grieving their daughters' circumstances, or as directing their voices and actions, their desires and pathways in life. I wrote, "The overwhelming feeling at the moment, in this room as in the ward, is something about the way mothers care for daughters, even grown ones who are just beyond their control, but always within their care, for whom they mourn and rage."

Later I asked Dr. P. and Mrs. R. about Lata's case, and they repeated her story, as they knew it. I asked what Lata herself said, what she wants. I did not get an answer, though I asked several times.

Dr. P. said, "She has an illness. She is not right—almost like a child, so one can't take her word. She is also very clever and manipulative and will say many, many things."

What Lata actually said was blocked by interpretations of its validity and moral value. I kept asking, "But what does she say she wants?," knowing what Lata had told the residents and me. Perhaps I played the same game as Dr. P., asking her to say something I knew she already knew.

"It is impossible to know, given her state of mind."

I was frustrated by the double bind—if Lata's state of mind discounted her ability to tell the truth about what she wanted, then how could "what she says" be anything but pathology, even if there was, diagnostically, "nothing wrong." Angry, I wrote that night, "This is not only a kind of obstruction of speech, it is way of discounting or dissolving a desire—and speaks to the [kind of] relationship between the two, especially in mental illness, especially in the medicolegal domain."

Communication between residents was markedly different from the way they spoke to and around Dr. C. Residents and assistants would assemble in his office by 9:00 A.M. to wait for his arrival, which was silently but portentously announced by his assistant. Preceding Dr. C., the young man hurried in with the doctor's briefcase and lunch basket. The room would grow silent until the moment when all stood up, brisk and flustered, as Dr. C. entered, the door held open by a man referred to as "the peon."

In reporting cases, residents' voices dropped. They leaned in, began (and sometimes ended) phrases with "sir," and wore the masklike gaze of the low-ranked, silent until spoken to or when sentences were cut off. Criticism was taken with a barely perceptible bob of the head, a quiet, affectless "yes, sir." Patients and their families were equally deferential, especially after Dr. C. yelled at them to sit up straight, put their feet on the floor, button up their shirts. Though a decade older, I adopted the submissive demeanor of the residents. I said sir; I spoke quietly; I asked few questions.

Early that morning, Dr. C. warned the residents about transference. There was a new patient in the female ward who said she could not return to either her *maike* or *sasural* because her husband beat her and her father mistreated her. The residents discussed her case, and Dr. C. said there was difficulty in assessing the truth of the situation. "You must pay close attention to how the patient speaks to assess if this is really true—a lot of the patients are often very manipulative. It may be a case of transference. She is among these young doctors. She may be exhibiting some signs of transference."

Later, Lata and her mother were brought to his office. In a typically large group (aside from Lata and her mother, I was the only other woman in a room with about nine or ten), Dr. C. turned to Lata's mother.

"What is the husband's name?"

"Amit T."

"But that is a Brahmin name, you are Brahmin, so what is the problem?"

"His age. He is forty-five."

He turned to Lata. "How old are you?"

"Nineteen."

"Did you go with this man of your own will?"

"Yes."

"How did you meet?"

"At home."

"At home?"

"He works in my home."

"You fell in love with a servant?"

"Yes."

Dr. C. asked about the makeup of Lata's family, a question Lata struggled to answer. Dr. C. frowned and, sarcastically, held up his hand and said, "What are the names of the five Pandav brothers?" then recited the heroes of the Mahabharata himself, suggesting these were names every young Hindu should know. "Why did you run away with that man?"

"I didn't run away. I went out [*ghumne*] with him."

Using subtle language rich with quiet euphemisms, Lata's mother explained that Lata had been living with Amit in a house with another man and that money was exchanged between the men.

"Why did you get her married to this man?"

"I didn't get her married to him."

Dr. C. looked at Lata. "How did you learn all of this behavior?"

"I learned it from my sister."

Dr. C. looked confused. Virinder leaned in. "Sir, since age fifteen she has been involved in sexual activities. She has reported this herself. She also has episodes of disordered behavior."

Dr. C. looked at Lata's mother. "Can't her older brother control her?"

"He lives far away." They discussed who else lived in the household.

Lata's mother told Dr. C. about Faisal. "Doctor Sahib, Amit took her, after the marriage, to a man named Faisal K., who kept her. She stayed there with both men for one month." Dr. C. looked at the marriage certificate, turning it over as though to check for forgery.

Lata said, "There is a lot of fighting at home. We live alone." Her mother shook her head with what looked like resignation to an untruth.

"Who fights?"

"My brothers and sisters."

"No, it's not like that," her mother said.

After a long pause, Virinder said, "Sir, in 2006 she had a psychiatric episode. She saw Dr. T. in private practice and later was admitted to [a psychiatric hospital]"

"The past episodes are immaterial," Dr. C. said curtly. "They do not matter to the issue of the marriage if they did not occur at that time. Marriage is a contract, and a person must have testamentary capacity to enter into a contract. So to see if the contract is valid you must prove that at the time of signing that contract the person is not well. The past episodes do not matter. Does she have testamentary capacity?"

Virinder nodded. "Her IQ is 85."

"An IQ of 85 does not go anywhere." It could not be considered to limit testamentary capacity.

"She exhibits infantile behavior." Virinder tried to establish Lata's childlike state.

"It does not matter. If it is a matter of the law we have to look at the state of her mind when the contract was signed, and there is no evidence of a psychiatric disorder at that time or now." He looked over to his assistant, a young doctor who recently completed his residency. "Right?"

"It may be unethical," he said, "but it is not illegal."

"We should get a checkup to make sure that she has had sexual relations."

Virinder replied, "She has been having sexual relations since she was fifteen, by her own admission."

Lata's mother added, "In that month when she ran away, she was also having sex with the Muslim."

Dr. C. turned to Lata. "Is this true?"

Her response was ambiguous and confusing, to the doctors and to me. "No, I was not with that man. My older sister exposed me to this behavior."

"This Muslim paid Amit to keep her," her mother said, "But if you ask her, she won't tell you this. I need to get her married to someone."

Dr. C. was looking at his desk. He looked at the residents. "The court paper is there. She can't get her married to someone else."

"I did not know that this affair was happening."

Dr. C. scolded her. "How could you not see this? Happening right in your own house, you keep this male servant, how did you not know?"

"Doctor Sahib, my eyes were closed."

Dr. C. addressed the residents. "There is no *matlab* [meaning to be gained] from her IQ or from her psychiatric background. In order to make the marriage null and void they can prove that this man has another wife. That he married already and did not get a divorce. Or if there was no marriage and she wants to make the complaint that he has used her in this way she can prosecute the husband, she can take the divorce, but the mother cannot. It has to come from her side." They discussed other avenues available to Lata's mother, assuming that the marriage should be ended in one way or another. Dr. C. went on explaining that it was Lata's mental state and psychiatric status at the time of her marriage that was crucial. "Marriage is essentially legal," he said, "and she has entered a legal arrangement willingly."

"Her sister's husband also kept another wife," Dr. C.'s assistant said.

Dr. C. looked perplexed. His look seemed to channel my own scrambled thoughts, as I scribbled in my notebook, "what *would* be a feminist approach here??" On the one hand, a decision about Lata's marriage and possible victimization was being made by a group of men; on the other hand, their adjudication seemed to fall short of judging or disciplining Lata's aberrant life and decisions. Were they respecting Lata's decision or missing an unfolding crisis?

"The point is," Dr. C went on, "we have to remain neutral. We cannot say this was an illegal marriage. There must be psychotic symptoms at the time of the marriage, must say that she cannot sign the contract, that she does not have testamentary capacity."

Looking at Lata and her mother, he said, "*Jao* [go]." There were still several days left of the observation.

One day, on my way home, I bumped into Lata's mother in the yard, returning from the food stalls beyond the gate. We stood in the shade of an old banyan tree festooned with red ribbon offerings and spoke about Lata's circumstances.

"She has destroyed her future," she said. "I keep thinking about it. I have so much tension from thinking and worrying about her future." She hoped to marry Lata "properly," "in the right way," to settle her into a solid life in a decent family, and hoped to begin to find a good husband when they returned to their village. "But now she says she is married to Amit and wants to stay with him. And the Muslim, too. Amit has procured girls for him in the past. This is what he does. This affair will ruin her life. But if I can make her a good match, she will have a future."

She described the way Amit had "taken advantage" of the family before, getting her husband to take out an insurance scheme before his death, and convincing Lata to sign over money to him—eighteen thousand rupees in total.

"You must worry a lot," I said.

"What is worry? A worry in your mind goes directly up to God."

Lata and I spoke often in the female ward, and her mother and I had conversations both on the ward and in the hallways and walkways between buildings. Concerned about her daughter's future, she wanted desperately for Amit to be out of their lives.

"This will ruin her life," she said. "It has been difficult for me, with my husband no longer living, but it will destroy her life. And now, see her, she doesn't bathe for days. She eats and drinks almost nothing. . . . Her father was a priest, we are a good family. This is a terrible stain."

She hoped to find for Lata a "good man who would take care of her," and knew that though Lata could seek a divorce on her own, her daughter was unlikely to initiate it. "If this marriage can be annulled," her mother said, "I can make her a good match."

In the ward, she described the time she caught Lata with a cell phone given to her by Amit, from which Lata had phoned Faisal.

"I grabbed the phone from her with my own hand, but Amit said, 'However many phones you take from her, I'll keep giving her more.' He must have given her two, three, four. I think there is a phone there still."

Lata interrupted. "I hated living there. Her thing was, 'Don't talk, don't do anything, don't go anywhere. Don't do anything. Behave yourself [*Sidha rahe* (literally, stay straight)].'"

Her mother continued, explaining how Amit and Lata had phoned Faisal and had him come take them away in the middle of the night.

Lata again interjected. "Amit and I left for this reason: because she was giving us trouble."

"What trouble?" I asked.

"Yelling. A lot of yelling. Yelling abuses. And she made us do so much work."

We discussed the kinds of housework a person has to do in life, and Lata said, "I wanted to be able to get out a little bit, and he said, 'Come on, let's take her out.'" It was unclear whether she meant Amit or Faisal.

When she learned that an official marriage certificate existed, Lata's mother realized she would have to file a court case. "I thought of all the difficulties this would cause me. I am a woman alone. I am a widow. I am a farmer. How would I pay for it? I would have to sell things in the house."

"Did you go to a lawyer?" I asked.

"I went to a lawyer, but he didn't listen. He said she is an adult. She got a court marriage."

"How did you find out about the court marriage? Did they tell you?"

"We did it secretly," Lata answered. "But she knew before."

"How could I know before, child?"

"Before getting a court marriage, she was always saying, 'Get out of here, get out of here.' She was always yelling at me to get out of her house," Lata said.

"Why did she say this? Why did you say this?"

"Who knows? What can I say?" her mother said. "The reason she left is because she wanted to be out and about, she left me so that she could meet Faisal."

"Yes, yes," Lata agreed.

"And I thought this is wrong. Meeting men. This is wrong."

"Why did you marry Amit?" I asked, "Why did Amit marry you?"

"For this reason. Because he gets work out of me. For this reason," Lata said plainly. "But she doesn't want me . . . she says I shouldn't do this."

Lata's mother described the way she went to Faisal's house when she learned Lata was there. "There was a lot of yelling, I said, 'We are Brahmins, and he is a Muslim . . .'"

Lata again interjected, "Amit, Faisal, and I were all living together. Like husband and wife."

"All three of you?" I asked.

"All three of us. She was yelling and saying, 'I'll have you killed, I'll have you killed.'"

"To whom?"

"To Amit and Faisal."

"Look, we are Brahmins, he is Muslim. And he kidnaps girls. And why should he have my daughter? He is forty-five years old. And I am supposed to let them be married?"

Lata began to sound annoyed, "But with him I got everything I needed. Food. I got clothes. And I am supposed to stay at your house and be sad?"

"Why? Why are you sad at my house? The name of the game is insurance. The name of the game is money." She alluded to the fact that Amit had taken out an insurance policy on the family, circumstances I couldn't quite decipher. "Society casts out these kinds of girls. Can they sit with their sisters, with their daughters, with their mother and father?"

As she spoke, Lata protested. "Who cares about society? I did this out of love."

We discussed what Lata might do in her future. Lata's mother said she had completed high school, perhaps she could be a teacher. "But this will be a very long problem. She has destroyed her life. No one can help. Not her mother, not her brother, not her father. I want her to have decent karma. I want her to be able to perform rites. These things are very important. To be able to protect your life, your karma."

After Lata's mother got up and left to begin preparing food, Lata and I continued to talk. She described the way even in childhood she had felt alone, that there was always "fighting all around" her. "They all fought. My work was just to look, to understand, that's all. Now, if I go home there will be trouble."

"About what?"

"About him."

Since she came to the hospital, Faisal had helped her, sending her clothes and gifts. They spoke on the phone regularly. "Otherwise," she said, "I have nothing."

I asked how she met Faisal. Her sister had introduced them, she said. They were friends.

"How did that happen? Why did she introduce you?"

Lata spoke softly. "To work. To go out. To go with everyone. To get things. It was my sister who taught me this work." She laughed.

"How do you feel about it?"

"I'm in the habit now. This is why I do it. Sex, etcetera. They give me things." She pointed to her necklace and her new *selwar kameez*. Speaking vaguely and euphemistically, Lata said this "work" would support her if she were ever "alone." The matter came up in clinical questioning too. "A person needs to eat, to clothe herself."

Our conversation came around to the event with the houseguest, her rape by her brother's friend. "I had sex when I was twelve," she said. "He was my brother's friend, and he came over to drink with him. He came into my room one night. But I chose it. I didn't like it. It hurt. But I wanted it, too." Her little-girl voice slipped into a giggle.

At some point in my final month at Nehru, I decided it would be a good idea to compile from my notes a series of narrative cases, to build as stories the circumstances of women I had met in busy, confusing, and fragmentary encounters. Lata defied this effort. In part this was because of confusing details, not least of which involved her own elliptical language and changeable views, what her mother called "Lata's lies." In part it involved incomplete circuits of knowledge in the hospital, things that were and were not passed on, were and were not said. In part it was because I had difficulty locating power in the fact that, in spite of intense surveillance, doctors found no evidence of a mental illness. In part, to be sure, it had to do with the difficulty I had accepting Lata's decisions and stated desires, with my own filter of judgment. And in part it had to do with sheer moral complexity.

Part of me was relieved that residents found nothing diagnosable in the fact of Lata's sexuality, though much of what they did pathologized it, and much of what she said unsettled us. Another part of me wished diagnosis *had* been made, that more attention, not less, had been paid to Lata's symptoms, to her ways of speaking, to the unspoken possibilities of her past. I was sympathetic to Lata's need to find a kind of independence and, in general, to women's choices to enter into sex work, but doubted that she would find happiness or freedom in prostitution for Amit and Faisal. I wished Lata rid of Amit and Faisal even as I wished her to be able to love whom she wanted. I hoped for relief for her mother even as I hoped Lata could establish a life of her own and get the care she seemed to need.

I rehearsed ways of forging connections between details. Several obvious stories asserted themselves. I thought them through on rickshaw rides home from the hospital and tried to craft them on my computer at night. But each failed to contain the whole story. To begin with one detail, or subordinate another in a paragraph amid others, would be to tell Lata's story with one moral emphasis; to reorder details would create an entirely different account. Each was a critical narrative, an account of crisis in which something was wrong. But the something differed in each case. Each relied on a different set of supporting elements—scholarly critiques, histories, critical stances, received wisdoms about women's lives in India, and more and less subtle evaluations of violence—outright violence, violence related to love, and more and less subtle coercions.

And each came to a different conclusion about the justice or injustice of Lata's nondiagnosis. Did Lata fall through the cracks because a medical establishment failed to find disorder? Or did her case show clinicians' sensitivity to the messiness of love, coercion, and the points in between? Did doctors side with Lata's traffickers in finding nothing wrong, or with her mother, who objected to her daughter's unconventional life, in their advice to her?

While all the cases I encountered were difficult to tell, Lata's, more than any other, suggested the need for a particular hermeneutic, a timbre of understanding that saw description (or ethnography) less as illuminating via deep inquiry than as demanding attention to the momentary, loaded, stake-claiming, and transference-ridden processes of telling, less illuminating in the strength of its coherence than revealing in the gaps between incompatible ways of telling.

Almost immediately on returning to Boston, as my own life and stories continued to fall apart around me, I began to write about Lata, first in a struggle to summarize that coherent account for my own records, and then as an essay for a conference. After presenting the piece and going through the usual routine of cutting, revising, and rewriting, I sent the essay to a prestigious anthropology journal. Some of the reviews were positive. But one—which, the editor said, contributed to its ultimate rejection (after declaring the piece indecipherable, the editor suggested I "try a feminist journal" instead; it was later published as Pinto 2012)—stated, in a tirade about my "postmodern" interest in uncertainty ("The author writes that ethnographic work is difficult. I *know* this"): "The author seems to have lost contact with any reality outside of his or her own language games." It was a phrase I committed to memory for its brash epistemological confidence. I shared the review with a friend, also an anthropologist, who said, "How lucky that person is to inhabit a reality beyond language games."

Of interest to me, of course, was not the *fact* of ambiguity in Lata's case. (To be sure, this is something we "know" about anthropology and medicine.) The details of that ambiguity—the things those difficulties exposed about clinical practice, about love, sex, and violence at this particular place and time—were revealing and disturbing. Evidence passed through many social and moral filters—mine, the doctors', Lata's, and her mother's. All were important to document, but not just for the sake of saying, "look, a filter!" Instead, in the gaps between disjointed and inconsistent stories were specific revelations about medical and legal practice in India as it pertained to women. Also in those gaps were questions about everyday means of getting by, about people coping with undoing, demanding closure but evading the forms in which it was offered.

One way of making Lata's case, of diagnosing her circumstances, suggested she was overscrutinized by medical personnel and that her unconventional decisions were evaluated medically. These evaluations seemed to align with family efforts to discipline daughters, including family interventions in love marriages or chosen unions, and might have offered tacit support to the greater and lesser violence enacted by families when a couple marries against their designs (often across religious or caste lines). A story emphasizing these points might suggest a line of critique connected to efforts to preserve female expressions and protect choice in marriage, activism that emphasizes the truth-value of speech and the rationality of free choice in the face of efforts (usually by kin) to challenge both. It would be buttressed by the fact that legal practice in India has historically opposed female agency to community solidarity (Mody 2002). But a story told this way misses several elements. First, though Lata's sexual actions, as well as her dress and behaviors, were made the subject of medical evaluation, the fact that she was not assigned a diagnosis (for her sexual behavior or anything else) makes it difficult to argue that clinical interest in women's sexuality is successfully a way for female desires to be made over by a medical gaze into psychiatric disorder. Second, a story told this way assumes that parents object solely to cross-community marriages, avoiding the ways Lata's mother's objections related to Amit's age and his possible control over Lata. Finally, this kind of account may take the surface value of Lata's expressions *too* seriously, ignoring past (and hidden) violence—the troubling things Lata "does not report," the murky and not so murky facts of coercion.

Another way of telling the story suggests that Lata was sick, perhaps made so by trauma, and that the extent of her suffering was unacknowledged by a medical paradigm that refused to acknowledge violence and sexual predation. This way of telling Lata's story implicates a cultural discourse that renders victims responsible for violence perpetrated upon them. And it involves efforts to contest those assumptions, critical dialogues on trafficking and rape. In more sensationalist moments, women figure in these discourses as victims rather than bearers of agency. On the surface, this does not appear to contradict the first story. But subtler attentions do two things—first, they expose the compromising effects of sexual violence on the stability of clinical and legal formulas for truth (and the way sexual violence shows those formulas to be inherently unstable) (Leys 2000). Second, they show, in India, the way rape figures as a symbolic category (a threat to the kinship, community, even the nation) while being impossible to acknowledge individually in a setting where rape can mean social death (Das 2006). In this account, women's voices occupy a position of instability, lives bear things that cannot be said, and truth can be compromised not only by the psychic effects of trauma (the stories people must tell themselves to get on with life in a world that will not recognize their victimization), but also by the clarity of institutional discourse (that paints victimized women as signs of the nation, for example; Das 2006). Telling Lata's story in this way sees pathology in unusual speech and truth in lies. In it, speech is unreliable as a testament to "what happened." Instead, it looks beneath surfaces of expression for the facts of trauma. But such an account empties Lata's language of truth and denies her the ability to express what she really wants—to stay married to the man she "chose," to engage in sex work.

As I wrote in that article, the one lost in its own language games, in each way of explaining "what happened" in doctors' inability to diagnose Lata with mental illness, a different piece of the picture interceded, a "Yes, but . . ." itching at the story.

> At the moments at which the authority of interpretation is assumed (Lata's marriage is valid . . . ; Lata's marriage is a sign of disorder . . . ; Lata's marriage is strange but not sick . . .), the interpretation cannot be completed—one of the symptomatic facts intercedes (. . . but Lata may have been raped and trafficked; . . . but Lata wants to stay married; . . . but no one is listening to what Lata is saying). . . . In each [account] are different senses of not only what might be wrong with Lata's social world or mind, but what may be at stake in her marriage. If sexual agency is at stake, also at issue is Lata's ability to speak for herself and make her own choices, unconventional though they may have been. But if those choices, in their very aberrance, represent an agency compromised, at times traumatically, over time, security is in question, and Lata's interests far from locatable in her speech. (Pinto 2012: 134)

For the doctors, different pasts functioned differently. Sexual agency was permissible in their considerations. It was a sign of personality (deemed unchanging). But sexual victimization (which might have predicated possible pathology) was not allowable as it could only refer to periods other than that of Lata's marriage. One way to explain this bifurcation would be to blame legal demands on clinical practice. Trauma (and especially Lata's response to it) may have been disregarded because, first, it was a past pathology and past pathologies were inadmissible, and second, because it did not pose the kind of crisis that would have a bearing on testamentary capacity (for better or for worse; see Leys 2000). And Lata was not in the clinic to be treated, only observed.

At the same time, Lata's doctors were working as cultural brokers, treating patients and observing individuals in a cultural system whose limits they recognized. They made decisions according to the values of the kinship and gender orders in which patients lived. This was not because they felt those systems to be right or true but because the systems posed overwhelming facts of life, terms of living that would not go away when patients left the clinic. Thus, they took seriously Lata's mother's desire to get her married into a respectable home. They grappled with the fact that by not diagnosing Lata, she would be consigned, in all likelihood, to a life of risk, shame, and struggle, one mitigated somewhat if her choices could be shown not to be her own.

But I sensed something else at work, something involving a split in the kind of subject a woman could be—victim or agent, truth teller or liar. This became evident in doctors' confusion about how to deal with Lata's past. Social crises over female sexual desire (its scrutiny) and sexual violence (its inadmissibility) are certainly part of an apparently cohesive gender ideology (typically consolidated in the notion of honor killings). But for Lata, when this ideology entered clinic and court simultaneously, it exposed opposing ideas about the relationship between language and truth, a division that depended on where and how sex figured as part of the history. That seemingly coherent cultural gender ideology fragmented, putting Lata—"what she reports"—at a point of contradiction. Amid efforts to give credence to "the things Lata says," doctors' scrutiny of her desires (which she expressed) and disinterest in the violence in her life (of which she spoke more evasively) brought to light contradictions in what might otherwise seem coherent moral frames. Such contradictions made less explicable the nature of agency, language, pathology, and, indeed, norms—at the point that female sexuality and sexual violence entered the clinic in the same person, one who is both desiring agent and victim, or a different compilation of both at any given point in time.

In other words, for me, as for doctors and social workers, "what Lata says" became impossible to evaluate, made so by the moral and gender structures in which Lata was situated. "Lata's story," even if it wasn't told, could only be imagined as a coherent thing according to incompatible ways of reckoning a woman's word in relation to "the truth." These ways of reckoning were not entirely products of a sexist gender ideology; they were equally the products of efforts to reform and combat that ideology and its effects (rape, trafficking, forced marriage, etc.). "Lata told a lot of lies" because there was no way, at the juncture of these moral codes, for her to "tell the truth." And so, "what she said" had to be taken seriously, even though it sounded strange and frightening.

Another element came into my efforts to sort out what was so troubling about this situation (and, indeed, about Lata herself). That was confusion. Lata's case may have fallen apart in the clash of components of a larger gender ideology and efforts to combat it, but at the same time, it unfolded as a specific kind of clinical process—one beholden to medical pedagogy. The detailed observations of Akhil, Virinder, and Azim were consumed by the demands of reporting and the hierarchical and performative context in which they occurred. It struck me that, unlike Moksha, where language moved in the sparest terms, here, amid all the possible lanes of communication, a game of "whisper down the line" was in constant motion, up and down staircases and hallways, through windows and doors. This was true even in the presence of the subject and her historian. Lata's performances of speech were read and evaluated in a context in which all speech was performative, all speech was under scrutiny, all speech was tentative and experimental—none more so than the speech of the residents themselves, reporting in tense interactions with their domineering physician.

While we can examine ideological drives behind clinical scrutiny, we can also ask about the kinds of speech that communicate what is "seen." In north Indian hospitals, where it is precisely overcrowding and poor conditions that produce good diagnosticians, good seers, and good readers of human behavior, clinical conditions shape the economy of language that guides diagnosis—time-strapped practitioners, intensely hierarchized practice in which language can only be communicated "up", and crowded wards with a lack of privacy and the constant circulation of partial stories.

Were there more time to consider them, it is possible that subtleties of affect and behavior, memory and fantasy could contribute to an understanding of Lata's experience. But whether due to conditions or structures of communication, pathology was impossible to keep straight, especially in terms of what parts of the past counted when it was precisely the truth about the past that was at stake.

On the one hand, we could argue that Lata's (non)diagnosis pathologized female sexual agency. On the other, we could see it as ignoring the possibility of compromised female agency. But both possibilities assume a system with enough time or space for ideology to "work." This requires overlooking conditions in which diagnosis is an unstable process of telling and retelling, and in which constraints on time and speech and the structure of pedagogy might swamp ideological motivations. In the language games of diagnosis, pieces of information circulated through a complex web of engaged, critical, and self-conscious actors playing designated roles in the process of medical education—a process that was, by residents' and doctors' estimation, so good because the system around it was so flawed. I wrote,

> The more I tried to pin down power in Lata's story, the more her situation demonstrated that disciplinary power can have threadbare patches, not because subjects are not adversely affected by the convergence of law and medicine, but in the ways they are impacted. Discomforting details expose the way norms might be regulated in clinical terms at the same time that they show the limits of a normalizing gaze, the way care can fail (if it did) in the space between averted gazes—blind spots—and overly attentive ones—surveillance. They show that legal, clinical, and kinship structures may impact subjects less by sharing the enforcement of norms, intentionally or accidentally, than in contradictions and unlikely convergences, ways that are diffuse and involuted, fragmenting the possible positions a person might occupy, the possible stories she might tell about herself.
>
> . . . This form of power may be disciplinary, but it is also power in and of disintegration—the disintegrating ability to know, the disintegrating ability to name, the disintegrating ability to find a coherent subject, all in the spaces in which something—knowing,

naming—is reached for. It happens through the limits of diagnosis—at its verges, performing less the infrastructural work of scaf-
folding norms than the more caustic work of showing norms to be
fungible and intimacies vulnerable. (Pinto 2012: 138)

And, I would now add, allowing for the possibility that hope can be a
hollow undertaking involving some degree of self-deception.

When Lata came to Nehru, a young woman had been staying on the ward
for nearly two months. Hema, brought in as a "destitute" by the police,
was under magistrate order to receive psychiatric care. The social workers
located her parents, and though they had asked to take their daughter
home, doctors, worried that Hema's parents would neglect her, refused,
referring to the court order stating that doctors' permission was required
for Hema to be released. Threatened with a fine if they did not care for
their daughter on the ward, her mother and father alternated days in the
hospital.

Prior to coming onto the unit, Hema's life had involved movements
toward and away from home. Treated for schizophrenia, she spent six years
on and off antipsychotic medications, during which time she often left
home, sometimes quietly wandering off to return days later, sometimes in
dramatic escapes, jumping from the roof. Earlier in the year, she disappeared at a Kali temple during an outing with her mother. Twenty days
passed before Hema's parents filed a missing person report. Four months
later, the police picked her up wandering in a neighborhood far from home
and brought her to Nehru. As well as signs of mental illness, Hema had
symptoms of a sexually transmitted disease, and residents suspected she
had been sexually assaulted. She did not communicate, was emotionless
and unreactive, but slept normally. For fifteen days, she stayed on the ward
while residents tried to glean information about her family. "There was
nothing wrong really," Virinder said, "She ate, dressed, bathed, nothing
wrong except she did not communicate. She only said, 'I will not go
home.'"

After our first meeting, I wrote in my notes that Hema appeared "sad
and angry, in a pink embroidered *selwar-kameez*, laying on the bed and not
looking at us, not wanting to get up either. Her feet were peeling badly on
the soles, and her mother seemed concerned about that. [The resident] said
that it was from poor washing, and they said, no, she is washing well. [He]

asked her to get up and walk and she refused, and when they tried to pull her up to her feet she yelled out and flailed her arms. Otherwise, she was quiet and sullen looking."

When her parents were found and past prescriptions provided, doctors gave Hema a diagnosis of "thought disorder" and treated her with antipsychotics and ECT. The drugs had little effect, and though there were initial signs of improvement with ECT, after the sixth application, her condition deteriorated. She had begun speaking but now stopped; she had started bathing herself but now refused to leave her bed. Doctors changed her medication from olanzapine and risperidone to clozapine. Seeing no improvement, they wondered if her drug resistance indicated advanced syphilis.

When the festival of Holi came around, the doctors gave Hema's parents permission to take her home. After a few days, however, her parents brought Hema back in a wretched state. Nearly catatonic, she had stopped eating, bathing, and communicating, urinated in her clothing, and lay in bed, awake but unresponsive. Dr. C. asked if something had happened at home. With evident anger, he reminded her mother of events. "A girl, twenty-six, unmarried, meets the police. There has been no FIR [first incidence report], no complaint. The police take her to hospital, the family doesn't worry, we think the courts sent her here to get a test. She went home for Holi, came back worse. Did people in the family say something to her?"

"No, she had a fever."

"There is no connection between fever and mental problem. So what happened in those three days after Holi? I'm not blaming you, but I have to tell you what is in my mind. Why is there tension? Is she not loved at home?"

As residents tried to determine if Hema's psychosis was the result of external or internal causes, they began to note her father's strangely overattentive behavior. He even bathed her, they observed, and could frequently be seen touching her and rubbing her back, behaviors they found odd and inappropriate. "There is something definitely wrong with the father," Dr. C. said, "but there is no way we can really know." He advised I avoid being alone with him. As time went on and Hema's case was discussed, doctors' and residents' assertions that we could not know "what happened at Holi" or "what happened at home" came to mean just the opposite.

What we know about diagnostic categories is that they are constructed, historical, and imperfect, while they are also the currency in which medical care deals. Knowing this, we ask of contemporary life why so much about human behavior is placed on a diagnostic grid. According to Michel Foucault, "the case" and the subjects it envisions are chief products of modern power—results of the clinical gaze, systems of measuring and categorizing bodies, persons, and populations in the interest of discipline, on the one hand, and knowledge creation, on the other (2003a).

But there may also be something to be learned about things that enter the diagnostic gaze and leave it all but untouched, even as we question what cultural or political practices make us sense that "something is wrong." In Lata's case, diagnosis was layered—the clinical diagnosis fed into a legal diagnosis, both of which involved critical social diagnoses and fed the anthropological diagnosis. The same might also be said, to an extent, of Hema. Here, in the sense of "not getting it," we return to Lacan's inaugural conundrum about truth telling and the unconscious, about the impossibilities of awareness and expression, paradoxes present in all knowledge, including self-knowledge. Lacan writes, "All I can do is tell the truth. No, that isn't so—I have missed it. There is no truth that, in passing through awareness, does not lie. But one runs after it all the same" (1978: vii). At the moment at which "*one knows*" (Lacan's emphasis) oneself to be "in" the unconscious, one is severed from that knowledge by the conditions of knowing. In the vibration of perception, we move back and forth across an ontic chasm, just as Lacan, in his introductory phrases, moves back and forth across the space of the lie that plagues the effort, his and ours, to tell the truth.

The spirit of having "missed it" infused my efforts to make a case of Lata. It may do the same for other cases in a medicolegal system in which the intersection of intimacy and agency, or intimacy and violence, is at issue in the management of mental illness. As is so clear in Moksha, though postasylum mental health reform in India has taken up a language of human rights, women's movements in and out of clinics are brokered in other languages, notably those related to relationships, and legal structures related to marriage. Into this split, in which stakes are debated one way in policy and given life in others through jurisprudence, come the difficulties that Lata's stories trip over: the challenge of disentangling violence and intimacy, the uncomfortable idea that distinctions between the two can be complex and blurry. For Lata, a range of (possible, never quite certain) overlapping intimacies and violences—between mother and daughter, siblings, lovers, and others—demarcated the boundaries of pathology and, in effect, undermined them.

"Missing it" may bring certain things to light. Through symbolic and moral arrangements of gender and sexuality, in legal, medical, and social scripts, Lata's history of sexual assault was transformed into a focus on her sexual agency. Similar elisions happened more baldly in other cases, and, on rereading my own notes, I realized I had documented several cases like Hema's in which sexual violence, including violence by family members, was spoken of by being rendered unknowable. Incest was all but impossible to speak of. Evidence of sexual abuse and assault asserted itself in the clinic, in the form of young women brought in by families as well as those who were brought to Nehru as destitutes. When doctors mentioned such possibilities, they often reverted to expressions that knowledge was impossible: "We cannot know for sure." And often it was. But in reviewing my notes, I came to feel that expressions of lack of knowledge ("We cannot know what happened") were often ways of expressing the opposite sentiment ("We know just what happened").

Doctors' motivations are as complicated and layered as those of patients and their families. Freud wrote of his patient Irma, whose pains he had been unable to treat, "It occurred to me, in fact, that I was actually *wishing* there had been a wrong diagnosis" (2010 [1901]: 142). In his dream, Irma's body (her mouth) and scars (white patches) were revealed (opened) to him, indicating Freud's anxiety about determining whether her illness was hysterical or organic. At issue in the dream (which inaugurated Freud's theory of dreams as wish fulfillment) was the enterprise of diagnosis itself, the status of which emerged in layers of interpretation: in the effort to "keep at bay" interpretation, the dream's wish-fulfilling element becomes clear (1965: 151). The revealed desire (for a false diagnosis) packs itself inside the larger undertaking of dream analysis, which is inside the enterprise of diagnosis, itself within the domain of medical practice. At the kernel of nestled enterprises is anxiety over the incomplete cure and the personal desire of the diagnostician/dream interpreter/dreamer. Revelation of the dream's hidden meaning opens up a web of action, agency, and pathology, incorporating Freud, his patient Irma, and his fellow physicians. If a desire impels this dream, Freud notes, it is the larger desire of medicine.

Reading the dream of failed diagnosis alongside Marx's *Capital*, Slavoj Žižek notes a homology between dream and commodity (1989). Both are structured around levels of what can be seen or known to lie within, around a shared structure of eruption. This structure is the shape of the symptom, borne out in the product that is diagnosis, as in the interpretation of the dream. Here, knowledge of what lies beneath is defeated by its own availability. The processes of diagnosis—of deciding what is wrong by uncovering (a quiet refrain, a hidden story, the source of a symptom, the root of a dream) or exposing (the fantasy behind the symptom, a clinical act as a moral negotiation)—and the threat of breakdown it involves depend on the eruption of the symptom. This is true also for other kinds of diagnosis (criticism, for example, or deconstruction), practices that "consist in detecting a point of breakdown *heterogeneous* to a given ideological field and at the same time *necessary* for that field to achieve its closure, its accomplished form" (Žižek 1989: 21; emphasis in original).

This means that "as soon as we try to conceive the existing social order as a rational totality, we must include in it a paradoxical element which, without ceasing to be its internal constituent, functions as its symptom—subverts the very universal rational principle of this totality" (Žižek 1989:23). This structure is evident in the production of the case as well as the diagnosis. The appearance of the unlikely enacts a breakdown on that coherent account. But this is not all there is to say. In the irrational element and the story's demise are specific configurations of power. Thus, in my accounts that failed to make a case from Lata's time in Nehru, in the moments at which a story congealed, it could no longer produce a viable female subject. But in conflicting lines of failed stories, something was to be learned about sex, agency, and violence in clinical and legal circumstances in north India.

The irrational element speaks to the way configurations of power contain points at which all threatens to dissolve. In Nehru, in Freud's dream, and in my failed accounts, nondiagnosis and the knowledge found in lack of knowledge play out the same paradox: at the moments at which the authority of interpretation is assumed, the interpretation can no longer produce its own object. For Lata, sex chosen, forced, or coerced is like Irma's pains—the symptom that holds it all together and tears it all apart. Lata's case, and its failure to hold together, involves more than the limits of the language of diagnosis (its inability to account for the complexity of life, for instance). It extends to the symptomatic nature of the process itself.

Of course, Lata's time in Nehru was not a dream. Nonetheless, in different efforts to get close to experience—efforts to make a case, to say "what

is wrong"—an element of dream life drifts in. Lata's difficult story impli-
cated the authority of analysis and the social relations that go into its production, the diagnostic desire to say what, if anything, is wrong. Its
interruptions point to the way the Indian clinic involves social processes
that are built upon—even as they cannot cope with—a fractured and frac-
turing female subject. This clinical process, in the process of reaching
toward women's experience, will very frequently, by the necessities of its
own coherence, miss it.

Years later, I wrapped these difficult details into a paper, if not a case, that
would boil down and distill out details, harnessing difficulty for a larger
point, the argument; ultimately, this would become part of my tenure file
and secure me a place in the academy. My sense that Lata's case told about
the violences inherent to love (as well as violences that were just plain
violence) had become a bitter joke between myself and the man I secreted
myself away with in that difficult month. And my sense that it spoke to the
violences of the necessary—sometimes life-saving—acts of naming (as well
as more plain exploitations) grew ever more ironic as I worked my way to
job security. I only managed to complete the paper when I pulled myself
out of the morass of that relationship and when the axe of academic scrutiny—my own diagnosing—hung over me in the form of tenure review.

Recognizing the ever-thickening layers of irony, I wrote the following
words about Lata:

> It is possible to wonder if there is something at this specific junc-
> ture of dissolutions and conflicting possibilities—of law, politics,
> and critiques thereof—that, while making some subject positions
> impossible, namely a truth-telling voice at the crux of sexual agency
> and sexual victimization, also makes some rather uncomfortable
> things possible to imagine, namely the constrictions inherent to
> love, or the particular equation of suffering and pleasure that is the
> constraint of will. This is also the work of kinship; for women in
> India such improvisations may already be an integral part of normal
> life, something readily apparent in forms of expression in which
> women push back against restrictive patriarchal structures (Raheja
> and Gold 1994); in systems in which sex is exchanged for money
> and, in the process, notions of marriage unsettled, mocked, and re-
> articulated (Nanda 1999; Reddy 2005; Oldenburg 1990; Ramberg

2006), and in a range of ways women elucidate awareness of their status as objects of exchange in normative kin structures as part of the contract of love. None of these nuances, however, are so easily reckoned in the life of the law.

. . . There were many moments of care in Lata's case—between mother and daughter, Lata and her young physicians, Lata and the constable, and Lata and Faisal (to whom Lata spoke on the constable's cell phone every day). Each relationship also involved vulnerabilities, constrictions, and bad faith, moments of disintegration and periods of shoring up. For almost everyone concerned, coercion bled into what would seem to be its opposite, and freedom contained the stain of abandonment. A mother's effort to override her daughter's decision involved a protective urge even as it represented the will and well-being of the kin unit. Both husbands' coercive behavior was woven into signs of love. Clinical minuets mirrored domestic ones—dances at the crux of love's overlap with suffering and the possibilities for both in violence's need for recognition. Shared scrutinies of disordered intimacy emphasized kinship and love at their—entirely normal—points of breakdown, incipient or realized, even as they borrowed from the moral grammars of normative gender. Lata's actions and reactions not only represented an impossible subject at the juncture of gender constrictions, they may also have represented resolutions, or at least knittings, she herself employed—matters that had less to do with disciplining subjects than with getting on with life. As such, even—or especially—at their points of impasse, converging regimes of law/authority may have provided room, at the limits of diagnosis, for configurations of care and constriction, freedom and abandonment, ethics and understanding, illegible in other schemes. Indeed, Lata's illegibility—undoubtedly intentional at times—may represent an effort to make intimate life possible in its most impossible moments. (Pinto 2012: 138–139)

But then, perhaps, in that way of telling a story by telling stories, making a case by making cases, I erected even more distancing scaffolds of language, though I was trying, through that (and this) artifice, through building up rather than unearthing, to find something solid. Perhaps in so doing,

I underestimated Lata's exploitation. Perhaps I underestimated the importance of her low intelligence or her girlishness, or the role of trafficking or effects of rape. Perhaps I had inadvertently downplayed the way Lata's mother clearly—and vocally—made Faisal's religious identity part of her objections. Then again, listening again to my interviews, I wonder if I may also have discounted Lata's rational thinking—her "choice"—about sex work. Even now, as I reread my own words and revisit those of everyone involved in Lata's case, it remains clear that, once again, even in elaborating a hermeneutic of missing it, I have missed it.

Chapter 6

Ethics of Dissolution

> The amorous catastrophe may be close to what has been called, in
> the psychotic domain, an extreme situation.
> —Roland Barthes, *A Lover's Discourse* (1978)

One afternoon, Mrs. P. phoned Mrs. M. to invite us to a talk at the university by a feted alumnus, a psychiatrist relocated to the United States, where he now held a high position in a professional psychiatric organization. Arriving late, we were ushered into the packed room and shown to seats at the front as the lengthy introductions got under way. The speaker introduced his topic—threats that modernity posed to mental health. The force of his argument fell on divorce and the impact of rising divorce rates on mental well-being. The United States, a country he described as rampant with frivolous divorces, was his example, epitomized by a patient who had been "married and divorced eleven times" (a Vietnam War veteran with posttraumatic stress disorder, whose marriage habits he saw as a sign less of his disorder than of the times). Lauding India for its strong unions, he warned of lax approaches to marriage and their consequences for mental health and, indeed, the nation.

During a reception after the talk, conversation stayed close to divorce and the "cultural value" placed on marriage in India. A professor observed that in some families in the United States, parents put children in Indian schools so they keep the good habits of Indian culture. The speaker agreed. He had seen many families who, inside the home, "keep the culture, do the *pujas*, keep the traditions, they teach their children the morality and the cultural ways, and things like that in our culture we don't have this thing of eleven *shadis* [marriages]."

He went on, "Look, many people criticize the Indian marriage system, and it can be criticized, but I am actually a proponent of it. Here when you get married you get married for life. My parents were married for life, my grandparents were married for life, I am married for life, you are married for life, but over there, you see how it is. There is so much divorce, half of all marriages."

I asked the speaker about his experiences in America and said I felt his examples were extreme. "Even we [meaning Americans] would find eleven marriages to be shocking."

"It's an extreme case, but it makes the point," he said.

In the car later, I said I thought the talk had been good but that the cases were unrealistic. I doubted whether it was even possible for one person to marry so many times.

Mrs. M. and Mrs. P. said they liked the examples in spite of some exaggeration. They held the audience's attention, Mrs. P. said. "They made it spicy." This may well have been the speaker's intention; he praised what he expected were his audience's views and values.

His point of view was not unique. A short newspaper article from around that time described a campaign to raise public awareness of mental illness and quoted one of the campaign's organizers. "Ms. Justice Mishra said psychiatric illness was often caused by the breakdown of joint families, unemployment, an inferiority complex, fast pace of modern life and negative impact of modern culture" (*The Hindu* 2007). Here a familiar compression of factors associated with mental illness—modernity, family breakdown, economic malaise, a "fast"-paced life, cultural change—reiterated another myth, that families do not break down unless afflicted by large-scale social and cultural (read non-Indian) forces. In such statements was a critical turn: from individual distresses related to families that break down (because families sometimes break down), distresses that might relate to the ways the burdens of those normal breakdowns are distributed (not to their abnormality), to distresses caused by the widespread breakdown of "the Indian family," the idea, that is, that a dissolving family is a moral threat.

Not long after Eve started school, she began to talk about her desk mate, Karuna. I heard the name over and over—Karuna's lunches, the bows in Karuna's hair, how she and Karuna had failed to provide a correct answer (the definition of CPU) to "Computer Sir" and were hit on the hands with rulers. I found Karuna's mother one afternoon. Like stones amid a flood of children out the gate, Sonali and I introduced ourselves across the tide of little heads and arranged to get our daughters together to play. After our first afternoon of tea and biscuits on the rooftop veranda, we began to take morning walks around the neighborhood.

Sonali was separated from her husband, though not divorced. Hearing about my work, she had much to say. I mentioned depression (*udasi*) and said I wondered if it might have something to do with conditions in the home. This ignited her. Animatedly, she agreed: women are at home all day; they have no one to talk to, no one to share their troubles with, especially in the husband's house. "Often they can't go out, so the tension builds up in their heads and can make anyone crazy. Sometimes you feel like your head will explode."

I was reading a Hindi novel at the time about the suffering of a woman whose husband was unaffectionate and dismissive. The novel dwelt on the suffering of unactivated longing, the pain of being ignored, and the main character's efforts to find an outlet for that sorrow in artwork. I described this to Sonali, saying I thought the book was good, if heavy-handed. She said it was not an exaggeration. "Men are unlikely to return that affection, but a bit of care and human sensitivity has to be there. A husband needs to demonstrate affection for his wife in a caring way, not just to want sex at night and then ignore her during the day."

Two years earlier, after five years of marriage, Sonali had left her husband and returned to the city with Karuna. Here, they lived in an apartment with Sonali's parents, brother, and younger sister. She spent some time during the day helping out at her sister's beauty salon, but most of the time she stayed around the house. She did not have a paying job but enjoyed the time she spent at the salon.

People had told her she should get a divorce "because then I could have a second marriage" (suggesting this was the only reason to get a divorce), but she was not interested in a second marriage. "How can you explain to your child that this is your new father?"

She was happy on her own, happy as a "single mother" (for this, she used the English phrase). Her husband loved her daughter and still saw her a few times a year, but she would not go back. "He is a Hitler type," she said, strict about household conditions, uncaring and disinterested. "At the beginning it was fine, in the marriage," she said, but after five years she could no longer tolerate his domineering personality.

It was still difficult for her to be back in the city and strange to be living permanently with her parents. "No one says anything directly, but everywhere they say, 'That's the one who had a divorce.' They think badly." Even our walks were a challenge. "If I go out for a walk or something, people associate it with my not being married." Living on her own with her daughter was not an option and, in spite of "tension" caused by the close conditions, it was nice, she felt, to live with others.

Her mother thought she should return to her husband. "Men gradually change," she had told her. "They slowly get better after some time."

But, Sonali said, "If I then get a divorce after twenty years, where will I be?"

Just outside Mrs. M.'s house, a woman lived on the edge of the street. Though I first took her to be in her sixties, I later learned she was at most in her early forties. She situated herself along a perimeter wall the height of a man and defined her area with fabric—clothes on her body in layers, the bundle underneath her, a blanket around her head. On the fringe of a street thick with commerce, barbers, food sellers, and hawkers looked after her, in one way or another. A widow in one of the bungalows let her use her spigot to bathe, and shopkeepers gave her food, though they also complained about the trouble she caused—staring at customers, demanding money, yelling at passersby.

Sometimes if spoken to she said nothing. Other times she offered her hand, her name, erudite English, and her educational qualifications: "M.A. fail."

Her name was Reena, and not only did those around her look after her, they also curated her story, or parts of it, trading pieces of narrative to explain her state. As a teenager she fell in love with a boy from another religion. Both families objected to the affair, and the boy married the girl his family chose for him. After this, Reena failed her university courses and had a psychotic break. Her family took her to Nehru, where she got medical attention. But she soon relapsed and, refusing to go back to the hospital, moved onto the street a few blocks from her home. According to people in the neighborhood, her family ("a good, educated family"), had tried to convince her to come home, but she preferred to stay on the street. Reena's family eventually moved away, though a brother returned periodically to give her money. Medical students from Nehru tried to convince her to come in for treatment. She refused that, too.

As many put it, it was because of the affair that her "mind went bad." It was unclear whether the root of the trouble was the loss she suffered or the inappropriateness of the pairing. Some denied the latter, others hinted at it. Loss and improper love were as easily entwined as madness and lost love.

Doing this work, I often felt I was in a windstorm of narratives—some converging, some competing, some shaded with subtlety and edged with critique, some painted in bold strokes of fantasy. This was especially true of things related to love, marriage, or illness and unwellness—anything in which a whiff of change might be in the air. Just as there were points at which close concern with life's messier eventualities undid bold plots, at other points lines between critique and mythical discourse blurred. Taking people seriously for their critical views seemed to be just as important as being cautious about the force of familiar narratives.

A web of possible stories exists to account for the lives of women in this book. There is no disentangling them all, though it is worth pursuing some of their curious lines. Stories of progress and decay may be among the most immediate. Both were pungent in the lecture at the university. They were far less putridly present in things I was told by doctors at Nehru and in reflections shared by Ammi's family. Though they may seem to compete, progress and decay are not incompatible ideas. They often arise simultaneously, together invoking what Lawrence Cohen calls the "persistent sense of 'India' as an irrevocably split world" (2007: 105). Where love is concerned, progress overlaps with agency, and especially adheres to the idea that India is on a steady path toward "love marriages," unions freely chosen and based on romantic love, leaving behind the traditional arranged variety. This moral axis of agency—to what extent unions involve it or show its constraint—is, of course, a too-easy story at odds with the many different forms marriage can take in the gray area between "arrangement" and "love," not to mention unions that evade that binary altogether. Decay, too, can be found in the idea that with too much individual choice and too little family involvement, people become isolated, bonds become fungible, and morality declines (or in the fantasy world in which divorce does not [yet] happen in India). In both trajectories, sex and marriage add "spice" to big ideas about time and space, involving the repeated "localized invocation of a lost world" (Cohen 2007: 105).

There are ways of portraying love and madness other than those involving progress or decay, abandonment and repression. The 1969 film

Khamoshi shows a patient in a psychiatry ward made insane by lost love and healed by the attentions of a nurse who has been directed to pretend to be in love with him. As his state improves, her act becomes real, so that by the time he is well (and realizes he does not love her) *she* has gone mad. Love here is both therapeutic and undoing (with an interesting gender breakdown). It can be made and unmade, both feigned and felt. Its impact on the psyche is at home with modern clinical sterility, and its destabilizing power is juxtaposed with an ability to heal.

Another vector brings in rationality (whose orienting role in psychiatry is well documented), a culturally specific idea involving individuated personhood, clarity of perception, and notions of utility, productivity, and value (Martin 2009: 55). In principles of consent at the heart of medical ethics, the rational person, entitled to the rights of citizenship, is one whose perceptions and decision-making abilities involve unobscured neutrality (Petryna 2009). However, as Emily Martin observes among those diagnosed with bipolar disorder, distinctions between rationality and irrationality can be unclear in lives, not to mention in popular valorizations that laud the economic value of irrationality (2009).

In South Asia, across a wide range of texts and imaginaries, boundaries of rationality are crossed all the time in descriptions of love. Religious practice and poetry portray devotional love of a deity as a form of acute suffering; the position of lover to the beloved is analogous to devotee and god; and in the epics, gods go crazy with love just as people do. Stories of lovers like Leila and Majnun, and Hindu epics portray more and less permanent insanities wrought by loves lost and found. In Urdu poetry, passionate love can involve catastrophic destruction (*fanaa*) of the self (and the lovers in question), themes reflected in film plots with tragic endings (Anjaria and Anjaria 2008); and mad love is a trope in Bollywood blockbusters, rationalized through family acceptance, but celebrated in song and dance. In this formulation, romantic love is irrational but not unthinkable, desirable and dreamt about. Love can make a person crazy; crazy love is a sign of madness; neither is beyond possibility.

But rationality is not abandoned. A hint of something I call "rational love" appears (Pinto 2011). In one iteration, it makes use of the arranged/love marriage spectrum, where it lives on the side of family-chosen (arranged) unions. Here, passionate love is selfish, disordered, and disordering (and prone to breakdown), while rational love is slow-growing, stable, and self-sacrificing. But things can line up differently. The 2008 film *Love Aaj*

Kal (Love These Days) imagines two romances. In the first, set in England in an era of transnational travel and conversation by text message, partners have a "no strings attached" approach to love. Decisions are made rationally, determined by necessities of time and place. The second story, set in India in the 1960s, involves a love-struck couple whose passion overrides familial obstacles. Though initially portrayed as outmoded, logic-defying love trumps the modern, rational approach, making crazy love definitively Indian, and passion is shown to be viable and enduring.

In legal proceedings, things fall into still different places. In contested marriages, rational love is established biologically: a decision to marry can be legitimated by proof of maturity (and the rationality an adult is understood to possess). Bone testing determines age and, thus, rational consent, and psychiatric observation establishes the ability to have chosen a union in full capacity of mind (Dhanda 2000). Divorce, custody, and nullification cases depend less on a person's rationality in entering a union than on the way mental illness prohibits the ability to fulfill marital duties. In cases of fraud in marriage, medical histories determine whether a spouse had a mental illness at the time of the marriage, which would call into question the purpose of marriage, while divorces can depend on whether mental illness amounts to cruelty. In marriages contested from the outside, individuated rationality establishes the ability to choose whom to love, while marriages challenged from the inside deliberate definitions of marriage (Dhanda 2000).

Thus, women come into clinics amid imaginaries that can be loosely grouped into (at least) four categories: ideas that (1) mental illness jeopardizes intimacy, (2) love can cause madness, (3) wrong love is a sign of madness, and (4) rational love is impoverished. Each crosses continua of normal/abnormal, arranged/chosen, past/future, progress/decay, rational/irrational in different ways, and each carries different social, moral, and even political weight. Each may intercede in clinical life differently as well, participating in the ways cases are made, and differing in the impact each perspective has on decisions made along the way to the final framing of a "case."

In each is a vitalizing idea, sometimes put in medical terms, sometimes expressed in curvatures of story and memory, sometimes in anger and outburst: with attachment comes a certain agony. Others have noted that love and mental illness (not just "madness") share conditions of dissolution and loss. Roland Barthes writes, citing Donald Winnicott: "The psychotic lives in the terror of breakdown (against which the various psychoses are merely defenses). But 'the clinical fear of breakdown is the fear of a breakdown which has already been experienced (*primitive agony*).' . . . Similarly, it seems for the lover's anxiety: it is a fear of a mourning that has already occurred" (Barthes 1978: 30).

As in the scrutinies—unfinished though they may have been—in Lata's case, or Sanjana's, or of other women whose feelings about marriage became biological signs, while psychiatry may hinge on delineating what is rational about love from what is not, it also addresses love as unstable and destabilizing, defying rationality while being something less than pathological, capable of absorbing a spectrum of unusual, abnormal, or damaging behaviors and demands. In this perspective is room for a kind of acceptance of strangeness, of the different forms behavior and emotion can take, but in it may also be space and means for blocking certain realities from view, for privileging one aspect of experience over others, thereby continuing cycles of harm. In (or against) the pulse of master narratives about love and madness, the challenge is to leave space for the *jugalbandi*, the play and riffing like the musical pairings in a raga, in ways of knowing what is wrong, while sustaining the possibility for critique, even outrage.

At the university, a woman who was a professor and activist for women's rights said,

> You mention the divorced women in the psychiatry wards, but also, if you did a broad survey, in both normal and abnormal situations, you would probably find that a lot of divorced women are happier. They may have their own set of problems, but all of those deep internalized problems of the marital household, of marriage have gone away. . . . In India, so often you hear the comparison to the West, the stupid superiority about marriage. People will say, "Look over there, everyone is getting a divorce, but here we have so much less divorce, almost none." But they don't recognize the drawback of that, the suffering that goes into that, the suffering behind the facade. Maybe some marriages should not continue, but still the idea is there even among very educated people that divorce is a big problem that afflicts Western countries but not India.

She described the dependent position of women within the family, a financial and emotional condition as well as a state of identity that distances women from their own desires. Women's emotional struggles might be discounted or subordinated to family concerns, they have less ability to speak out, and they constantly suppress desires. "Those without clear psychiatric problems may be contained within the family such that either problems will go unrecognized as psychiatric or as needing treatment, or it is the family context itself that can make minor aberrations into major ones."

"Women here can't imagine living independently," she said, "So the stakes are very high."

> The anxiety is multiplied many times by the threat of losing one's children, because husbands will indeed snatch children away; in the case of a divorce, they are very likely to take them, and then a woman is in a terrible situation. Either she puts up with it, or she goes through years of long litigation that she may be in no position to go through; it is costly, it takes time, and in the meantime, years are lost. Women are almost paralyzed. Either they become mad or they become very religious. If a relationship is bad, there are only two ways: either [a woman] lives under guilt or has flourishing desires, both things make them abnormal.

A number of people, when I mentioned my research, joked that "in this country, all women are psychiatry cases." A lawyer working for a legal advocacy organization said, "All violence survivors are mental patients, in fact you can probably say that all women are mental patients." Against an overwhelming popular discourse that said that Indian marriages are strong and Indian society (and minds, souls, and families) strong because of them, was a fierce counterdiscourse that saw oppression, control, and dependency in marriage. While divorce and mental illness might be stigmatized, this view observed that it was less the case that India's strong marriage culture was under threat by Western influence than that *normal* marriage was maddening, important for many women's material survival but a source of grave distress. In this view, divorce may involve cultural shame or stigma but it may also be liberating, offering escape from difficult or dangerous conditions, freeing desires and providing new avenues for connections, as well as predicating loss. The problem is in the conditions that accompany it rather than its cultural value, conditions like the loss of custody of children, drawn-out legal processes, difficulty finding a place to live or work to do, or the disapproval of kin.

Interceding in ideas about the madness of love, feminist critiques, which state that the institution of marriage is maddening, are less interested in the way love just *is* crazy-making than in the conditions of dependency in which women live, conditions that can drive a person to illness. These views are grounded in historical considerations of the ways marriage practices relate to the economic and political configurations of colonialism and post-colonial nationalism. They note the ways existing countersocieties—of courtesans, for example—expose the constraints on movement, the dependency on men, the formulas of exchange in which women are goods which condition normative marriage (Oldenburg 1990). They debate the idea that to be feminist is to embody individualism, observing that many women— "native," "non-Western," "subaltern"—"are excluded from any share in this . . . norm" (Spivak 1985: 244). Or, conversely, they encourage legal measures to protect women's individual status (Kumar 1997; Agnes 1999). Feminist critics observe the way women in marriage (child brides, *satis*) and women on the edges of marriage (widows) have long been made pawns in larger debates about nationalism, religion, and the self-determination of men, and how they have been made signs of bigger things—religion, home, the nation (Spivak 1985; Mani 1998; Chatterjee 1993; Agnes 2011; Das 1996). Films like *Fire* portray middle-class domesticity as denying female desire, and responses challenge such portrayals as depending on limited ideas about same-sex love. Feminist scholars observe that, contrary to popular wisdom, divorced women forge new connections and build social worlds rich with movement and possibility (Aura 2006), and single mothers find myriad creative ways to build lives and families (Mehrotra 2003).

In contesting the idea that Indian feminists are, by definition, "Westernized" for rejecting cultural values defined as "Indian," Uma Narayan movingly observes that it was not her Western education that made her critical of the institution of marriage but the emotions, attitudes, and experiences of her own kin—tears she witnessed being shed, comments and stories she overheard in her own childhood home. Her mother, when criticizing her, "forgets how widespread and commonplace the cultural recognition is in India that marriage subjects daughters to difficult life situations, forgets that my childish misbehaviors were often met with the reprimand, 'Wait till you get to your mother-in-law's house. Then you will learn to behave'" (Narayan 1997: 9). For many women—activists, scholars, and others—the maddening effects of marriage, given the cultural and legal circumstances of India, remain a pressing reality.

Among critical narratives, another, more and less academic, more and less feminist theme appears from time to time, seeming to explain the desperate situations in which some women find themselves. Abandonment is an idea that interjects itself in all of the cases that appear in this book. However, though a vibrant discourse, it seldom functions here as a reliable end point of analysis. For anthropology, abandonment is an idea that works in conjunction with critical ideas about the regulation of norms; Foucauldian concepts like biopower and governmentality are grounded in the idea that modern power works through self-discipline, through real and metaphorical architectures by which people discipline themselves and each other to accommodate moral codes. Those who fail these mechanisms of surveillance may be not cast out as much as relegated to catchment areas, through the modern expressions of an asylum logic that shape everyday life and logics of care.

In India, as I have noted, discussions of mental illness often come around to abandonment, embodied by "dumped women." Many conversations about divorce—as in discussion of the plight of widows—see it primarily as a vector to abandonment rather than something from which women may benefit. Where many within and beyond contexts of activism or scholarly feminism speak of connections between mental illness and the strains of Indian marriage, academic reflections on psychiatry, in India and elsewhere, seldom verge toward the vagaries of love, or kinship and its condensations of togetherness and apartness, but lean toward the idea that medical and cultural systems protect society from the threats of the abnormal, the contagion of the disordered and violated. These ideas refract through a prism of progress. In more resistant moments they involve semi-engaged states of partial inclusion, abandonments that have liberating components and produce new intimacies in exclusion, countersocieties of sex workers, widows, and *hijras*. Or they invoke the abject, those seen as lacking society altogether—inhabitants of asylums, women on the street. Love might be posed against abandonment as redemptive and transformative or as a sign of freedom and self-fulfillment. Or, if kinship facilitates abandonment, love might be *opposed* to kinship, which is seen as an agent of order, evaluation, constraint, and exclusion.

In its intellectual genealogy, the critical idea of abandonment involves reordering notions of inside and outside, inclusion and exclusion. For

Foucault, expulsion is precisely what modern power does *not* do. He describes the seventeenth-century shift in state responses to disease from the expulsion of lepers to the regulation of plague, that is, from exclusion to quarantine and eventually therapeutics. From this emerged a logic of abnormality mediated by medicine and law, mechanisms that generated new forms and conditions for control. Focusing scrutiny on desire, these mechanisms had everything to do with "the family." Evaluations of normalcy established complicity between families and institutions, as families turned over their defective members and, in the process, reproduced the institution of the family. As the family became the site and mechanism of surveillance, it was also its field of evaluation—are people good enough for kinship? (This can be seen in the reproductive logic of eugenics.)

Foucault writes that "the norm's function is not to exclude and reject" (2003b: 50). This may not be its function, but anthropological evidence holds that this is its effect, that biopolitical mechanisms that seek to regulate life are designs for abandonment, less by casting unwanted members out of society than placing subjects into new and restricted interiors. Therapeutic structures can amount to, in João Biehl's phrase, "zones of social abandonment," receptacles for the "ex-human," those adjudicated according to notions of humanity and value (Biehl 2005). Abandonment is, like "letting die" (Foucault 1973), the end point of biopolitical triage, and has as its condition a twin crisis—confinement. In many feminist uses of concepts of normalization and control, confinement and isolation are emphasized as counterparts to abandonment—the yellow wallpaper effect (cf. Gilman 2006 [1899]). Here, homes are like asylums, and normalization converges with consumption, inclusion (in domesticity) collapses with exclusion (from public life).

From this twinning of abandonment and confinement as effects of normalizing logic comes a range of ethical stances. One, more critical and academic, is oriented toward therapeutic markets and the governing effects of intervention. Another is found in human rights language and adopts a more basic sense of abandonment, including things beyond the biopolitical purview—explicit exclusions from society, and forms of life that are anything but "bare." Though critical stances overlap, they can also be read as counterpoint: one involves an effort of deconstruction to expose abandonment where it might be masquerading as something benevolent; the other considers crises in plain sight. Both are important in showing linked-up strategies for managing life, for finding wolves in sheep's clothing.

As in these stories, there are many points at which the analytic of abandonment not only evades more liberatory and hopeful aspects of life, efforts that push against its teleologies; it also may not tell us enough about the shape of crisis. It is with the latter that I am most concerned: what understandings of conditions of life, power, and therapeutics are not possible in this framework? Here, I find Lata, Sanjana, Amina, Kavita, and Ammi, and crises both vivid and ambiguous, connections that skirt the abandonment analytic and its liberatory countergestures, or moments that summon those hermeneutics but in the final instance leave nowhere for them to stick. There is a need to explore crises, afflictions, and suffering in other terms, to seek the blurry edges of this characterization alongside the ways it may be put to use—not only by anthropologists, but by actors with a clear stake in the outcomes of its application, the doctors in Moksha, for example, or Ammi's family, Amina's daughters, or perhaps Kavita herself.

For now, though none of this absolves us of the need to consider abandonment as both an "old" social affliction and a condition of late capitalism and its therapeutic politics, I draw a dotted line around the analytic while keeping "abandonment" vivid as a term in motion, an idea with force—and, in Sanjana's case, dire effects—in the places through which it passes. In addition, I draw a dotted line around "rationality" and "normalization" as analytics, as one might around the idea that the strength of Indian society lies in the strength of Indian marriages.

In spite of the artifice involved, let us imagine a grid (another way of organizing master narratives) consisting of two intersecting axes, one a line between freedom and confinement, the other between care (or what we might also call integration or belonging) and abandonment. In these overlapping lines is a convergence of two ethical formulas—one tracing degrees of agency, the other degrees of attention. These formulas, overstated for the purposes of this exercise, are nonetheless discernible in ethical arrangements guiding psychiatric practice. Many analyses and processes arguably seek to discern where people and circumstances fall along these axes: when freedom is or should be limited, or when care (or belonging) is replaced by abandonment. At what point is involuntary commitment required? Are patients part of families and communities, or have they been discarded? Is there, in schemes of attention, a concomitant exclusion of others deemed unfit?

If we were to chart circumstances and decisions as places on this schema, we might find that a line can be overlaid on this axis tracing a

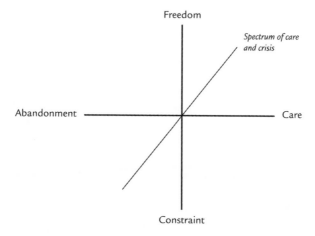

Figure 1. Ethical Grid.

spectrum between ideal conditions (in the upper right corner, at the convergence of freedom and care) and ethical crises (in the lower left, with confinement and abandonment), from sites and practices of the asylum and its worst abuses (lower left) toward community care (upper right), with the messiness of family and clinical life happening in between (Figure 1).

It is possible to see many ways in which people and institutions implicitly make use of this grid: in admissions proceedings in psychiatric institutions, in evaluations of conditions of care, in involuntary consent procedures, in negotiations of whether to institutionalize a loved one, in understanding one's own place in relation to others—spouses, children, parents, communities, the state. Such evaluations depend on the idea that movement along these axes requires schema of evaluation—of social norms, in some cases; feelings in others; actions and behaviors in others. Certainly, they can be applied to the lives of women in this book.

But, much as I try, these axes do not explain many things that happened in Moksha or Nehru, both those that had peaceable outcomes and those that felt unjust, those that settled in resolution and those that enhanced suffering. This grid is less fulfilling as a diagnostic tool in places where, while official formulas might navigate distinctions between freedom and constraint, care and abandonment, everyday practice comes up, again and again, against the limits of these axes. This is not simply to say that ideas like abandonment and freedom were fetishized or insufficient, in Moksha and Nehru, in that vague land of master narratives or in academia. Ideas of freedom, abandonment, care, constraint, integration, and confinement were more than academic abstractions; they were put to use in the ways people thought and spoke about themselves, their kin, their physicians, and their patients. What is more important to emphasize than their insufficiency is the way, were we to deploy them, they would line up in unexpected and uncomfortable ways. In practice, I observed, a zenith overlapped with a nadir, a "good" term segued into a "bad." This was not the case with the terms at the opposite ends of the spectra; that is, it wasn't that distinctions between freedom and constraint grew blurry, or care deteriorated into abandonment, but rather the end points of different continua seemed to collapse into each other. Freedom became difficult to distinguish from abandonment, integration from constraint. In practice, certain abstractions were difficult to tell apart, and people worked to make sense of the slippage. Different questions become pertinent: Where does freedom end and abandonment begin? What arrangement of care/constraint, or freedom/abandonment can a person bear? How might a person inhabit spaces of integration and control?

This category collapse happened both in relationships and in clinical practice. It happened, especially, when those things overlapped (though each axis pertains to both clinical and family life). Thus, in women's psychiatric care in north India, work—of knowing, treating, and living—involved relationships and therapeutics simultaneously, but this work happened other than where ethical arrangements (and academic apparatuses for understanding them) might turn our attention. The vitally important work of finding a way through a life with others, and of illness and healing, happened at points at which freedom and abandonment, or care and confinement were not easily distinguished. This was a choreography that families and clinics shared. Indeed, when I locate the circumstances of Sanjana, Ammi, Lata, and others on our grid, I find they trace a diagonal perpendicular to the one tracing asylum abuses to community care; that is, the line runs from lower right to upper left (Figure 2). Along this line, our original two axes collapse, but not in a way in which "good" converges with "good" and "bad" with "bad."

This line involves important ethical work, work to make right, to do good. It is also a location of crises, some old and seemingly familiar—long-term involuntary commitment, the enforcing of moral and kinship norms, the eclipsing of certain violences—and others harder to locate, such as Ammi's solitary and florid existence, Lata's uncertain illness.

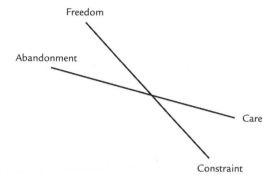

Figure 2. Ethics in Action.

These are also spaces of love stories and stories of love come undone, of overlapping dissolutions of minds and relations. They are spaces of divorce as liberating and as crushing, of parenthood as vulnerable and tenuous, of exploitation masquerading as affection, of recognition as a justification for exclusion, of rehabilitation as aloneness, and of long-ended marriages curiously continuing in the happenstances of old age. Importantly, we can feel in them the consequences of kinship's vulnerabilities for women. Though we are not excused from the need to talk about abandonment, or freedom and self-determination, or undue constraint, thinking in a collapsed grid, we can see that in times of breakdown people navigate forces in their lives along axes other than those by which care is typically evaluated. Freedom or even self-determination may not be clear indexes of the "good." Constraint may indicate more than limitation. For women in north India, these blurry lines are negotiated all the time. Freedom comes with a whiff of abandonment. A woman unmoored, "free" from kin, is threatening; what might be called "independence" might be a lonely, sad existence, while integration in family life does not come without constraint. Some of these overlaps involve systematic social conditions about which we might be concerned, things we might like to see changed; some are the stuff of life with others; all are shared improvisations of kinship, illness, wellness, and medicine.

In this exercise in artifice and interpretation we nonetheless come to a different way of accounting for "what is wrong," an alternate set of explanations for things immediately legible as crises and those in the grayer areas.

And so, another argument follows: efforts and movements related to women's mental illness in India are not, or not only, about managing what is deemed abnormal so much as they involve coping with aspects of life that are very normal, if in heightened form. When clinical and familial negotiations coincide at the points at which freedom and abandonment, and care and constraint collapse, the work of knowing relations coexists with efforts involving their intense, but seldom abnormal, dissolutions. This is not to say they do not involve desperate circumstances, crises, and abuses. But these are not necessarily generated by motivations of normalization or according to grids of legibility.

Judith Butler asks, in a discussion of the play *Antigone*'s relevance for the contemporary governance of intimacy, "What new schemes of intelligibility make our loves legitimate and recognizable, our losses true losses?" (2002: 24). In such schemes, Butler suggests, lie a confluence of knowing (or establishing as knowable) and governing relations and, by extension, of establishing as knowable forms of loss and desire. In Moksha, Nehru, and households, in the aura of stigma, or things like it, where emotions come under scrutiny for their disruptive and defective capacities, we may encounter attempts to enforce the limits of permissible love (and permissible states of being). In doctors' efforts, this might appear as legitimization of forms of being and loving or of the production of a threatening domain beyond recognition. For families it might involve ways of being that disrupt normative conditions of kinship. We might ask how biopolitical arrangements allow and disallow forms of life (Foucault 1990), and, at the same time, "how . . . kinship secures the conditions of intelligibility by which life becomes livable" (Butler 2002: 3).

But another approach to intimacy and distress focuses attentions less on recognizing "right" and "wrong" relations than on the kinds of knowledge that emerge from relations in general. Into this might fall a range of modes, mores, and meanings of recognition. Indeed, "recognition" might be seen to be an inconsistent presence, involving different sets of actions and perceptions. In India, this may mean, much as Cohen argues in locating the idea of "bad families" in accounts of senility, that critical understanding comes less by looking at the maintenance of the ideal family in Indian cultural terms, or notions of right and wrong, legitimate and illegitimate love, than at how, why, by what means, and with what consequences bonds fall apart, not as a break from Indian ideals or a decline into Westernized modernity, but as something at once banal and complex (Cohen 1999).

According to Marilyn Strathern, contemporary scientific practice and Euro-American kinship share a cultural project in which knowledge is based on "relationality," that is, "know[ing] things by their dependence on other things" (2005: 12), using relations "to explore relations" (2005: 7). Pairing kin and clinical work somewhat differently than the Foucauldian model, and yet again differently from Butler's interest in formulas for recognition and legitimacy, Strathern shows clinical knowledge and kinship to share negotiations of interdependence and knowability, in a range of forms of varying causes and effects. Here, "recombinant kinship" replaces the idea of "the family" as a fixed entity with the patterned messiness and messy patterns of love, duty, relatedness, and future making; with condensations and dissipations, layering and fissioning, restorations and ruptures, knitting and fraying.

Though elements differ, there is a method in this for thinking about the ethical dimensions of psychiatry and kin life in north India. Such an approach allows us to focus on how relational knowing (in scrutinies of Sanjana's emotions and Lata's relationships, in narrations of Ammi's life, in Amina's daughters' sense of her progress) and recombinant relations (in the changing configurations of Ammi's family, in Amina's remade family life, in Lata's tenuous arrangements) involve the normal work of dissolving bonds. Indeed, kinship seen as recombinant allows room for divorce and other dissolutions to be seen not solely as wrong, stigmatized, or posed against the (intact, Indian) family, but as part of the family's moving fibers.

At the same time, this shared dance of unbinding and remaking, of knowing things through relations in motion, brings to light unevenly distributed burdens. In circumstances in which divorce and illness mean that women lose contact with children, there are no intermediary care facilities, and women are overwhelmingly dependent on male kin, women bear dire consequences of relations' undoing. It is not just the stigma of divorce or mental illness, or the wrongness of their loves, that intervene in women's psychiatric care, it is, perhaps more trenchantly, the forces and effects of dissolution that establish the gendered stakes of mental illness.

Whereas Butler asks what forms of attention, legal and clinical, are paid to those who "confound" the norms of kinship (Butler 2002: 24), in Moksha, Nehru, and elsewhere we are pressed to ask something different: what forms of living emerge for those situated at the point of kinship's (never quite nonnormative) dissolution, not for the way they defy its norms, but for how they bear the effects of its undoings? While clinical scrutiny of love and marriage may have a place in psychiatry's disciplinary attentions to women, it does so unevenly, less as an aim than an effect, embedded in other goals and contingencies.

Or we might take things from the opposite direction to see in expressions that appear to push the limits of "normal" behavior (and people did use the word "normal" all the time) the outcome, more than the cause, of the precariousness of relations, of the way things always threaten to go to pieces.

Or, recalling Sanjana and Lata, we can make an even stronger argument: the clinical mustering of the *idea* that certain people are abandoned on the basis of their stigmatized status or illegible love has the effect of effacing women's needs, desires, and concerns about their own lives. Indeed, it can efface the possibility that they might imagine establishing an independent existence. In contexts in which marriage is both a clinical tool and an idiom of social embeddedness (the opposite of abandonment), women's life possibilities are delimited by clinical recourse to abandonment or normalization as explanations and critical tools: "We keep her here because her family won't have her."

There is a need to sustain skepticism about the liberatory gestures of accounts of medicine that depend on an analytic of abandonment, say, or to invocations of unilateral visions of Indian culture, either its "treatment of women" or its "strong families." In troubling ideas about secrecy and exposure, Eve Sedgwick expressed displeasure with Foucault's repression hypothesis (the idea that the nineteenth century, rather than being a time of repression, was an era of flourishing discourse on sex, a flourishing that amounted to a new form of disciplinary power) and its deferred liberatory promise: "I knew what I wanted from it: some ways of understanding human desire that might be quite to the side of prohibition and repression, that might hence be structured quite differently from the heroic, 'liberatory,' inescapably dualistic righteousness of hunting down and attacking prohibition/repression in all its chameleonic guises" (Sedgwick 2003: 10). This discomfort can be extended to the liberatory promise of unencumbered desire and unsurveilled integration that may result from (if not be present in) applications of Foucauldian theories of biopower to medical practice, to hunting down and attacking abandonment in all its chameleonic appearances. Thinking, then, to the side of regulation and askew of abandonment, I find myself drawn again and again to other movements, to metaphors of breakdown, and to the idea that there might be an ethic to be found in and by way of dissolution.

In the introduction, I described a threefold set of breakdowns—of minds/bodies, relationships, and narratives—suggesting that crises in women's psychiatric care can be approached in their simultaneity. On our revised ethical grid, locations of category collapse can also be those of breakdown and, thus, of intensified life, stakes, and conditions. While one inclination would be to look at the ways things are rebuilt, or rehabilitated, I find it is useful to pause in dissolution, to imagine it less as an aberration from which people seek to recover than as a condition in its own right, incipient or realized, to focus on the habitation of breakdown as much as (or more than) on making anew (or remaking).

These are also locations of the specific form of kin work that is storytelling, which brings this discussion to less concrete but no less consequential considerations, to dissolutions of language and to another question I opened with: why does care for women with mental illness in India produce crises in narration, stories that fail to hold together? For Sanjana and Amina, narration was unstable because of the instabilities and unevenness of clinical efforts, particularly those related to "delusion"; for Kavita it was unstable because of the way her disorder was itself rendered a disturbance of truth telling; for Lata it was unstable because of conflicting diagnostic narratives about sexuality, violence, and truth; for Ammi it was unstable because of the momentary, contingent, and multiple ways of establishing a story as a form of relating. And, so, I turn now to more esoteric language, language that, while "lost in its own language games" draws together fields of dissolution into something like an ethic, or at least a method for understanding.

I see two approaches. The first comes from applications of psychoanalysis to systems of power. Let us revisit Lacan's conundrum of truth telling, the way knowledge of what lies beneath can fail in its moment of consolidation. Lacan's esoteric comments interrogate the value of the analytic act of uncovering, locating the structuring of awareness in efforts to know, and finding a particular and valuable kind of understanding in the epistemological void of "missing it," in knowledge's inevitable dissolution at its point of accomplishment. This is a position not unlike that described by Donna Haraway as "situated knowledge" (1988), but with a perhaps more cynical sheen, addressing the partialness and contestation of knowledge, but leaning most heavily on failures to know and knowledge's inevitable structures of deception. Going beyond the fact of dissolution to the means of dissolving, explanations find conditions of dissolution to be revelatory of specific forces. Here, knowledge is constituted *through*, not against, "missing it," and impossible stories help us interrogate structures for knowing. They tell us about the stories that diagnosticians (including this feminist anthropologist) tell themselves. In this frame, when it comes to accounts of "what is wrong," dissolution is a condition of both existence and knowledge, one whose structure can be read for its structuring elements. We might imagine accounts (explanations, diagnoses, ethnographies) as movements, rather than things, and the process of storytelling as enclosing (rather than closure). In every case discussed here are such asymptotic processes, unfinished movement in tension with the finality it reaches for.

In asking what is at stake in our ethnographic worlds, as we are rightly urged to do (Kleinman and Kleinman 1991), we may, through our best intentions and efforts, place a particular demand on those worlds, one that depends on a certain degree of truth telling and coherence. Such a demand, feminist ethnographers caution, should also recognize lying and concealment as tactics (Visweswaran 1994), and see ligaments of repression, protection, or desire reaching from psyches into speech. Likewise, as Arthur and Joan Kleinman point out in their seminal essay, there is a negotiated quality to stakes, something temporal and immediate (1991). In all of this, ethnographic truths spoken to power may not live on the surfaces of what is spoken or perceived, or might not be solely in the depths, what is uncovered through fathoms or beautifully described. There might be much to learn about the conflicting nature of stakes from accounts that flutter but fail to take flight—that obfuscate, contradict, and fall apart—and much to gain from the conditions of those dissolutions.

A second way of thinking about the dissolution of stories (like minds and relations) relates to things more phenomenological and aesthetic than to structures of knowledge or motivation. As I have referred to throughout these chapters, Deleuze's early writing on twentieth-century film pursues the epistemological status of representations that are indirect, plural, unclear, or condensed. He describes film as offering means of representation that locate truth in unsteady images, and narration as a thing of dissipation, as dissolving established relationships between time and movement and story and completion, and replacing chronological narrative with an intensity of aural and visual episodes (1989: 22). In contrast with the sense, as in Ricoeur, of narrative as offering order, reason, and meaning to chaos,

Deleuze described representations that disorder and destabilize. Neither truth nor knowledge are legible here, and in overturning the relationship of language to truth, "description stops presupposing a reality and narration stops referring to a form of the true" (1989: 133); "the real and the imaginary, the actual and the virtual, chase after each other, exchange their roles and become indiscernible" (1989: 127).

How do we locate this approach to the dissolution of narrative, and its epistemological possibilities, in the lives described here? If the structural breakdown of coherent knowledge (the psychoanalytic epistemology of "missing it") allows us to gain a better sense of Lata's time in Nehru, something slightly different is gained in thinking about Sanjana, Amina, and Ammi. In the crafting of these cases, clinical truths, legal truths, kinship truths, and ethnographic truths were produced through flows of unstable time and language. That instability pointed to other conditions that shaped lives and stories—the breakdowns of kinship and love, the delicate space between abandonment and freedom, clinical ways and circumstances. There were things that were true and knowable in each case but that appeared only in relief, by peripheral vision.

In parallax, specific social conditions come into view, especially in the *ways* that narration might be separate from action or dissipated across narrators (Deleuze 1989: 101). In Moksha, this involved truths formed amid the instability of language to tell it, breaches between what doctors said and what was possible for patients. These involved fewer aberrations from clinical procedure than they did forms for clinical practice. The many ways people spoke about Ammi showed that "knowing" Ammi was itself a kind of rehabilitation, but one conditioned more by perpetual dissolutions and reconfigurations of kinship and stories than by the perceived abnormality of mental illness. In both contexts, while truth was at stake, it was at the same time emptied of its value.

Importantly, this is not only the mode of the artist (or the mad); it is also the language of the clinic. It brings to mind the collapse of the actual and virtual felt in wards or in doctors' and clinicians' speech, suggesting this to be a kind of habituated form. Thus, Deleuze's descriptions of narrative dissolution are not to be mistaken for the "right" or "good." Rather, they provide a locus of attention, a method for perceiving, access to crises as much as to possible ways of being and telling. Whereas in the psychoanalytically inclined approach to dissolution, articulating stakes might involve acts of power, in the sense of dissolution offered by Deleuze, stakes may come to light as incomplete and momentary emergences. Or they may not "come to light" at all so much as be visible through layered optics in which distortion is a kind of truth and description tells something other than "what happened."

An ethical perspective attentive to dissolution addresses selfhood and relations as matters of movement, condensation, and dissipation rather than points of arrival. It is not just a method for knowing but also one for writing. Some circumstances might call less for an effort to "tell the whole story" than the creation of gaps, breaks, and absences. This involves a more effortful approach, one that doesn't so much show as push cases to their inevitable incompletion, one that "introduces voids" and "rarifies the image" (Deleuze 1989: 21). For me, in finding my way through the overlapping dissolutions I encountered in homes and wards, in making ethical sense of them, representations had to not only find (or account for) but make (or at least widen) holes, especially in the places where seamless wholes might be attempted. Doing so told me about the contexts I was exploring. It told me about crisis; it helped me come closer, if never to arrive at, "what was wrong."

An even more fundamental condition of language became relevant in not only looking at layered dissolutions but trying to account for them in writing. Writing in and of catastrophe involves, as Maurice Blanchot observes, a "writing that is the end (without end) of knowledge, the end of myths, the erosion of utopia" (1995: 47). It involves "experience of the loss of the mastery of the self" (Blanchot 1993: 9). Ethical positions must begin, Blanchot observed, from this notion of writing, or language, as inherently a form of loss (a kind of eternal "missing it"; 1993: 3). Here, as in creating holes, is an effort to rethink the valorization of narrative, to ask that "words cease to be arms, . . . means of salvation," to find in writing the habitation, rather than conquering, of "disarray" (1995: 11).

Ultimately, ethics of dissolution are found in overlapping spaces where things come undone, not in their shoring up but in the ways undoing happens and how it is inhabited. This involves evaluating crises as layered undoings—the undoing of language relates to the undoing of relations, which relates to the undoing of states of being. It is specific, ethnographic work, a tool for locating small, detailed, and possible causes rather than grand and overarching schemes. And so, in the spirit of small explanations, in these cases, at the end of the asylum in India an ethic of dissolution draws us to the following recognition. By way of psychiatric care, women in India bear dire consequences of dissolved bonds and the ends of love. Such dissolutions involve the way relationships are at stake in other relationships. They speak to a larger vulnerability in women's position in kinship arrangements. This includes the burdens women bear of the precariousness of kinship in general (rather than the way certain forms are established through the recognition of legitimate life). These vulnerabilities are deftly interwoven with mental illnesses; each ratchets up the effects of the other.

In making sense of both the big disasters and the murk of what is livable, an ethic of dissolution accounts not only for right and wrong, legible and illegible forms of love, but also for the ways love can be crazy, catastrophic, and undoing. It considers the habitation of dissolution not just as efforts to shore up or stave off undoing. And the dissolution of stories around love and madness shows genuine crises (both obvious and ambiguous) to be less the result of normalization, stigma, or ostracism than of a million moments of more and less ordered, more and less managed, more and less attended to dissolutions of selves, relationships, and efforts to tell about them, in which conditions of precariousness are part of what it means, for women especially, to be bound to others. At their most dire, such conditions can allow and entrench violence and containment. In other moments, there may be in them room for peace and expressions of outrage, for new bonds, even friendship, and new kinds of movement, even dance.

But something remains elusive. In an ethic of dissolution, perhaps this is just it. There is little solace and no liberatory potential in seeking small details and conditions, only context and content in the inevitability of dissolution. The task at hand is just to disarticulate the ways dissolution is inhabited, the forms it takes, the conditions it sets, to observe how the process of reaching for—freedom, care, love, relationships—is filled in with action as things come undone, and how undoing impacts people in different ways. In this, too, for all concerned, there is room for the self-deception involved in movements and decisions, for the limits of the mastery of the self. In it is a sense of ethics as asymptote, of effort that is a kind of habitation, of movements toward intimacy (or freedom, or self-knowledge, or other-knowledge) and the nagging sense one can never really accomplish it, not without large and small catastrophes along the way. But we try to get as close as we can.

One afternoon, in all likelihood when I had returned from Moksha, though my notes give no indication, Eve and I were called to the courtyard where a mango-wood fire had been built, faded cushions arranged, and photographs of Mrs. M.'s late husband strung with garlands of night queen. Mrs. M.'s middle-aged daughter, visiting from Delhi, and Mrs. P. gathered for a *havan*, a purification rite marking Mrs. M.'s husband's birthday. Mrs. M. sat on a mattress higher than the rest, her red eyes to the fire and Sanskrit, her billowed and sheltering back to the picture on the shelf, to the night queen garlanding a face whose round youth was obscured by wings of mustache. She smiled shyly from atop a body like a mountain.

We were all wives or widows, all but Eve and the priest readying the fire, though I knew myself to be a secret half-wife and grew anxious about my playacting, worried about my ability to spoil the ceremony with brokenness.

Synchronized with the priest's syllables, we threw shaved sandalwood and sugar into the fire and watched as droplets of ghee and water cast from our fingertips burst into tiny feather bombs of steam. I wondered what thoughts we threw into the fire with them—recollections, perhaps, of things like expectation and regret. We heard about Ram and Sita, and betrayal and loyalty, exile, abduction, return, and trials by fire. The priest talked about difficulty, how life needs death as day needs dark and moving needs ceasing. I watched the bursts of spark as splinters fell into the fire, and noticed the shavings that missed the sacrifice and gathered on the floor.

A certain convention of ethnographic writing now says I should finish the story, and return to what happened next, to an arrival or a departure, foolishness or learning, broken loves or new ones, and, especially, to the ever-sustaining light that is Eve or the one soon to come who, as I write, dances against my insides.

But better, perhaps, to introduce a final void, an inhale of invention alongside those I have exhaled along the way, neither to invoke the idea that there is a more "true" truth, a more real reality in the lives of the women I write about, nor to suggest that all I have is my own (or anyone's) experience. In this sink of stories of love and dissolution is also a cistern of selves, of artifice, effort, and resignation, and catastrophe and calm in the idea that there may well be some truth to be told, though not one that does not lie, or connections to be made with others, though not ones that can ever be fully accomplished.

"But one runs after it all the same."

Bibliography

Abrams, Minnie. *The Baptism of the Holy Ghost and Fire.* Maharashtra: Pandita Ramabai Mission, 1906.

Abse, D. Wilfred. *Diagnosis of Hysteria.* Bristol: John Wright and Sons, 1950.

Addlakha, Renu. *Deconstructing Mental Illness: An Ethnography of Psychiatry, Women
and the Family.* New Delhi: Zubaan, 2008.

Agamben, Giorgio. *Homo Sacer: Sovereign Power and Bare Life.* Trans. Daniel Heller-
Roazen. Stanford: Stanford University Press, 1998.

———. *State of Exception.* Trans. Kevin Attell. Chicago: University of Chicago Press,
2005.

Agnes, Flavia. *Law and Gender Inequality: The Politics of Women's Rights in India.*
Oxford: Oxford University Press, 1999.

———. "From *Shah Bano* to *Kausar Bano*: Contextualizing the 'Muslim Woman'
Within a Communalized Polity." In *South Asian Feminisms.* Ed. Anika Loomba
and Ritty A. Lukose, 33–53. Durham: Duke University Press, 2011.

Akhtar, Salman, and Pratyusha Tummala-Narra. "Psychoanalysis in India." In *Freud
Along the Ganges: Psychoanalytic Reflections on the People and Culture of India.* Ed.
Salman Akhtar, 3–25. New York: Other Press, 2008.

Anjaria, Ulka, and Jonathan Shapiro Anjaria. "Text, Genre, Society: Hindi Youth Films
and Postcolonial Desire." *South Asian Popular Culture* 6, no. 2 (2008): 125–140.

Attewell, Guy N. A. *Refiguring Unani Tibb: Plural Healing in Late Colonial India.* Hyd-
erabad: Orient Longman, 2007.

Aura, Siru. "Agency at Marital Breakdown: Redefining Hindu Women's Networks and
Positions." In *Culture, Power and Agency: Gender in Indian Ethnography.* Ed. Lina
Fruzzetti and Sirpa Tenhunen, 171–203. Kolkata: Stree, 2006.

Barthes, Roland. *A Lover's Discourse.* Trans. Richard Howard. New York: Hill and
Wang, 1978.

Benjamin, Jessica. "The Primal Leap of Psychoanalysis, from Body to Speech: Freud,
Feminism, and the Vicissitudes of the Transference." In *Storms in Her Head: Freud
and the Construction of Hysteria.* Ed. Muriel Dimen and Adrienne Harris, 31–64.
New York: Other Press, 2001.

Berkeley-Hill, Owen. "The Anal-Erotic Factor in the Religion, Philosophy, and Character of the Hindus." *International Journal of Psychoanalysis* 2 (1921): 306–338.

Biehl, João. *Vita: Life in a Zone of Social Abandonment.* Berkeley: University of California Press, 2005.

Blanchot, Maurice. *The Infinite Conversation.* Trans. Susan Hanson. Minneapolis: University of Minnesota Press, 1993.

———. *The Writing of the Disaster.* Trans. Ann Smock. Lincoln: University of Nebraska Press, 1995.

Blavatsky, Helena P. *The Secret Doctrine.* London: Theosophical Society, 1888.

Butler, Judith. *Antigone's Claim: Kinship Between Life and Death.* New York: Columbia University Press, 2002.

Carstairs, G. M., and R. L. Kapur. *The Great Universe of Kota: Stress, Change and Mental Disorder in an Indian Village.* Berkeley: University of California Press, 1976.

Chatterjee, Partha. *The Nation and Its Fragments: Colonial and Postcolonial Histories.* Princeton: Princeton University Press, 1993.

Clément, Catherine, and Julia Kristeva. *The Feminine and the Sacred.* Trans. Jane Marie Todd. New York: Columbia University Press, 2003.

Cohen, Lawrence. *No Aging in India: Alzheimer's, the Bad Family, and Other Modern Things.* Berkeley: University of California Press, 1999.

———. "Song for Pushkin." *Daedalus* 136, no. 2 (2007): 103–115.

Corin, Ellen, Rangaswami Thara, and Ramachandran Padmavati. "Living Through a Staggering World: The Play of Signifiers in Early Psychosis in South India." In *Schizophrenia, Culture, and Subjectivity: The Edge of Experience.* Ed. Janis Hunter Jenkins and Robert John Barrett, 110–145. Cambridge: Cambridge University Press, 2004.

Curtis, Heather. *Faith in the Great Physician: Suffering and Divine Healing in American Culture, 1860–1900.* Baltimore: Johns Hopkins University Press, 2007.

———. "A Sane Gospel: Radical Evangelicals, Psychology, and Pentecostal Revival in the Early Twentieth Century." *Religion and American Culture: A Journal of Interpretation* 21, no. 2 (2011): 195–226.

Dangar-Daly, Claud. "The Psychology of Revolutionary Tendencies." *International Journal of Psychoanalysis* 11 (1930): 193–210.

Daniel, E. Valentine. *Fluid Signs: Being a Person the Tamil Way.* Berkeley: University of California Press, 1987.

Das, Veena. *Critical Events: An Anthropological Perspective on Contemporary India.* Delhi: Oxford University Press, 1996.

———. "The Signature of the State: The Paradox of Illegibility." In *Anthropology in the Margins of the State.* Ed. Veena Das and Deborah Poole, 225–252. Santa Fe: School of American Research Press, 2004.

———. *Life and Words: Violence and the Descent into the Ordinary.* Berkeley: University of California Press, 2006.

Das, Veena, and Renu Addlakha. "Disability and Domestic Citizenship." In *Disability in Local and Global Worlds*. Ed. Benedicte Ingstad and Susan Reynolds Whyte, 128–148. Berkeley: University of California Press, 2007.

Das, Veena, and Ranendra K. Das. "Pharmaceuticals in Urban Ecologies: The Register of the Local." In *Global Pharmaceuticals: Ethics, Markets, Practices*. Ed. Adriana Petryna, Andre Lakoff, and Arthur Kleinman, 171–205. Durham: Duke University Press, 2006.

Davar, Bhargavi V. *Mental Health of Indian Women: A Feminist Agenda*. New Delhi: Sage, 1999.

Deleuze, Gilles. *Cinema*, volume 2, *The Time-Image*. Trans. Hugh Tomlinson and Robert Galeta. Minneapolis: University of Minnesota Press, 1989.

Deleuze, Gilles, and Félix Guattari. *Anti-Oedipus: Capitalism and Schizophrenia*. Minneapolis: University of Minnesota Press, 1983.

Dempster, Elizabeth. "Women Writing the Body: Let's Watch a Little How She Dances." In *Bodies of the Text: Dance as Literature, Literature as Dance*. Ed. Ellen W. Goellner and Jacqueline Shea Murphy, 20–38. New Brunswick: Rutgers University Press, 1995.

Derrida, Jacques. *Specters of Marx*. New York: Routledge, 1994.

Desjarlais, Robert. *Shelter Blues: Sanity and Selfhood Among the Homeless*. Philadelphia: University of Pennsylvania Press, 1997.

Devereux, George. *From Anxiety to Method in the Behavioral Sciences*. The Hague: Mouton, 1967.

Dhanda, Amita. *Legal Order and Mental Disorder*. London: Sage, 2000.

Didi-Huberman, Georges. *Invention of Hysteria: Charcot and the Photographic Iconography of the Salpêtrière*. Trans. Alisa Hartz. Cambridge: MIT Press, 2003.

Doniger, Wendy. *The Bedtrick: Tales of Sex and Masquerade*. Chicago: University of Chicago Press, 2000.

Dube, K. C. "Unlocking of Wards, an Agra Experiment." *Indian Journal of Psychiatry* 5, no. 1 (1963): 2–7.

Ecks, Stefan. "Pharmaceutical Citizenship: Antidepressant Marketing and the Promise of Demarginalization in India." *Anthropology and Medicine* 12, no. 3 (2005): 239–254.

Ernst, Waltraud. *Mad Tales from the Raj: The European Insane in British India, 1800–1858*. New York: Routledge, 1991.

———. "Colonial Lunacy Policies and the Madras Lunatic Asylum in the Early Nineteenth Century." In *Health, Medicine and Empire: Perspectives on Colonial India*. Ed. Biswamoy Pati and Mark Harrison, 137–164. New Delhi: Orient Longman, 2001.

———. "Madness and Colonial Spaces—British India, c. 1800–1947." In *Madness, Architecture and the Built Environment: Psychiatric Spaces in Historical Context*. Ed. Leslie Topp, James E. Moran, and Jonathan Andrews, 215–238. New York: Routledge, 2007.

Esdaile, James. *Mesmerism in India and Its Practical Application in Surgery and Medicine.* London: Longman, Brown, Green, and Longmans, 1846.

Fabrega, Horacio. *History of Mental Illness in India: A Cultural Psychiatry Perspective.* Delhi: Motilal Banarsidass, 2009.

Fassin, Didier, and Richard Rechtman. *The Empire of Trauma: An Inquiry into the Condition of Victimhood.* Trans. Rachel Gomme. Princeton: Princeton University Press, 2009.

Flueckiger, Joyce Burkhalter. *In Amma's Healing Room: Gender and Vernacular Islam in South India.* Bloomington: Indiana University Press, 2006.

Foster, Susan Leigh. "An Introduction to Moving Bodies: Choreographing History." In *Choreographing History.* Ed. Susan Leigh Foster, 3–24. Bloomington: Indiana University Press, 1995.

Foucault, Michel. *History of Sexuality*, volume 1. New York: Verso, 1973.

———. "Of Other Spaces." *Diacritics* 16, no. 1 (1986): 22–27.

———. *Madness and Civilization: Insanity in the Age of Reason.* New York: Vintage, 1988.

———. *Psychiatric Power: Lectures at the College de France 1973–1974.* Trans. Graham Burchell. New York: Picador, 2003a.

———. *Abnormal: Lectures at the College de France, 1974–1975.* Trans. Graham Burchell. New York: Verso, 2003b.

Freed, Ruth, and Stanley Freed. "Spirit Possession as Illness in a North Indian Village." *Ethnology* 3, no. 2 (1964): 152–171.

———. "The Psychomedical Case History of a Low-Caste Woman of North India." *Anthropological Papers of the American Museum of Natural History* 60, no. 2 (1985): 101–228.

Freud, Sigmund. *The Interpretation of Dreams.* Trans. James Strachey. New York: Basic Books, 2010 [1901].

Garro, Linda C., and Cheryl Mattingly. "Narrative Representations of Illness and Healing." *Social Science and Medicine* 38, no. 6 (1994): 771–774.

Gilman, Charlotte Perkins. *The Yellow Wallpaper and Other Writings.* New York: Bantam Dell, 2006 [1899]).

Gilman, Sander, Helen King, Roy Porter, G. S. Rousseau, and Elaine Showalter. "Introduction: The Destinies of Hysteria." In *Hysteria Beyond Freud.* Ed. Sander Gilman, Helen King, Roy Porter, G. S. Rousseau, and Elaine Showalter, vii–xxiv. Berkeley: University of California Press, 1993.

Good, Byron J. *Medicine, Rationality, and Experience: An Anthropological Perspective.* Cambridge: Cambridge University Press, 1994.

Good, Byron and Mary-Jo Delvecchio Good. "In the Subjunctive Mode: Epilepsy Narratives in Turkey." *Social Science and Medicine* 38 (1994) 835–842.

Hacking, Ian. *Rewriting the Soul: Multiple Personality and the Sciences of Memory.* Princeton: Princeton University Press, 1995.

Halliburton, Murphy. "'Just Some Spirits': The Erosion of Spirit Possession and Rise of 'Tension' in South India." *Medical Anthropology* 24, no. 2 (2005): 111–144.

———. *Mudpacks and Prozac: Experiencing Ayurvedic, Biomedical and Religious Healing.* Walnut Creek, Calif.: Left Coast Press, 2009.

Haraway, Donna. "Situated Knowledges: The Science Question in Feminism and the Privilege of Partial Perspective." *Feminist Studies* 14, no. 3 (1988): 575–599.

Harlan, Lindsey, and Paul Courtwright, eds. *From the Margins of Hindu Marriage: Essays on Gender, Religion, and Culture.* Oxford: Oxford University Press, 1995.

Hartnack, Christiane. "Vishnu on Freud's Desk: Psychoanalysis in Colonial India." In *Vishnu on Freud's Desk: A Reader in Psychoanalysis and Hinduism.* Ed. T. G. Vaidyanathan and Jeffrey J. Kripal, 81–106. Oxford: Oxford University Press, 1999.

The Hindu. "Public Awareness Campaign on Psychiatric Diseases." October 14, 2007.

Jackson, Michael. *Paths Toward a Clearing: Radical Empiricism and Ethnographic Inquiry.* Bloomington: Indiana University Press, 1989.

Jain, Sumeet, and Sushrut Jadhav. "A Cultural Critique of Community Psychiatry in India." *International Journal of Health Services* 38, no. 3 (2008): 561–584.

———. "Pills That Swallow Policy: Clinical Ethnography of a Community Mental Health Program in Northern India."?*Transcultural Psychiatry* 46 (2009): 60–85.

Jenkins, Janis. "Introduction." In *Schizophrenia, Culture, and Subjectivity: The Edge of Experience.* Ed. Janis Hunter Jenkins and Robert John Barrett, 1–28. Cambridge: Cambridge University Press. 2004a.

———. "Schizophrenia as a Paradigm Case for Understanding Fundamental Human Processes." In *Schizophrenia, Culture and Subjectivity: The Edge of Experience.* Ed. Janis Hunter Jenkins and Robert John Barrett, 29–61. Cambridge: Cambridge University Press, 2004b.

Kakar, Sudhir. *The Inner World: A Psychoanalytic Study of Hindu Childhood and Society.* Delhi: Oxford University Press, 1981.

———. *The Colors of Violence: Cultural Identities, Religion, and Violence.* Chicago: University of Chicago Press, 1996.

Kapila, Shruti. "Masculinity and Madness: Princely Personhood and the Colonial Sciences of the Mind in Western India, 1871–1940." *Past and Present* 187, no. 1 (2005): 121–157.

Kasbekar, Asha. "Hidden Pleasures: Negotiating the Myth of the Female Ideal in Popular Hindi Cinema." In *Pleasure and the Nation.* Ed. Rachel Dwyer and Christopher Pinney. Delhi: Oxford University Press, 2001: 286–308.

Kinsley, David. *Hindu Goddesses: Visions of the Divine Feminine in the Hindu Religious Tradition.* Berkeley: University of California Press, 1986.

Kleinman, Arthur. *Social Origins of Distress and Disease: Depression, Neurasthenia, and Pain in Modern China.* New Haven: Yale University Press, 1986.

———. *The Illness Narratives: Suffering, Healing, and the Human Condition.* New York: Basic Books, 1988.

————. *What Really Matters: Living a Moral Life Amidst Uncertainty and Danger.* New York: Oxford University Press, 2006.

Kleinman, Arthur, and Joan Kleinman. "Suffering and Its Professional Transformation." *Culture, Medicine and Psychiatry* 15, no. 3 (1991): 275–301.

Kumar, Radha. *A History of Doing: An Illustrated Account of Movements for Women's Rights and Feminism in India 1800–1990.* Delhi: Zubaan, 1997.

Kumar, S., and R. Kumar. "Institute of Mental Health and Hospital, Agra: Evolution in 150 Years." *Indian Journal of Psychiatry* 50 (2008): 308–312.

Kurtz, Stanley M. *All the Mothers Are One: Hindu India and the Cultural Reshaping of Psychoanalysis.* New York: Columbia University Press, 1992.

Lacan, Jacques. *The Four Fundamental Concepts of Psycho-analysis.* Ed. Jacques-Alain Miller, trans. Alain Sheridan. New York: Norton, 1978.

Leys, Ruth. *Trauma: A Genealogy.* Chicago: University of Chicago Press, 2000.

Luhrmann, Tanya. *Of Two Minds: The Growing Disorder in American Psychiatry.* New York: Alfred A. Knopf, 2000.

Lunbeck, Elizabeth. *The Psychiatric Persuasion: Knowledge, Gender and Power in Modern America.* Princeton: Princeton University Press, 1994.

Mandelbaum, David G. *Women's Seclusion and Men's Honor: Sex Roles in North India, Bangladesh, and Pakistan.* Tempe: University of Arizona Press, 1988.

Mani, Lata. *Contentious Traditions: The Debate on Sati in Colonial India.* Berkeley: University of California Press, 1998.

Marrow, Jocelyn. "Psychiatry, Modernity and Family Values: Clenched Teeth Illness in North India." Ph.D. dissertation, University of Chicago, 2008.

————. "Feminine Power or Feminine Weakness? North Indian Girls' Struggles with Aspirations, Agency, and Psychosomatic Illness." *American Ethnologist* 40, no. 2 (2013): 347–361.

Martin, Emily. *Bipolar Expeditions: Mania and Depression in American Culture.* Princeton: Princeton University Press, 2009.

Mattingly, Cheryl. *Healing Dramas and Clinical Plots: The Narrative Structure of Experience.* Cambridge: Cambridge University Press, 1998.

————. "Reading Minds and Telling Tales in a Cultural Borderland." *Ethos* 36, no. 1 (2008): 136–154.

McCarren, Felicia. *Dance Pathologies: Performance, Poetics, Medicine.* Stanford: Stanford University Press: 1998.

Mehrotra, Deepti Priya. *Home Truths: Stories of Single Mothers.* New York: Penguin Books, 2003.

Metzl, Jonathan. *Prozac on the Couch: Prescribing Gender in the Era of Wonder Drugs.* Durham: Duke University Press, 2003.

Mills, James H. "Modern Psychiatry in India: The British Role in Establishing an Asian System, 1858–1947." *International Review of Psychiatry* 18, no. 4 (2006): 333–343.

Mitchell, Juliet. *Mad Men and Medusas: Reclaiming Hysteria.* London: Penguin, 2000.

Mody, Perveez. "Love and the Law: Love-Marriage in Delhi." *Modern Asian Studies* 36, no. 1 (2002): 223–256.

Mol, Annemarie. *The Body Multiple: Ontology in Medical Practice.* Durham: Duke University Press, 2002.

Monroe, John Warne. *Laboratories of Faith: Mesmerism, Spiritism, and Occultism in Modern France.* Ithaca: Cornell University Press, 2008.

Moore, Lorrie. "People Like That Are the Only People Here: Canonical Babbling in Peed Onk." In *Birds of America*, 212–250. New York: Knopf, 1998.

Mukharji, Projit Bihari. *Nationalizing the Body: The Medical Market, Print and Daktari Medicine.* London: Anthem Press, 2009.

Mulvey, Laura. "Visual Pleasure and Narrative Cinema." *Screen* 16, no. 3 (1975): 6–18.

Nabokov, Isabelle. "Expel the Lover, Recover the Wife: Symbolic Analysis of the South Indian Exorcism." *Journal of the Royal Anthropological Institute* 3, no. 2 (1997): 297–316.

Nancy, Jean-Luc. *The Birth to Presence.* Trans. Brian Holmes and others. Stanford: Stanford University Press, 1993.

Nanda, Serena. *Neither Man nor Woman: The Hijras of India.* Charlottesville, Va.: Wadsworth, 1999.

Nandy, Ashis. *The Intimate Enemy: Loss and Recovery of Self Under Colonialism.* Oxford: Oxford University Press, 1983.

———. *The Savage Freud and Other Essays on Possible and Retrievable Selves.* Princeton: Princeton University Press, 1995.

Narayan, Uma. *Dislocating Cultures: Identities, Traditions, and Third-World Feminism.* New York: Routledge, 1997.

Nunley, Michael. "Why Psychiatrists in India Prescribe So Many Drugs." *Culture, Medicine and Psychiatry* 20, no. 2 (1996): 165–197.

Obeyesekere, Gananath. *Medusa's Hair: An Essay on Personal Symbols and Religious Experience.* Chicago: University of Chicago Press, 1981.

Oldenburg, Veena. "Lifestyle as Resistance: The Case of the Courtesans of Lucknow, India." *Feminist Studies* 16, no. 2 (1990): 259–287.

Pandolfo, Stefania. "The Knot of the Soul: Postcolonial Conundrums, Madness and the Imagination." In *Postcolonial Disorders.* Ed. Mary-Jo Delvecchio Good, Sandra Hyde, Sarah Pinto, and Byron Good, 329–358. Berkeley: University of California Press, 2008.

Petryna, Adriana. *When Experiments Travel: Clinical Trials and the Global Search for Human Subjects.* Princeton: Princeton University Press, 2009.

Pinto, Sarah. *Where There Is No Midwife: Birth and Loss in Rural India.* New York: Berghahn Books, 2008.

———. "Rational Love, Relational Medicine: Psychiatry and the Accumulation of Precarious Kinship." *Culture, Medicine, and Psychiatry* 35, no. 3 (2011): 376–395.

———. "The Limits of Diagnosis: Sex, Law and Psychiatry in a Case of Contested Marriage." *Ethos* 40, no. 2 (2012): 119–141.

Porter, Roy. "The Body and the Mind, the Doctor and the Patient: Negotiating Hysteria." In *Hysteria Beyond Freud*. Ed. Sander Gilman, Helen King, Roy Porter, G. S. Rousseau, and Elaine Showalter, 225–285. Berkeley: University of California Press, 1993.

Povinelli, Elizabeth A. *The Empire of Love: Toward a Theory of Intimacy, Genealogy, and Carnality.* Durham: Duke University Press, 2006.

———. *Economies of Abandonment: Social Belonging and Endurance in Late Liberalism.* Durham: Duke University Press, 2011.

Rabinow, Paul. "Artificiality and Enlightenment: From Sociobiology to Biosociality." In *The Science Studies Reader*. Ed. M. Bagioli, 407–416. New York: Routledge, 1999.

Raheja, Gloria Goodwin, and Ann Grodzins Gold. *Listen to the Heron's Words: Reimagining Gender and Kinship in North India.* Berkeley: University of California Press, 1994.

Ramberg, Lucinda. "Given to the Goddess: South Indian Devdasis, Ethics, and Kinship." Ph.D. dissertation, University of California, Berkeley, 2006.

Reddy, Gayatri. *With Respect to Sex: Negotiating Hijra Identity in South India.* Chicago: University of Chicago Press, 2005.

Roland, Alan. *In Search of Self in India and Japan.* Princeton: Princeton University Press, 1991.

Rose, Nikolas. *The Politics of Life Itself: Biomedicine, Power, and Subjectivity in the Twenty-First Century.* Princeton: Princeton University Press, 2007.

Rubin, Gayle. "The Traffic in Women: Notes on the Political Economy of Sex." In *Toward an Anthropology of Women*. Ed. Rayna R. Reiter, 157–210. New York: Monthly Review Press, 1975.

Rumi, Jalal al-Din. *The Essential Rumi.* Trans. Coleman Barks. New York: Harper Collins, 1995.

Salerno, Roger A. *Landscapes of Abandonment: Capitalism, Modernity, and Estrangement.* Albany: SUNY Press, 2003.

Sedgwick, Eve Kosofsky. *Touching Feeling: Affect, Pedagogy, Performativity.* Durham: Duke University Press, 2003.

Showalter, Elaine. *The Female Malady: Women, Madness, and English Culture, 1830–1980.* New York: Pantheon Books, 1985.

———. "Hysteria, Feminism, and Gender." In *Hysteria Beyond Freud*. By Sander Gilman, Helen King, Roy Porter, G. S. Rousseau, and Elaine Showalter, 345–452. Berkeley: University of California Press, 1993.

Simpson, Bob. "Bringing the 'Unclear' Family into Focus: Divorce and Remarriage in Contemporary Britain." *Man* (n.s.) 29 (1994): 831–851.

Sousa, Amy. "Pragmatic Ethics, Sensible Care: Psychiatry and Schizophrenia in North India." Ph.D. dissertation, University of Chicago, 2011.

Spivak, Gayatri Chakravorty. "Three Women's Texts and a Critique of Imperialism." *Critical Inquiry* 12, no. 1 (1985): 243–261.

Stoller, Paul. *Embodying Colonial Memories: Spirit Possession, Power, and the Hauka in West Africa.* New York: Routledge, 1995.

Strathern, Marilyn. *Kinship, Law and the Unexpected: Relatives Are Always a Surprise.* Cambridge: Cambridge University Press, 2005.

Taylor, Julie M. *Paper Tangos.* Durham: Duke University Press, 1998.

Thara, R., Shanta Kamath, and Shuba Kumar. "Women with Schizophrenia and Broken Marriages: Doubly Disadvantaged." *International Journal of Social Psychiatry* 49, no. 3 (2003): 225–232.

Trawick, Margaret. *Notes on Love in a Tamil Family.* Berkeley: University of California Press, 1992.

Valéry, Paul. "Philosophy of the Dance." In *What Is Dance?* Ed. Roger Copeland and Marshall Cohen, 55–102. Oxford: Oxford University Press, 1983.

Visweswaran, Kamala. *Fictions of Feminist Ethnography.* Minneapolis: University of Minnesota Press, 1994.

Wajeman, Gerard. "The Hysteric's Discourse." *Lacan Study Notes* 6, no. 9 (1988): 1–22.

Winter, Alison. *Mesmerized: Powers of Mind in Victorian Britain.* Chicago: University of Chicago Press, 1998.

Young, Allan. *The Harmony of Illusions: Inventing Post-traumatic Stress Disorder.* Princeton: Princeton University Press, 1995.

Zika, Charles. *Exorcising our Demons: Magic, Witchcraft and Visual Culture in Early Modern Europe.* Leiden: Brill, 2003.

Žižek, Slavoj. *The Sublime Object of Ideology.* New York: Verso, 1989.

Index

abandonment, 35, 105, 150, 242, 250; asylum era and, 13, 14–15; confinement twinned with, 249; in ethical grid, 250–51, *251*; ethics and, *253*; freedom and, 3, 4, 29, 30, 236, 259; kinship and, 74, 76; patients' desires and, 106; regulation of norms and, 248; social embeddedness as opposite of, 256; state's role in, 55; suffering and, 89

abduction, 204, 209, 210

Abrams, Minnie, 178

addictions, 52, 136

agency, 6, 23, 144, 158; compromise of, 228; crises in, 181, 188, 190; dramas of control and, 197; female agency and community solidarity, 225; intimacy and, 232; sexual, 33, 226, 227

Agra Mental Hospital, 2, 44–45, 50, 60; family decision to commit patients to, 62–63; history of, 54–55; teasing threat about being sent "to Agra," 15, 54; conditions in, 53; visitors to, 48

Antakshiri (singing game), 79, 91

anthropology, 5, 31, 121, 224, 250; on abandonment, 248; hysteria diagnosis and, 159, 160–61, 179–80

antipsychotics, 90, 98, 165, 167, 168, 186, 203; catatonic reaction to, 206; drug resistance, 231

anxiety, 79, 169, 190, 245

Aronofsky, Darren, 196

asylums, 4, 19, 75; asylum era, 13, 14, 18; in colonial India, 16, 82; end of, 15, 260; history of, 22, 162; renamed mental hospitals, 17; shift from containment to treatment, 54

aversion therapy, 166

Ayurvedic medicine, 177

Barthes, Roland, 238, 244–45

behavior modification, 28

Benjamin, Jessica, 195

benzodiazepine, 186

Bhool Bhulaiyaa [The Labyrinth] (film, 2007), 182–85, 188, 197

Biehl, João, 249

biology, 23, 24, 98, 176; dissolution of bonds and, 114; female biology and hysteria, 177

biomedicine, 21, 24

biopolitics, 30, 249

biopower, 25, 28, 248, 256

biosociality, 24

bipolar disorder, 138, 211

Black Swan (Aronofsky film, 2010), 196

Blanchot, Maurice, 13, 87, 112, 260

bodies, 6, 145, 146; biology of, 24; body multiple, 26; meaningful action and, 144; pharmaceuticals and chemistry of, 19

Bollywood movies, 7, 184, 196, 208, 243

Bose, Girindrasekhar, 16, 179

Brahmin caste, 40, 57, 202, 217; contested marriage and, 210, 221; doctor from, 205

Breuer, Josef, 23

Brouillet, André, 195

bureaucracy, 72, 121, 154

Butler, Judith, 254, 255

Capital (Marx), 233

capitalism, late, 14, 25

card games, 130, 131, 142, 143

caregiving, 5, 14, 60, 104; asylums as central nodes of, 17; caregiver narratives, 47; consent to, 77; crises of, 22; "local ecologies of care," 19

Acknowledgments

Many people who deserve thanks for their help and guidance on this book will have to remain nameless due to my intention to conceal, as much as possible, details about places and people. I hope they know who they are and realize how much I owe to their wisdom, kindness, and assistance. Most important are the women, families, physicians, and caregivers who let me into their homes and lives and allowed me to trail them during their stressful workdays. Also important were the friends, fictive kin, colleagues, and fellow scholars who guided me through this research, making introductions, giving advice, and facilitating connections. A deep aquifer of gratitude and love exists for the woman who, in these pages, I call Mrs. M., not only for her help, companionship, and inspiration, but for her adoring attention to Eve. Special thanks are due to the young man who took me on the back of his motorcycle to shrines every Thursday evening. In Delhi, gratitude is, as always, owed to Janet and Kanwarjit Chawla, Kachina Chawla and Pitamber Sahni, and the entire Chawla clan for their generosity, intelligence, and warmth.

Many have read and/or commented on versions and parts of this manuscript on its way to completion. I am grateful for the insightful comments and thoughtful advice of Amahl Bishara, Lucinda Ramberg, Katherine Lemons, Sarah Willen, Byron Good, Mary-Jo DelVecchio Good, Arthur Kleinman, Alistair Donald, Sadeq Rahimi, Chris Dole, Rich Jankowsky, Susanna Trnka, Lisa Wynn, Alexander Edmonds, Rachel Newcomb, Thomas Strong, Kirsten Scheid, Cristiana Giordano, Isabelle Clark-Decès, Alexander Keefe, and anonymous reviewers for several journals. A particular debt of gratitude is owed to Robert Desjarlais for midwifing many of these chapters, not to mention everything I wrote for my tenure application, and to to Susannah Heschel for her help and support on the hysteria work. I am grateful to Tufts University for providing me with a Junior

Faculty Research Leave year in which to pursue this work, and to the Center for Humanities at Tufts for supporting my work in 2008–2009, when I drafted Chapter 1, "Rehabilitating Ammi." Thanks are owed to those who invited me to give talks and presentations and provided thoughtful, critical audiences: Isabelle Clark-Decès, Craig Jeffrey, and Jane Dyson at Princeton University, Saiba Varma at Cornell University, Julia Kowalski at University of Chicago, Byron Good and Mary-Jo Delvecchio Good at Harvard University, Andrew Nicholson at SUNY Stony Brook, Sarah Lamb at Brandeis University, Sarah Willen and Don Seeman at Emory University, Susannah Heschel at Dartmouth College, Jason Danely at Rhode Island College, and Steven Parish at University of California, San Diego. For painstaking research assistance, I thank Douglas Pet and Tamara Turner. It would not have been possible to stitch fragmentary notes into stories, arguments, and ideas without my students, who continue to push me to think in new, sometimes frightening, and always exciting ways. At the University of Pennsylvania Press, I thank Peter Agree, Noreen O'Connor-Abel, and two anonymous reviewers for their guidance and truly remarkable observations and comments.

Chapter 4, "Moskha and Mishappenings," began life as an essay for an edited volume ("Movement in Time: Choreographies of Confinement in an In-Patient Ward," in *Senses and Citizenship*, ed. Susanna Trnka, Julie Park, and Christine Dureau [New York: Routledge, 2013]).

At home, many have put up with the weeks and months of distraction, moodiness, and melancholia that come with writing a book of this sort. And many have, through their attentions and labors, provided invaluable hours for writing. Thanks to Team Eve: Marianna Papageorge, Gladys Helzberg, Mariah Gruner, and Alexis Daniels, and Team Thea: Anna Larson Williams and Emily Wyner. My parents, Mary and Bruce Pinto, as always, offered their time, care, labor, and pride to this project, and my sister, Kristina Pinto, shared her intelligence and unfailing wit.

These words have been difficult to write, and they have made me a less than pleasant person at times. For this and so many other reasons, I am fortunate for and undeserving of the limitless love and confidence of Dennis Michaud, who helped me cross the wobbly bridge out of the state described here and who has shown me that love can be stable, sane, and inviolable. Likewise, infinite gratitude to my darling Eve for inspiration, companionship, laughter, trust, and love, and for putting up with my distraction in the days when I have been in the thickest thickets of writing.

This was our journey, and I am blessed to have had her at my side, in my lap, in my arms, or within earshot for much of this, and sorry, so sorry, she was there for some of it. Though Thea was here only for the final phases of this work, I am grateful for her smiling presence and for the sense of new beginnings she brings. To those in my life whose darker moments and sadder days make appearances in this book, I am sorry. These mad words were born in love.